memoralia

THE MEMOIRS OF RICHARD BURGIN

Memoralia: The Memoirs of Richard Burgin
Copyright © 2017 by Diana Burgin

All rights reserved. No part of this book may be used or reproduced in any form, electronic or mechanical, including photocopying, recording, or scanning into any information storage and retrieval system, without written permission from the author except in the case of brief quotation embodied in critical articles and reviews.

Cover Photo for *"Memoralia,"* Richard Burgin conducting the Boston Symphony Orchestra with soloist Samuel Mayes, 1958. *Whitestone Photo*

Book design by Jessika Hazelton

Printed in the United States of America
The Troy Book Makers • Troy, New York • thetroybookmakers.com

To order additional copies of this title, contact your favorite local bookstore or visit www.tbmbooks.com. Also available through amazon.com.

ISBN: 978-1-61468-390-2

memoralia
THE MEMOIRS OF RICHARD BURGIN

*Former Concertmaster and Associate Conductor
of the Boston Symphony Orchestra*

Compiled, Edited, Arranged and Introduced by
Diana Lewis Burgin

CONTENTS

VII | LIST OF ILLUSTRATIONS
IX | INTRODUCTION TO MEMORALIA
    by Diana Lewis Burgin

MEMORALIA PART I

2 | Beginnings 1897-1908: Winetzky, Lotto, Markees, Joachim
11 | The St. Petersburg Conservatory 1908-1914. Leopold Auer
26 | Professional Activity In Russia And Scandinavia (1912-1920)
32 | How I Became Concertmaster Of The BSO

PHOTO INSERT I

37 | Before the Boston Symphony Orchestra, 1910 – 1920

MEMORALIA PART II

43 | The Boston Symphony Orchestra: Pierre Monteux (1920 – 1924)
44 | Koussevitzky (1924 – 1950)
53 | The Job of Assistant / Associate Conductor (1927-1966)
57 | The Berkshire Music Center
58 | Composers
59 | Schoenberg
62 | Hindemith
67 | Stravinsky
69 | Munch (1949-1962)
72 | The BSO Tour of the Far East (May-June, 1960)

PHOTO INSERT II

75 | Concertmaster and Associate Conductor of the BSO, 1920–1962

THOUGHTS ON MUSICIANS AND MUSIC
   83 | Conducting and Conductors
   85 | Virtuosi
   87 | Music Editing
   89 | Teaching
  101 | Musings on This and That

PHOTO INSERT III
  105 | After the BSO, 1966 – 1977

IMPRESSIONS AND MEMORIES OF RICHARD BURGIN
  111 | Leonard Bernstein   115 | Nathan Gottschalk
  111 | Malcolm Brannen   116 | Seiji Ozawa
  111 | Sarah Caldwell   116 | Willis Page
  112 | Ronald Carbone   116 | Charles Rex
  113 | Jerome D. Cohen   118 | Joseph Silverstein
  113 | Harry Ellis Dickson   118 | Robert Taylor
  114 | Joseph Gingold   119 | George Zazofsky
  115 | Lois Elfenbein Gosa

121 | ENDNOTES
125 | PRINT SOURCES
126 | DISCOGRAPHY – COMMERCIAL RECORDINGS
130 | PROGRAMS CONDUCTED BY RICHARD BURGIN AND THE BOSTON SYMPHONY ORCHESTRA, 1927-1967

LIST OF ILLUSTRATIONS

1. Burgin as a student at the St. Petersburg Conservatory, 1910.
2. Laureates of the St. Petersburg Conservatory, 1912 graduates.
3. Auer's class in summer in Loshchwitz, Germany.
4. Leopold Auer, 1915.
5. Scandinavian composer, Christian Sinding.
6. The Young Concertmaster in Scandinavia, 1910's.
7. Advertisement for violin strings, endorsed by Richard Burgin, 1920's.
8. Burgin, Koussevitzky and the BSO in the late 1920's.
9. Burgin and Posselt, newlyweds at Tanglewood, July 14, 1940.
10. Igor Stravinsky, 1940.
11. Burgin with Bohuslav and Charlotte Martinu and Gregor Piatigorsky, 1941.
12. Paul Hindemith playing the rebec.
13. Koussevitzky and Burgin, 1940's.
14. Burgin and his daughter, late 1940's.
15. Ruth Posselt and Richard Burgin welcomed at the airport in Warsaw, June 1949.
16. Burgin holding his two-year-old son, Richard, at Koussevitzky's birthday party, Tanglewood, July, 1949.
17. Posselt and Burgin rehearsing the Bach Concerto for 2 violins with the BSO in Symphony Hall, 1949
18. Burgin rehearsing the student orchestra at Tanglewood.
19. Burgin and Heifetz, at Tanglewood, July 1949.

20. Posselt and Burgin, 1954.
21. Charles Munch and the BSO in Leningrad Philharmonic Hall, September 1956.
22. Burgin conducting, 1958.
23. Burgin and Leonid Kogan, late 1950s.
24. Richard Burgin and Alfred Krips.
25. Munch, Burgin and members of the BSO being greeted in Japan, May 1960.
26. Burgin rehearsing the chorus for Mahler's Symphony No. 2, 1962.
27. Joseph Silverstein, Erich Leinsdorf, Richard Burgin at Tanglewood, 1962.
28. Munch and Burgin, Tanglewood, 1962.
29. Flyer for the Florida International Music Festival, 1966.
30. Edward Kilenyi and Richard Burgin, 1967.
31. Florestan Quartet at Florida State University.
32. Richard Burgin at his home in Tallahassee, Florida.
33. Burgin conducting a rehearsal of students at a Congress of Strings, 1967.
34. Bowing an imaginary violin, Congress of Strings, Cincinnati University, 1970.
35. Burgin at the conferring of Honorary Degree on Gregor Piatigorsky, FSU. June, 1970.
36. Burgin conducting student orchestra for a Benefit at FSU, April, 1972.
37. Richard Burgin and members of the International Conducting Symposium, Jacksonville University, May, 1975.
38. Burgin at Master Class in New School, Sarasota, Summer, 1977.

Introduction to *Memoralia*
Diana Lewis Burgin

There is no better way to introduce readers of this book to Richard Burgin (1892-1981), and his importance in the world of 20th century music, than to quote the following remembrance of him, written in October 1981 by the eminent pianist and Burgin's former colleague at Florida State University, Edward Kilenyi.

"What did Richard Strauss, Stravinsky, Sibelius, Hindemith, Rachmaninov, Joachim, Auer, Heifetz, Piatigorsky, Prokofiev, Martinu, Schoenberg – and other men of genius just as disparate – have in common? Close, collegial and friendly relations with ... Richard Burgin.

"It would be a grave mistake, however, to assume that Burgin's importance lay mostly in his associations with such dazzling friends. Rather, these greats were attracted to him on account of his tremendous musical gifts and marvelous, winning personality and wisdom. For forty-two years he was concertmaster of the Boston Symphony, one of the country's top orchestras, and for twenty-one years, its Associate Conductor. After he retired from the BSO, Florida State University had the glory of having Burgin on its Music Faculty as Professor of Violin, Conductor of the Chamber Orchestra, and member of the Florestan Quartet during the years 1963-72.

"Born in Warsaw, and trained in Berlin and St. Petersburg, he became a guiding light in musical culture from 1920. During the summers, when he taught at the Berkshire Music Center, and at numerous Congresses of Strings, there was hardly an American musician, who did not benefit from his inimitable training in orchestral playing, conducting, and chamber music. As a violinist, he was second to none among all the great concertmasters. As a conductor he was so aware and enthusiastic about new music that his list of American (and several world) premieres includes such diverse works as Mahler's Third Symphony, Schoenberg's difficult scores, and the compositions of the constantly changing avant-garde.

"Although distinctions were showered on Richard Burgin throughout his life [including induction into the American Academy of Arts and Sciences (1947) and the French Legion of Honor (1954) as well as the reception of the Bruckner-Mahler Society Medal (1951) and numerous honorary doctorates], no great musician remained so consistently and sincerely modest. During his years at FSU, I never heard him raise his voice at a rehearsal or after a concert. The only occasion he did raise his voice in anger ... occurred while playing his beloved game of bridge."

Burgin's long and multifaceted life in music spanned the greater part of the 20th century, from 1903 when he made his debut as a child prodigy with the Warsaw Philharmonic, until shortly before his death in April 1981 when he played his last professional performances in the Boston Opera Orchestra. Music was Richard Burgin's life. When asked if he planned to retire after being forced to leave the faculty of Florida State University – because of his age – in 1972, he exclaimed, "Never! As long as I can play the violin and conduct, I will do so." As Kilenyi noted, Burgin enjoyed close professional (and often personal) relationships with some of the world's greatest 20th century violinists, conductors, and composers. At the same time, several generations of his violin and conducting students have made careers in music, and many have won positions in major orchestras all over the world. His legacy to American students of the violin is still being passed on, from those he taught in the 1960's and 1970's to those they and their students are teaching today.

Burgin has not been forgotten; he has garnered his fair share of academic studies and personal memoirs from his students, his children, and his colleagues. Most recently, his ideas on violin playing and music making, expressed at a master class at the New School in Sarasota, Florida where he worked in the late 1970's, helped inspire the violinist and author of American detective fiction, Gerald Elias, to create the musical opinions of his amateur detective, Daniel Jacobus. Yet, Burgin himself never managed to write his own memoirs although he had the intention of doing so and was about to begin dictating them to me on the day before he suffered the stroke which led to his death three months later.

The present book represents at heart a collection of Richard Burgin's largely oral "memoirs," or *memoralia*, as he might have dictated them to me back in 1981. These *memoralia* come from tape recordings of Burgin's speech in various interviews, and quotations of his words in disparate printed sources, all of which I have been collecting into an archive over the years since his death. The main source is a transcript I had made, and have edited and re-ordered specifically for this volume, of Burgin's lengthy, free-flowing answers to the questions asked him by Dr. Elias Dann of Florida State University in a taped interview he conducted at Burgin's home in Tallahassee, Florida in June, 1974.[1] Into the framework of Dann's interview I have interpolated material from other "oral" sources, including two, shorter tape-recorded interviews; Burgin's directly quoted words in various articles about him that appeared from 1920 to the late 1970s; remarks he made and stories he told to colleagues and friends that have been quoted in print by them; some passages from his unpublished personal correspondence, which he would never have wanted to have published, but which I have risked airing, anyway; and stories I heard him tell *en famille*. I have organized and cobbled this material together, mixing and matching Burgin's own words on one and the same subject as they were quoted or recorded in different printed or oral sources and settings. The one rule I observed was to use only Burgin's own spoken or directly quoted words. A list of all my printed sources is given at the end of the volume.

Burgin spoke English fluently, if with an accent, but once I became fluent in Russian, I realized the degree to which his spoken English was syntactically and sometimes semantically a form of fluent Russian English. Therefore, in the interests of clarity, a quality Burgin greatly prized and always strove for in his playing, conducting, teaching and conversation, I have freely edited his syntax and word order while trying to maintain the rhythm and emphasis of his speech. My goal was to produce a coherent, readable, quasi-chronological, quasi-thematic first-person narrative in English of Burgin's words as spoken on tape or quoted in print over the years. The result, part-autobiography, part-reminiscences, and part-commentary, will hopefully sound like Richard Burgin to anyone who knew him.

I have divided *Memoralia* into three sections. In Part 1, the material of which comes mainly from the Dann tapes and was partially "versified" by me in my 1989 poetic biography, *Richard Burgin. A Life in Verse*,[2] Richard Burgin tells the story of his musical education from childhood through his years at the St. Petersburg Conservatory; talks about his first positions as concertmaster in

Scandinavia; and relates how he came to be concertmaster of the Boston Symphony Orchestra. Part 2 represents a miscellany of Burgin's reminiscences (from the Dann tapes and other published and unpublished sources) about various musicians he worked with and knew well (Pierre Monteux, Serge Koussevitzky, Charles Munch, Igor Stravinsky, Paul Hindemith, Arnold Schoenberg, and others); his thoughts about music, conducting, teaching and playing the violin, as well as other of his oft-repeated precepts, short anecdotes, and pieces of "wisdom." Each of the major segments of parts 1 and 2 is introduced by short biographical passages in brackets and italics that frame Burgin's recollections and stories. *Memoralia* concludes with a brief sample of other musicians' memories of Burgin.

Richard Burgin was known in musical circles as a great raconteur and many of his gently but pointedly ironic anecdotes passed into the musical folklore of the BSO and have been quoted here and there over the years since his retirement from the orchestra in 1967. Perhaps the key to his effectiveness as a storyteller lay in the urbane, dispassionate but quick-witted perspective from which he viewed the subjects of his stories and the unfailing self-irony and modesty with which he spoke of himself. His stories were disarming in the literal sense of the word – they brilliantly undercut any potential attack from a less-than-friendly interlocutor – but at the same time, they managed to hit their mark. Burgin's stories got *his point* across while never seeming to be *about him*. A man of considerable reserve, he also enjoyed being in company, where he radiated a quiet charisma. His wife noted of him after his death that he "loved to be sociable and see people, even people he didn't especially like."

When it came to talking about himself, Burgin was silent far more often than not. After his death, when I was trying to re-member his life in order to write his biography, I realized that what I didn't know far outweighed what I did. And, after all these years, I have learned very little more about his early life than I knew then. Therefore, I can vouch for the fact that what Burgin tells us in Part I of *Memoralia* represents pretty much all that is known of his first 28 years, with the exception of his first love and marriage to a talented pianist and graduate of the St. Petersburg Conservatory, Henrietta Borsh, a "great romance"[3] that ended in unhappiness and divorce, and then vanished from Burgin's professional biography.

Part II of *Memoralia* continues the story of Burgin's career in the United States, albeit indirectly, via his reminiscences of several of the musicians he worked with during his long tenure with the BSO and then, his years at Florida State University and so-called "retirement." In the remainder of this introduction, I shall provide a chronological and thematic context for Burgin's remarks in Part II, focusing on those aspects of his life and career which he underplays, or simply had no occasion to talk about, but which need to be at least mentioned in order to flesh out the picture of the musician and man he was. In particular I shall focus on Burgin's work as a conductor which remains even now the least known and perhaps under-valued part of his career in music.

Burgin's wife, the American virtuoso violinist Ruth Posselt, often recalled that her husband "loved to conduct." It would seem from the response to his conducting of composers, musicians, students, critics and audiences that the source of this "love" lay in the chance conducting afforded him to do what he deemed being a musician was all about, to serve the music. Burgin always insisted that the conductor was the only person on stage who wasn't playing an instrument, or producing sound, but was needed to facilitate the instrumentalists' production of the sound created by the composer. The goal of conducting was to express in sound what was written in the score. He always told his students, "We must start from the assumption that the composer knew what he wanted to say and said that in the score." Burgin's performances were often cited for their clarity, sense of proportion, musicianship, craftsmanship and lack of melodrama, histrionics and showmanship. As George Szell wrote in a letter to Burgin of January 16, 1943: "I just finished listening to your "Don Quixote" over the air and want to thank you and to tell you how much I enjoyed this moving and poetic rendering of the piece that I love so much. [...] Amongst many details that would deserve extra mention I must single out the exemplary clarity and plasticity of the F major 6/8 variation where both thematic strands came out consistently all the way through, particularly the upper one which, as a rule, is hopelessly drowned out by the sixteenth-motion all over the place – as you know. I never heard this spot nearly as transparent as tonight." [4]

Burgin expressed his aesthetic credo in his 1974 interview with Professor Dann: "In everything there should be freedom, and more than anywhere in art, but there's a point when freedom turns on itself; that happens when the individual player exaggerates his part or his importance, which causes him to lose all sense of proportion and then, freedom becomes distortion." This cherished belief made him deplore any excess, 'playing to the rafters', or lack of proportion which he detected in conductors and performers he otherwise might like and respect.

Burgin's own approach to conducting the orchestra was simple: " I know what I want, I know how to tell them what I want, and they give it to me, just as they give it to any other conductor, only maybe to me a little quicker."[5] Burgin often made an interesting comparison between an orchestra and a dramatic company. The orchestral players are like actors in a play. Each has his role and, in the final analysis, it is the actors who actually create the performance. But the director sets the pace, the tone, the emphasis of the play. From him the performers derive their characteristic style.

The characteristic style Burgin achieved with the BSO generally won enthusiastic applause from the musicians and the audience and earned high critical acclaim. By 1939 one Boston critic noted that "Mr. Burgin has become a very fine conductor indeed. His reading of [Richard Strauss'] "Don Juan" was one of the best within memory. The whole thing was clear; you could plainly hear several themes going on contrapuntally at the same time, and there were passion and atmosphere." (C.W. D, *The Boston Globe*) A few years later he was praised in *The Cleveland News* for "a fine dramatic sense, an expressive podium technique and a poetic temperament" in an "outstanding" performance of Brahms First."

Burgin's support of new music and innovative programs was often cited, but his performances of Mahler's symphonies aroused special critical enthusiasm.[6] The *Boston Globe* for March 31, 1951, wrote: "Mahler's Fifth had not been done here since 1940 and it was high time for another hearing. [...] When it all was over, Symphony Hall rocked with applause and some cheering, in which Mr. Burgin directed that all hands share. [...] In retrospect this concert ought to rank among the finest of the season." Four years later, the critic for *The Boston Herald* (October 29, 1955) noted: "Mr. Burgin had not only got up from a sick bed to conduct this concert, he had given one of the finest readings of Mahler's First symphony – or of any symphony – of his life. It was a remarkable feat for he not only gave this huge work a unity of style and mood; he gave it a tonal radiance of the most beautiful character. Mr. Burgin has made Mahler particularly his own; few other conductors save Bruno Walter seem to be so devoted to this tortured Austrian and so capable of penetrating his many mysteries." Burgin's performance of Mahler's Second Symphony in February 1960 was hailed as "a triumph not only for Mr. Burgin but for Gustav Mahler. We had just heard his Symphony No. 2 and it wasn't too many years ago that Mahler was generally considered something to avoid if possible." (*The Christian Science Monitor,* February 27, 1960). Finally, while regretting that Burgin's talent as a conductor had not been sufficiently known in New York, the critic of the *New York Times* remarked, "amends were made in Carnegie Hall yesterday afternoon when Mr. Burgin led the orchestra in the gigantic Third Symphony by Gustav Mahler and received a magnificent ovation for his achievement. It was an altogether superb accomplishment for Mr. Burgin, a personal triumph that was seconded by the way his colleagues reacted to his bidding. [...] His feeling for the special language of Mahler, as he made abundantly clear, is as deep and sensible as that of any conductor around today." (*New York Times*, January 29, 1962)

Harrison Keller, violinist and President-Emeritus of the New England Conservatory, in summing up Burgin's career as Associate Conductor, wrote: "As conductor, Mr. Burgin has shown his skill by successful performances of some of the most difficult and profound orchestral compositions. Had this artist of many talents been willing to glamorize himself, to seek flattering publicity, to cultivate the climate of a prima donna, he undoubtedly would have been wooed away from Boston to lead an orchestra of his own. Instead, fortunately for this city and the Boston Symphony Orchestra, his complete dedication to music and his deep devotion to serving the Orchestra and his colleagues have brought added distinction to this community."

Burgin's colleagues often testified to his incredible memory for music. In his capacity as conductor, both in rehearsal and performance, his mind could draw upon a neatly stored selection of solutions he had found for problems in actual performance, things he had observed in the efforts of conductors and players to make printed notes come alive (a similar problem-solving approach characterized his teaching as well). Burgin was especially speedy in grasping the intricacies of modern scores. Fellow musicians said that his quick and orderly musical memory also revealed itself in his prowess as a bridge player. (He was in fact a ranking bridge player in Massachusetts and played several well-known champions).

The flip side of Burgin's legendary memory for music was his equally remarkable forgetfulness in everyday life, which became the stuff of musical folklore in BSO circles. He would frequently forget his bow in all sorts of odd places and once he even left his Stradivarius on his commuter train. Another time, he journeyed to Concord, Massachusetts for a solo engagement and was amazed to find no one there aware of any such concert. A telephone call to Boston revealed that the recital was supposed to take place in Concord, New Hampshire. On another occasion, Burgin arrived at an auditorium for a performance and found the place locked and in darkness. After a bit of investigation he discovered he had turned up a month early.

Most mysterious of all was the concertmaster's congenital failure to have a mute with him – this was such a habit that the three violinists who sat nearest him always carried spare mutes ready to give him when after fumbling in his pockets he discovered he had forgotten his own. At one time, there seemed to be a promising solution to the problem of Burgin's mute. One of his outstanding violin students, Ma Si-Hon, who went on to a solo career and also played in the Cleveland Orchestra, devised a mute which could be permanently attached to a violin in a position where it was instantly accessible but did not interfere with playing when it wasn't wanted. All the violinists were excited when Ma showed them his invention. Everyone wanted one and everyone wanted Burgin to be the first to have one mounted on his violin. Expectation ran high as the orchestra approached the beginning of a passage for muted strings. The passage came and all eyes were on Burgin's fiddle. But the un-losable mute wasn't there. Alfred Krips, Assistant Concertmaster, proffered his usual spare.

Reporting on Burgin's retirement from the concertmastership in 1962, *Newsweek* magazine wrote: "When Richard Burgin showed up at a dinner in his honor in Boston last week at the right place, at the right time, and wearing the right clothes, his colleagues in the Boston Symphony Orchestra breathed a sigh of relief. [...] A violinist in the orchestra who is just about his size... was especially grateful that Burgin arrived for the dinner properly turned out in black tie. 'On a concert night when I see the personnel manager approaching me,' he explained, 'I just automatically start to undress.'"[7].

Since we have somehow moved into the realm of personal habits, this may be an appropriate place to say a few words about another, far more significant aspect, indeed the foundation, of Burgin's private life. Next to music, Burgin was devoted to his wife, his children and his home. Yet, for the first fifteen years of his life in Boston, there seemed little chance that wife and family would ever play the central role in his life that they ultimately did. Pursued unsuccessfully by several Boston ladies (one of whom sent him a dozen yellow roses before every Friday afternoon symphony concert for years), he had the reputation of being not only one of

Boston's most eligible, but also most die-hard bachelors! This reputation began to totter in the mid-thirties after Burgin met Ruth Posselt (1911-2007), whom his boss, Koussevitzky, characterized as "one of the greatest violinists of our time."[8]

Actually, Burgin had met Posselt for the first time back in April, 1923 when the 29-year old concertmaster went backstage at Symphony Hall to congratulate the 11-year old child prodigy after her Symphony Hall debut. Little did either of them suspect, then, that they would end up spending forty years of their lives together as husband and wife.

During the twelve years that passed until their next meeting in March 1935, the eighteen-year difference between their ages seemed to shrink. The Medford born Posselt had grown up and become a rising star on the concert stage, having attained to European fame as a virtuoso in the early thirties, and having just returned from a ground-breaking tour of the Soviet Union in late 1934 – one of the first American violinists to tour there. By then, Burgin had long since become a US citizen, solidified his position as concertmaster of the BSO and had recently been named assistant conductor. Then, in March, 1935 their respective musical orbits moved significantly closer when Posselt was preparing to play the Tchaikovsky Violin Concerto in Boston, her first appearance with the BSO and Koussevitzky.

In her eighty-third year, Posselt still would vividly recall the beginning of her and Burgin's relationship: "It was my first time with the Boston Symphony and I was still in my twenties. Koussevitzky was Russian, and world famous, and they said at that time he was a terror; I don't know if he was or not, but I was nervous. So, I decided to call Burgin up, - I didn't know him at all but he had the reputation of having a calming influence on Koussevitzky,

- and ask if he would have a few minutes to listen to some of the Tchaikovsky because, after all [...] . He said he would be delighted to. So I went to his house in Jamaica Plain with my pianist, Mary Tower, and I played and I played and he just stood there, smiling. When I finished playing, he said, "I think it's wonderful, I don't know what you're so worried about." I said, "I don't know if Koussevitzky will like this interpretation," and he said, "Anybody will love that interpretation. If you can play it like that, it's marvelous." And oh, that gave me so much confidence, I'll never forget that."

Boston concertgoers got their first view of an unexpected interaction between Burgin and Posselt during the performance of the Tchaikovsky, on Monday evening, March 25th. As reported the next day by Warren Story Smith in *The Boston Post,* it went like this: Miss Posselt's "playing last evening provoked applause that was more than commendation, applause that deserved the overworked characterization, enthusiastic. From Dr. Koussevitzky and his orchestra she received generous and eloquent support, *and from at least one member of it a very special service. In the course of the first movement a hair of Miss Posselt's bow became unloosened at one end and hung trailing down until Mr. Burgin arose from the concert master's chair and snapped it off while Miss Posselt in apparent unconcern continued her performance.*" [Italics mine: DLB]

The day after the concert, the orchestra's bass clarinetist, Boaz Piller, a long-time friend and supporter of Posselt's, invited Ruth for tea, and she said, continuing her story: "'Why don't you ask Richard Burgin, too, he was so nice to me.' Piller replied, 'Oh, I could ask him but he probably won't come, he doesn't like women, he thinks they're stupid.' But I said, 'I don't think he thinks I'm stupid, why don't you ask him?' So he did ask him, and Richard said he'd love to come. He already had a little yen for me, I think. Because we used to have tea after that, just he and I, whenever I was in Boston and we just talked back and forth, back and forth. I don't know, there seemed to be always something interesting to discuss. He could talk about European history, politics, mythology, he spoke four or five languages. I don't know, I was sort of captivated by all that."

The relationship developed slowly, from a collegial to a more personal friendship, then into a romance and finally, it blossomed into love. The moment that determined their future seems to have taken place at Burgin's house on Saturday, December 4, 1937, judging from a letter from him to her dated the following Monday: "Darling Ruth, Since you left me last Saturday I am in an exalted state of mind. Those wonderful words you spoke to me that afternoon are still ringing in my ears. They made me feel so sublimely happy that it seems like a dream. You see, sweetheart, for so many years I have been daydreaming about you that it seems hard to believe that this vision has turned into reality. I love you I love you I love you forever. Richard."

Boston was quite a prudish town back in the 1930's. It did not take long for the Burgin – Posselt "friendship" to become a favorite subject of "talk" in the society circles which patronized classical music, young virtuosos, and the BSO in the city. As Ruth told the story of how they came to get married, it happened like this: "Well, we couldn't stay apart. We used to stay together longer and longer. We'd have dinner, and we'd talk, and we hated to leave each other, you know, and once he brought me home, it was about 1:30 a.m., we parked the car in front of my house, and we were doing whatever we were doing, and then a police car came down the street, stopped, and flashed the light in the car and said, turning to Richard, 'What's your name?' He said, 'Richard Burgin.'[9] 'Richard Burgin, and I suppose that's Charlie McCarthy over there.'

Then, somebody saw me leave Richard's apartment with him around twelve o' clock, and that started some rumors, and one elderly society matron who had known me for years said to her friend, 'You know, I wouldn't be surprised if Ruth Posselt and Richard Burgin were living in sin!' Somehow, it got to Koussevitzky and Koussevitzky told Richard. The memory still lingered of Monteux having been forced to leave his post with the Boston Symphony because it was revealed he was having an extramarital affair. And so, when Richard told me the gossip about us, he said, 'You know, we have to do something, either we have to get married or we can't see each other, or if we see each other, we have to get home at 9 o' clock.' So we decided to get married." They went about it in rather an offbeat way.

They were married on July 3, 1940 by a justice of the peace in West Stockbridge, Massachusetts. That's not very original, but the site of their marriage was – the justice of the peace also happened to be a car mechanic, and so the ceremony took place in his garage. The Burgin-Posselt conjugal and musical union began in a country gas station, presided over by the town clerk in his greasy overalls. Later in July they were given a wedding breakfast by Paul Hindemith, who played the Wedding March on the French horn as the other guests beat time on pots and pans. The marriage proved fruitful in many ways. In 1943 their first child, Diana, was born, and four years later, they had a son, Richard. Perhaps, in tune with the irony of the Burgin family line, neither of the concertmaster's children became a musician.

Unlike many women virtuosos, Posselt did not give up her career on the concert stage after marriage or having children. In fact, her husband was probably the most active supporter of her career, encouraging her not to give it up even when she herself leaned in that direction. In addition, from 1941 till 1962, Burgin and Posselt were often musical collaborators, giving over thirty joint performances – he conducting, she appearing as soloist - with the Boston Symphony, including the world premiere of the Dukelsky Violin Concerto in March 1943 and the first Tanglewood, and then Boston BSO performances of the Khatchaturian Violin Concerto in August 1954 and October 1955. In 1949, they made a tour of Finland, Norway and Poland. In the fifties, they played and recorded together with the Cambridge Early Music Society. Finally, they played together in the Florestan Quartet at Florida State University where they were both on the faculty (1960's and 1970's), and made appearances at other concert venues in the United States and Canada. In American concert and chamber performance as well as in musical education Burgin and Posselt made their mark as a highly acclaimed and appreciated musical pair who were "more than welcome when they appear[ed] with the Boston Symphony Orchestra." As noted of their 1958 joint performance in Providence, Posselt "was given an accompaniment which was perfectly balanced in relation to her artistic conception of the solo. This usually occurs when a Posselt-Burgin appearance is scheduled." (Providence, January 25, 1958)

At the end of *Memoralia* Part II, Burgin focuses attention on his teaching career. His method of teaching the violin was based on what he called a "problem solving approach," which required of the performer, whether teacher or student, that s/he understand the composer's intentions in the work at hand and through experimentation determine how best to realize those intentions. One of his students at FSU remembered that he gave "no set or pat formulas either to making a sound, or to technical things or to musical things." Rather, he engaged the student in "a search and a process [of looking] for solutions to problems, guided by basic principles."[10] Those "basic principles" were strong rhythm, accurate pitch, and sound phrasing. His approach to technique varied with the student, but it, too, involved the student in a problem-solving process rather than insisting on acceptance by the student of the teacher's, or any single solution. Two things he emphasized with all students were the study of Bach; and attaining a thorough knowledge of common finger patterns. In sum, Burgin focused on training his students "to be good orchestral players… He prepared people not to be stars but to be team players, to contribute in a strong way, but also to blend." (Quoted in Robertson)

When he was a younger man Burgin had a reputation for being rather irascible and impatient with his students, but he seems to have mellowed with age. According to Robertson, his students at FSU found him extremely kind and tactful: "He accepted you for what you were, and he was always encouraging, never demeaning. He didn't show favoritism, exalting some students and belittling others," recalled a student who went on to play in the Cincinnati and Chicago Symphonies. "He was intense in his desire to help all students fulfill their absolute potential. No other circumstances mattered, no matter if he were going to fly that night to conduct the Boston Symphony [during his first four years at FSU he commuted from Tallahassee to Boston to fulfill his duties as Associate Conductor]: if you were taking a lesson, that was the focus of his universe, giving…the very best lesson he could," commented another student who won a position in the Atlanta Symphony. (Quoted in Robertson).

Burgin insisted on constant practice. He surprised many of his students by himself practicing daily, both the pieces his students were studying and things he simply worked on for his own pleasure, like the Berg Violin Concerto. When asked by a student who came for his lesson why he was practicing the Berg, Burgin said, "'because I love the piece and it's a great thing to practice.'" (Robertson).

At this juncture, we have come full circle as the cycles of student- teacher interactions have a way of doing, renewing themselves almost eternally. In the matter of practicing, Burgin apparently never forgot the example of his first teacher back in Warsaw, Jacob Winiecky, who simply loved to practice, and asked to have young Richard come live with him for six months, so that the five-year old "prodigy" could watch his teacher practice and become infected with the art.

Yet, Burgin's kindness, devotion and total commitment to his students did not in any way keep him from, and possibly even led to, his being strict and demanding during lessons. Sometimes he employed a form of what we now call "tough love," as in the following instance:[11]

"I'll never forget the lesson Richard Burgin taught me about the importance of accurate intonation in shifts. We were working on the first movement of the Beethoven opus 18 C minor string quartet and I missed a perfect fourth second finger shift on the G string. [...] On my miss-step his youthful excitement came to an abrupt halt as he turned to me and demanded I play that shift three times perfect, slurred, starting down bow with a full bow, up and back, all three perfectly in tune. I made it through the first two but unfortunately, missed the third one. Then, he growled at me with his thick Russian accent, 'Do it nine times.' I don't remember which one of those I missed, but at that point, he dropped his score on a chair quite forcefully and said, 'Now you do it twenty seven times,' and walked away. I do remember his short, rather stocky figure in baggy pants and a yellowing white short sleeve shirt walking away from us as we sat looking at each other, surprised and frozen for a few seconds. I quickly focused on my shift, my quartet members became busy with their 'dirty laundry,' and on his return, he looked at me and said, 'Now you play it three times perfect.' I had composed myself and thank goodness my accuracy was true, a smile returned to his face and we continued on."[12]

In the final analysis, Burgin seemed to agree with his "old teacher," Leopold Auer, that there really were no good or bad teachers, just good and bad students. Probably the greatest gift Burgin gave his students was his enthusiasm for and total immersion in the music he was performing or teaching. "The music was everything. It would have surprised him to get out of himself and see what we all thought of him. He never thought along those lines. He was very selfless, no ego-centrism whatsoever." (Quoted in Robertson) In return, his students rewarded him amply, I am sure, with their success in achieving positions in virtually all the leading orchestras in the United States, and in many cases, by becoming teachers themselves who to this day continue to discuss, amend and pass on to their students his suggestions to them of "problem-solving techniques." It is possible that namely as a teacher Richard Burgin made, and continues to make, his most lasting and truly living contribution to music. As one of his conducting students at the International Conducting Symposium in Jacksonville (May 1975) wrote to him: "You are an outstanding musician, teacher and human being. For the first time in my life I have seen it all in one person. [...] There is a lot to learn about conducting and a good deal of it is not music! But, from you, one can learn all."

MEMORALIA PART I

As I am Antonius my city is Rome, as a man – the whole world.

-Marcus Aurelius

[Richard Burgin was born on Sept 28/Oct 10, 1892 in Siedlice, a town with a large Jewish population 55 miles southeast of Warsaw in Russian Poland. He was the first of seven children born to his Russian-Jewish petit bourgeois parents who were first cousins. Richard's father, Moisey (Movsha), born in 1868 in Vilnius, was a sign painter and small-businessman and his mother, Ronia (Raska) Krzyzowska (b. 1870) was a factory worker and political activist before her marriage in 1892. Richard's father was a music lover, and according to family tradition, Moisey became aware of Richard's talent when, at a Warsaw concert they attended together, a member of the audience pointed out to him how the four or five-year-old boy sitting on his lap, was waving his arms in perfect time to the music. The die was cast, apparently. Richard began studying the violin, first with Jakob Winetzki, a member of the Warsaw Philharmonic's first violin section, then with the great virtuoso Izydor Lotto (ca. 1840-ca. 1936), thirdly, in Berlin, with Josef Joachim and his assistant, Carl Markees, and finally, with Leopold Auer at the St. Petersburg Conservatory (1908-1912).]

BEGINNINGS 1897-1908:
WINETZKY, LOTTO, MARKEES, JOACHIM

As far as anyone has been able to determine there were no musicians on either side of my family, going back for several generations.[13] My father was the dominant influence in my early life. He was a small businessman in Warsaw; he had a house painting business with a couple of workers. He also was very sociable and loved to play cards – once I remember, he had a toothache and had to go to the dentist. When he got there, the ache didn't seem so bad and since the dentist also liked cards they sat down for a game or two. They both got so involved that they played through the whole afternoon and my father came home for dinner with his tooth still aching.

But in addition to cards, my father loved music, loved it passionately. He would go to every concert he could and he would take me with him. Perhaps, he saw something in me that conveyed to him that I would love music also. At any rate, my violin studies started very early in my life. I'm very poor on dates, but I think I was about five and a half years old. I do remember my first teacher. He was a very kind and warm person, a member of the Warsaw Philharmonic, which at that time had a very good reputation. It was called the pride of Poland. I remember his name – Winetzky. I think he may have come to the United States much later in his life, I think somebody did tell me that he did, but I didn't see him although I wanted to, very much.

I liked him very much. And he liked me too, to such a point that he insisted I study with him in his house. He was not married; he had an old mother. He was a hard worker, he loved to practice. And he prevailed upon my parents, although he lived in the same town, to let me stay with him so he could teach me practically every day. He wanted me very much, and I liked him. So, I spent about six months in his apartment in spite of the fact that my parents lived in the same town. I had from him some of the advantages that Heifetz had from his own father, except that I am not Heifetz, and he probably was not Heifetz's father.

Winetzky felt he could do much more with me if I were in constant contact with him, and he also liked the fact that I could listen to him practice. He loved to practice. He could play for hours. He did nothing but attend his rehearsals and concerts and whenever he had the time, then he practiced. He also devoted a great deal of time to me. I think I was with him for at least three years.

Then, for some reason, maybe Winetzky left town or something like that, I got another teacher, whom I didn't like very much and whom my father absolutely hated. That was because he once saw him hit my hand when I played a note too sharp or too flat. My father couldn't stand seeing anybody hurting a young child. That made him wild. Once, it even happened he got into a real fight with a complete stranger on the street when he saw him hit his own child. So my second teacher did not last very long, only about six months. My father scolded him asking how he had dared to hit me although it wasn't very painful. But my father didn't approve of that at all.

When I was about nine, I got my third teacher, Izydor Lotto, the great virtuoso who had toured all over Europe. He was a pupil of Massart, the teacher of Wieniawski and of everybody who was anybody at that time, when, you know, everybody had to go and study with Massart. He in turn was a Kreutzer pupil, and he was an institution, really, because his pupils became famous all over the world: Vieuxtemps, Wieniawski, and all the famous names in Russia, in violin, all the virtuosi.

After traveling extensively, Lotto became professor at the Strasbourg Conservatory for many years, but eventually he returned to his home town, Warsaw. I don't know why he gave up traveling as a soloist – there were rumors that he had a nervous breakdown at one time. But if there was any truth to them, I don't know. Later, when I played for Joachim, he asked me whom I had studied with. He knew Lotto and asked me so many questions about him and his health that I had the feeling he was wondering whether he was still well.

Anyway, Lotto retired from the stage and lived in Warsaw. I know he was married and also had one son. Evidently he had saved up some money and didn't have to work too hard. He lived very modestly and occupied himself exclusively with playing violin for his own pleasure and composing for his own pleasure, too, although one or two of his pieces were published. Of course, it didn't take very long for young talented violinists in Poland to find out that he was there and many of them studied with Lotto, among them Bronislaw Huberman. Lotto was his first great teacher as a youngster. That was maybe ten or fifteen years before me. Joseph Achron, an extraordinary violinist, with phenomenal facility, also studied with Lotto and dedicated his *Suite Ancienne* to him. And Lotto was very proud of him because he loved students who could compose, the most important thing was to compose.

Achron also later studied with Leopold Auer and after the St. Petersburg Conservatory he devoted himself entirely to composition. He became one of the members of the group of young Russian-Jewish composers who were very interested in ethnographic material for their musical ideas. Many of Achron's things were published in Germany where there was general interest in traditional Jewish songs, some of which dated back to the time the Jews were thrown out of Spain, others of which were created in Poland.

Well, to get back to Lotto. He did not teach at the conservatory, he taught only privately. And from our point of view today, he was a very strange teacher. He would never have more than one pupil a day because it took him a whole day to live with a pupil. You would come in the morning and you would play all kinds of things for him, you would have lunch, then another lesson, and before dinner, you would give a concert. His wife was the audience, and you had to go through the whole procedure of a concert. You would come in from another room, from "the green room," and he would be the orchestra. You would tune up, and he would accompany you on the violin. That's how you would perform your program. Such things are now inconceivable. Although he had other pupils, we never met because Lotto never taught two pupils on the same day. When Raphael Bronstein, the well-known teacher, was my fellow student at the St. Petersburg Conservatory, it was only then I found out he had been a student of Lotto's too, and at exactly the same time as me! But he had his lesson on a different day.

Lotto's approach to music, like that of many French musicians who were educated in the Massart school, was very pictorial. There was always a story connected with anything you played whether it was Wieniawski's *La Legende* or a Vieuxtemps Concerto, or something by Sarasate. And you had to live the story, experience it, be involved. And he did succeed in getting you to do that.

I admired and loved Lotto very much both for his attitude and his phenomenal ability. He did not try, however, to explain things. Perhaps he could not. But he could demonstrate. Everything he wanted you to do was actually demonstrated to perfection by him. He was a phenomenal violinist who could pick up his instrument and play anything he wanted, the way he wanted to. Having come out of the Massart school, he had a lot to offer. But all you as his pupil could do, was to try to imitate him the best you could.

Later, I began to reflect upon Lotto's teaching and I sometimes wondered whether great performers, or people who have great natural ability, are necessarily the best teachers because, they have nothing to struggle with. Things come too easily to them. They cannot put themselves in the situation of somebody who is just an ordinary mortal, just an ordinary musician who is not trying to achieve immortality. They cannot understand what bothers such ordinary mortals. All they can do is demonstrate: "Here you are. That's how you do it!"

So, very often with Lotto I had to practice or play, or attempt to play, things which were way beyond my capacity. There were only two teaching "books" for him, one he labeled *Etudes* (that was Kreutzer) and the other was *Caprices* (Paganini). He didn't know about anything else in between. Kreutzer was the book one practiced every day and Paganini was the ultimate. Many Paganini caprices were way beyond me at that time, and they are still way beyond me!

By the age of about nine I had progressed sufficiently so that a decision had to be made about my future. My parents felt that I had talent but were worried about the question of how I was to make a living. The Jews were very restricted. They could not work professionally in Russia outside of Poland unless they possessed a diploma from a Russian university and for musicians, only "Rubenstein's diploma" would do, either from the conservatory in Moscow or St. Petersburg. So it was very important for every Jew to get into the university, or if he was an aspiring musician, into the conservatory and get a degree in order to have an opportunity to go out of their small circle of activity in Poland. My parents debated whether they should send me to St. Petersburg – hoping that I would be accepted there as a student of Auer – or to Berlin, which was then the center of the musical world. Everybody knew about the Berlin Conservatory (Hochschule für Musik) and Joachim, the violinist, who was a great artist. Perhaps, my parents thought, I could get in there. It was a toss-up in a way, but in any event, my parents were so poor they couldn't possibly pay, or help me out financially.

First, my father took me to St. Petersburg where I played for Auer and he was willing to accept me. Then, Auer also paid a visit to my father in Warsaw, and that was when my parents had to make a decision. I had nothing to say because I didn't know anything. My father consulted other people. Somehow, Berlin sounded much more glamorous then than St. Petersburg although St. Petersburg really was more practical from the point of view of being a Jew. A Russian diploma would have given me the opportunity to work in other Russian cities whereas a diploma from Berlin was not recognized – that was a "foreign" education. But my father decided for me to go to Berlin, nevertheless.

Of course, I was too young for the Hochschule. My father, who occasionally had to go to Berlin on business, decided to take me with him on one of his trips, hoping that somebody would find a way of having Joachim listen to me. This was in 1902 just before my tenth birthday. I even have a letter of Joachim's that he wrote after listening to me. I don't care much for *memoralia*, but this letter I do value.

I played the Vieuxtemps Concerto No. 4 in d minor. To me, Joachim was already an elderly man. Now, of course, I wouldn't say "elderly" – he was only 70 years old. He was then director of the Hochschule für Musik and not teaching anymore, but he listened to me. And he told my father that he would be very happy to take me. My father said, of course, that would be wonderful only he didn't know where he could find the money. Joachim replied, "Don't worry, I will see to it that he's well-provided-for." And he got some funds, and I stayed with him. My father made arrangements for me to live with my mother's relatives in Berlin. It was a happy two years. There were children of my age and I did well with my music.

Joachim had his assistant, Karl Markees, one of the teachers at the Hochschule, work with me. Every two or three weeks I would play for Joachim himself and afterwards, he would discuss my progress with Markees. I liked Joachim very much. He was wonderful to me, he just liked me, and he played cards with me. He loved to play cards; after he listened to me play, we would have a game of cards because I was very good at card games. And he enjoyed playing with me.

Of course, at that age I already began to have reactions to my teachers, very definite reactions. And I must say I found Markees rather dull. He was very pedantic, a taskmaster. I'm sure he was a very good teacher, just very scholastic. For instance, for three months, every day, I had to practice an E major Prelude of the sonata by Bach in a very strange way to develop my wrist crossing strings. He insisted that I hold my right hand close to a chair so that I wouldn't move it and be forced to bow only with my wrist and bending my fingers. Evidently, that was on Joachim's instructions, to develop the flexibility of my right hand which he probably thought was a little stiff.

Outside of Bach, the things I studied included etudes and scales, the standard works, and Kreutzer, which I had studied with Lotto. Also, the Spohr Concerto No. 2 in d minor, a beautiful work by the way, which I liked. But Markees's teaching was an entirely different world from Lotto's, an entirely different approach. When I think back now, I appreciate much more what Markees tried to accomplish. Whether I achieved that I don't know. I'm not a judge of myself. But he did try to make me develop muscles which were completely unused and to use the bow more with my fingers and wrist than with my forearm as a whole. And I think that being very strict about everything instills a certain kind of discipline which is very useful to anyone.

I stayed in Berlin for two years, and I was very well taken care of. Then came the Revolution, in 1905, the first big revolution. And things got very, very bad in Poland, very bad. The family was getting bigger and bigger and my father just couldn't make a living. He decided to immigrate to America and take me with him. He left the other children with my mother, hoping that later, he could make enough money to bring them across. Like every Jew in Russia he had relatives in America, his own brother [Leib] and his wife's brother.

So my father and I came to New York and spent almost two years here. But my father could not get used to the American way of life. First of all, probably, because in Warsaw he was his own boss. He had a couple of workers who worked with him, but he was the boss. Here, he couldn't even think of being the boss, he had to work for somebody else, and that hurt him. So, in general, life in America did not appeal to him.

He didn't have to worry about me because I was accepted at the German Conservatory of Music in New York. They helped me and I played there as a child prodigy, which I practically was. Of course, they were connected with the Männergesangverein, a very popular German choral society and also with the Liederkranz Society. I also played solos, all kinds of small pieces, with the

Liederkranz, for which they paid small fees. Besides playing with the Gesangverein, my first job as a youngster was to play with a group of very wealthy amateurs. The leader of this amateur group was a certain Filscheimer, a very wealthy man who loved to play chamber music. The group needed a violinist and somebody recommended me although I can not say that I really came recommended since I was only about 13 or 14 years old. But I was a very good reader. I love chamber music, quartets, and I actually learned the chamber music repertoire from those amateurs. They paid me, I think it was $5. an evening for about three or four hours, plus a meal, a wonderful meal.

But my father just could not adjust to life in America and when the revolution was over, he decided we'd go home. He couldn't bring over my mother and the other children, and it was the only way out. But then there was the question, what to do with me? I was already a young man, almost sixteen. Out of desperation, I, or my father, wrote to Auer who was in London at that time. He used to go always in the summer, in May and June, after the closing of the season, to teach in London. He'd return to Russia in October. My father asked Auer whether he would still accept me; mind you, already three years had passed since I played for him. We got a letter back from him and he said, 'Yes, I remember how he played for me in St. Petersburg. If he doesn't play any worse, I will accept him. But in order to find out, you will have to bring him to England and play for me there.' I thought that actually made sense since he couldn't just accept me.

And the ship we went back on, in May 1908, was the *Lusitania*. We landed in Liverpool and went to London and I played for him and he said, "All right!" I remember I played the Reger Sonata, solo sonata, because that's what I got to know in New York. Reger was then the new composer. He wrote eleven sonatas, seven in one opus and four earlier. He was very prolific. Well, that's how I got to St. Petersburg. That was an entirely different world, and I was also a different young man. I was in St. Petersburg for four years.

THE ST. PETERSBURG CONSERVATORY 1908-1914. LEOPOLD AUER

[When Richard Burgin entered the St. Petersburg Conservatory in 1908 he had already decided to forego the career of a virtuoso and strive for a concertmaster's position. This second turning point seems to have originated during Richard's first visit to America (1906-08) from which he returned to enter Auer's class at St. Petersburg. One of his class mates, Wolf Graffman, later recalled "young Richard's excitement when he returned from the United States. ... Everyone clustered around to hear his tales of the New World. 'And now I know exactly what I want to do for the rest of my life!' Richard announced. He then surprised his audience by elucidating, 'I want to be the concertmaster of the Boston Symphony Orchestra.'" Gary Graffman, concert pianist, from whose memoirs this anecdote comes, sums up: "For a long, long time – throughout the Boston Symphony's golden years under Koussevitzky and Munch – he had his wish, and I think he was a truly happy man. ... I [took] comfort for many years in the joyful serenity of Richard Burgin's presence behind me in the concertmaster's chair whenever I played in Boston."[14] After graduating with the Large Silver Medal in 1912, Burgin was accepted for graduate study in theory and composition with Alexander Glazunov. At the same time he took up his first concertmaster's post in Helsingfors under the direction of Georg Schnéevoigt.]

As a Jew, once I had been accepted by the Conservatory, I had the right to live in the city. My family was allowed to visit but only for a day or two without registering with the police. You could get a permit to stay there several days or even a week if it was on business, but then you had to leave. It was a ghetto. It was a ghetto within a ghetto. Of course, there were many Jews who were already living there, in Russia. And Jews from somewhere else who had served twenty five years in the army were also excluded from the restrictions. If you had devoted twenty five years of your life to Russia, then you were allowed to die there. But a person from outside of Russia proper, whose life was devoted to intellectual activity or art, he had to have a Russian diploma which proved he had the required education or could read and write, which was not true of all the Russians at that time.

I lived at first in various small apartments[15] with my uncle – my father's youngest brother who was just a few years older than me – who was an engineering student. We were always very poor and for weeks at a time we would eat only rolls and tea, without sugar, which was a luxury. We used to share a sugar cube, pass it around the table, each person would hold it up to the bottom of the glass as he took a swallow. We called this drinking tea *with sugar in sight*.

When I came to the conservatory very interesting things were going on. My first recollection of performing a new work dates back to the performance of Rimsky-Korsakov's "The Golden Cockerel" by the student orchestra at the conservatory. Although it was a student orchestra, it was equal to any professional orchestra because they had wonderful players in all sections. The conductor was Cherepnin, the composer and professor, who also conducted the regular opera in certain works. Cherepnin was assigned to put on the first performance of "The Golden Cockerel" with the conservatory orchestra right after Rimsky Korsakov's death (in 1908).

I have a very vivid recollection of this performance because the orchestra was very, very carefully prepared. There was a committee of composers in charge which included Glazunov and Shteinberg and all those who were either students of Korsakov, or had worked with him and knew him well. The production was the result of common discussion and agreement among the members of the committee; everybody had something to say or explain to Cherepnin. We rehearsed very long and carefully for a long period of time. Rimsky-Korsakov was highly regarded in Russia; I would say that after Tchaikovsky, he was considered *the* foremost Russian composer so the first performance of his last big work was a very big thing. All of us felt that we were participating in a very, very important musical event. At least, I personally felt that way.

I recall an amusing incident when I was a student at the conservatory. We were all very poor youngsters, mostly very poor. To buy music meant a sacrifice, you ate less for a couple of days in order to afford it and the prices were not anywhere near where they are now. So everybody had to borrow music until he saved enough money to buy it. Around the time of my second year there I decided I would like to study the Beethoven Concerto with Auer. The only copy I had was an edition by Helmesburg that I had somehow acquired when I was in Berlin though I had never studied it then because I was too young. Of course, the Beethoven Concerto was edited by every violinist who was known for something, but I wanted to look at Joachim's edition.

We had a very fine music library at the conservatory which was at the disposal of students. However, the head librarian was a real terror. He *hated* to give out music. To him, the printed score was an idol. If you took it in your hands, for him it was just a desecration of something holy. He was also of German descent, a bookworm, and unfortunately, he had a hunchback. Of course, it didn't take very long for the students to find a nickname for him. He was known among us as "the diminished fifth." I had one advantage over my colleagues in that I spoke German fluently although with him I had to speak Russian because that was a Russian conservatory. But he knew that I could speak German and therefore, being of German descent, he dealt with me a little more humanely than with all the others whom he considered "just riff-raff."

I went to the library and he said, "What do you want?" I said, "I'd like to get a copy of the Beethoven Concerto edited by Joachim." He said, "You mean to tell me you don't have a copy of the Beethoven Concerto and you want to study that? You don't own a copy?" "I do own a copy," I explained, "but I'd like to get the Joachim edition because I can't afford to buy another copy." "For what purpose do you want the Joachim edition? It's still the same Beethoven Concerto." I said, "Because I'd like to know about phrasing, fingering, bowing, you know, like every regular student of my age, I'm interested in bowing. It's not the music because the music is there." And he said, "Let me tell you that *any* violinist who is not capable of finding the fingering and bowing should not be playing the Beethoven Concerto." He gave it to me, finally.

But later, in retrospect, I thought there was something to what he said because he was trying to tell me that I was trying to play the bowing and fingering of the notes rather than trying to play the Beethoven concerto. I should first have known how I wanted it to sound and then I would find the fingering and bowing that would suit me. He was absolutely right. That dried-up hunchback who hated to distribute music really struck it right.

I was part of an excellent class at the Conservatory. Many of my fellow students have become very famous and deserve to be. But Auer's approach was just the opposite from Lotto's. It was class instruction. You played individually and usually you could spend about 20 to 25 minutes playing whatever you had prepared. Everyone was present unless he had a very good reason not to be. Not that attendance was obligatory, but it was an established tradition because that's the way we learned, from each other, by listening to each other. And actually, as far as I personally was concerned, that's the only thing I did. I learned not so much from Auer as I learned from my colleagues, listening to them.

Of course, you have an entirely different perception about the quality and the method of teaching when you are actually taking lessons than when you consider how you were taught in retrospect, and you really don't know which is the truer presentation of the facts because you can't help being influenced by your *own* ideas and by the time, by history, and by what has happened, and a great deal has been discovered since then. I won't even try to be objective since it's impossible. But one thing I always tell *my* pupils. One thing is definitely certain: No composer demands the impossible. It's only that all indications in music are relative. Everything is possible one way or other, you try to come as close to it as you can.

One thing about the Conservatory that I remember, we all had a terrific respect for the teachers, almost like it is now in Japan (early 1970s). The teacher was everything. Nobody dared to say anything against the teacher even when it was quite evident he was wrong. You could later discuss with your colleagues what was wrong with the situation, but not in class, to the teacher's face.

Yet, I must give Auer his due for one thing: he had terrific respect for the printed letter of the score. You didn't dare to change the letter of the composer. And this attitude is helpful to a student who is still young, in order to discipline him self and acquire this respect. That is also very important, to not be a freelancer all the time. So this, I must say, was a great asset in Auer's approach to which, as I recall, he made only one exception, and that was in his relation to Heifetz.

Heifetz's father, from whom he learned a great deal, was at the same time his greatest enemy, or at least, that's what he felt. He had a terrible attitude to his father who was, indeed, the ideal schoolmaster. His strict attitude to the printed word, that one doesn't dare to change anything that's printed, would seem to coincide perfectly with what Auer demanded from his pupils. But I recall one time, the only one, when this proved not to be the case. It happened at a private lesson at which I was present during the summer after I had already graduated (1912). Heifetz was playing for Auer an insignificant piece by Kreisler. In one of the variations, there was a descending scale from the high D, and Heifetz, who possessed a beautiful flying staccato, played it staccato instead of legato, as printed. The piece was new to Auer, so he just listened and you could see by the smile on his face that he enjoyed it. But Heifetz's father was very upset. He reproached his son, "How dare you change what Kreisler, the great violinist, has written?" Then he turned to Auer, I remember distinctly, and said, "Professor, do you know that he played that scale staccato instead of legato?" And Auer replied, "It's wonderful! Let him do it. He can't do anything wrong." Thus, he himself admitted that when there is a genius of this kind, there is nothing to teach him.

I was sort of like a big brother to Heifetz when he first came to study with Auer, in my final years at the Conservatory. And he never forgot how I managed to intercede in his fights with his father. Once when Jascha was going to play this very important concert, - he was quite young, - and it came down to what he was going to wear and his father said, 'I want you to wear short pants, and a soft collar and a flowing necktie.' Heifetz said he would have none of that. He said, "I want to play with a stiff collar and I want to play in long trousers." And they fought and they fought. And Jascha finally said, 'I'm not going to play or if I have to play, I'm just going to play terribly.' So the father called me in. He said, 'Richard, you speak to him, he doesn't know what it's all about. He's a little boy and I want him to be a little boy.' And I said, 'Look, he may be a little boy but he doesn't play like a little boy and if he wants to wear long pants, I think he deserves to wear long pants.'

With the exception of Heifetz, Auer was a disciplinarian, but he was also a great artist. He was particularly wonderful in the quartet class, which took place on Friday mornings. Auer really loved his chamber music and his whole attitude was completely different. He wanted as many as possible to play. Since I loved chamber music too, I didn't need to be urged to attend the class and in fact, I never missed it. And there were of course others who enjoyed it. Yet many of my colleagues, who were virtuoso minded, regarded chamber music as a kind of obligation. Auer detested those who didn't come to quartet class, and they would pay for it, somehow. And in the class itself, he could get very mean. Once, one of my colleagues had his violin damaged when Auer threw the score at him. He had meant to hit him, but hit his violin instead, which resulted in a major repair job. He had become upset because the player had done something that from his point of view was musically absolutely incorrect.

Once, I remember, Auer directed his rage at me. My colleagues and I had prepared the Beethoven Opus 59, No. 1, a very difficult quartet, which I already knew. (I was already the established "educated musician" because I knew all those quartets – not *all* of them, not the late ones of Beethoven, but the opus 59 and 18 I knew.) So we were playing Opus 59, all very interested, and Auer was standing nearby at a table, completely absorbed in the music. He was just listening and looking at the score. Suddenly, at a very touching moment where the violin plays grace notes – insignificant embellishments, or so I thought at the time – suddenly his voice like thunder came at me from behind, "You carpenter! Carpenter!" In Russian, that was the worst thing a violinist could be, the lowest you could sink, professionally, when you could only saw wood. It's like saying in German, "Cobbler," although Hans Sachs was one. And of course, I looked up at Auer very innocently because I didn't know what he was referring to. I thought I was playing in time, playing the notes, and I just looked at him with an expression as if to say, 'What's wrong? What is it?' And then he glared at me, wanting to explain something, and all my colleagues had stopped playing too. Thunderous words came down on me, just as if he was hitting me from the back saying, "Do you know what you are playing? Those are tears! Those are tears! He is crying, here." Evidently, he was convinced the music depicted some specific feelings or emotions at that point.

But, chamber music was where Auer really gave you the feeling you had an artist with you. There isn't much I can say about the classes, though. One played the Tchaikovsky Concerto, then another would play it, and it was merely a question, when it was your turn to play the Tchaikovsky, of 'what can I do that won't be the same as my colleagues have done and that will make sense?' Because everything had been explored already, a certain tradition had developed, and everyone played more or less the same, except for little details. Some students developed a certain specialty. There was a pupil – I don't even remember his name – who would come to class only about twice a year. And whenever he played, he played the E major Vieuxtemps concerto, because he had an extraordinary staccato. There was nobody who could play staccato like him. And Auer would derive a great deal of pleasure listening to him play staccato. When he'd get to a point in the last movement, where it's full of staccato up and down scales, Auer would say, "Will you try the staccato at the frog? Down bow?" He'd play it both ways and Auer was always astonished. It was something he never could do. He never had the staccato. And that staccato was that student's specialty. But Auer got wise to him and said, "Well, it's nice of you to come again, but when will you play another piece?" For two years he had forgiven him because he enjoyed listening. That student then disappeared completely from the musical horizon.

It was only in the chamber music class that you felt you really had an artist in Auer. And he remained an artist well into older age. I heard him play the Tchaikovsky concerto, which he loved, when he was already in his sixties. He played it sitting down, and in this particular performance, I especially recall his presence of mind. In the slow movement, the interlude between the opening part and the e flat major section, where the orchestra plays with the soloist the main subject, which is then imitated by the flute, at that moment the flute did not enter. Auer began to play the flute part and then the flutist came in. There is an example of a wonderful presence of mind which also illustrates that Auer was an old-time musician, who depended much more on his ear than on the score. It's a well-known fact that he sometimes conducted from the violin part rather than from the score even though he knew the score all right.

My own relationship with Auer was, of course, strictly professional. When I was his student, he had a certain respect for me because I was the one who would bring to class works by composers who were not very well known. For instance, I played and brought to class Sinding's Third Concerto, which nobody knew about. Auer was always interested even if he didn't know the piece. He was interested in what was being written outside of Russia.

Auer did show favoritism and express opinions about his students, but it was very difficult to say why he had the feelings he did, at least at the time when I studied with him myself. In general, he dealt with all students who were more or less talented with the best of intentions. It was only when a student didn't quite come up to his expectations that he became very antagonistic, gradually, like a disappointed father. At the same time, when he had a genius like Heifetz, he did not even teach him. He just derived great pleasure from listening to him.

Auer liked Mischa Piastro, a very promising violinist, very, very much. He had very great hopes that Mischa would succeed in making a career. Auer still had his connections with the German impresarios. He wrote a letter strongly suggesting that they give Mischa a chance in Berlin since at that time nothing counted but Berlin. If you wanted a career as a soloist, you had to go to Berlin and give a recital or a concert.

Mischa played in Berlin one year after Jascha had made his debut there in 1912. When he came back he told me, "You know, Richard, something has happened in the world of music. When Jascha played there, he made such a sensation as a child prodigy that after the concert all the married couples in the audience could do was to run home and see whether they could not make another baby."

Mischa was nice but sometimes he had moods. I think he became very disappointed in life that he really didn't do what he hoped he could do. He could have, but it didn't turn out that way for him. After Heifetz it became harder for virtuosos. But I think that's life. It gets harder and harder.

As to Auer's opinion on the relations between students and teachers, I remember another remark he made when we met outside of Russia during the Revolution.[16] I asked him about several of my colleagues who had stayed in Russia after I left. He gave me all the news and also made a remark which has stuck in my memory. On one hand, he expressed disappointment with some of the students he had had who didn't quite live up to his expectations; and on the other hand, he praised others who did very well after they left the conservatory. These reflections led him to make the following comment: "It seems that there are no good or bad teachers; there are only good or bad pupils because while they are studying, they are all promising to one degree or another, but the moment they leave the teacher, some of them get better and others get worse." He had concluded that it all came down to whether the student was talented or not talented.

That may have been an oversimplification, but the fact remains that Leopold Auer had been a member of the faculty of the St. Petersburg Conservatory, the concertmaster of the ballet, and very active as a soloist for roughly 20 years and it had hardly occurred to anybody to study necessarily with him because he was famous as a teacher. During all that time he was highly regarded as a violinist, but he was not what you would call a famous teacher until he got a young boy, a child prodigy, Elman, who really made him famous. So it isn't the teacher who makes a student famous, but the student who makes the teacher famous. After Elman became world famous, violinists flocked to the conservatory to study with Auer not because it happened to be the best conservatory at the time, but because he had been Elman's teacher. So it is Elman who made Auer famous. And Auer's remark that there are no good or bad teachers, only good or bad pupils is not only correct, but very modest in that he did not see himself as an exception.

Although my main professional activity started after I had graduated from the conservatory (1912), I did have engagements and experience as an orchestral musician, concertmaster and soloist while I was still a student. In the winter we would occasionally get a request to participate in Koussevitzky's orchestra when they played in St. Petersburg and needed extra people (he brought his orchestra from Moscow). I remember playing in his orchestra for a performance of Scriabin's Third Symphony, which was then a new piece, and *Prometheus* too, and a performance of Mahler's Fourth Symphony. The Mahler, which was very new, made an indelible impression on me. Since that time I became crazy about Mahler. Nobody existed for me but Mahler, especially the Fourth Symphony. So in the winter occasionally we would get to know newer works.

Also, every year, in Petersburg, it was traditional to perform Bach's St. Matthew Passion in German. An orchestra was engaged specially for this annual event. The conductor there liked me and hired me to be concertmaster. I think I have played the St. Matthew Passion more often than any other work because it was always a "must" in all the cities I happened to be in, especially Protestant cities.

* * * * *

While still a student at the conservatory I also got my first professional chamber music experience. As I already said, because of what I had learned of the repertoire from playing with those amateur musicians in New York, I was considered by my colleagues at the conservatory the only one who actually *knew* all those quartets we prepared in class. Well, the Piastro brothers, Mischa and Josef (pseudonym Borissoff), had a quartet (I don't remember who the cellist and violist were). When Mischa went to Berlin, his brother was left without a violinist and wanted to continue the quartet. He asked me whether I'd like to join his quartet. I was very pleased because I had great respect for him, and also, of course, for Mischa, whom I loved very much. Since I was still a student, I thought it was very nice of him to select me. I played second violin with him in the quartet for the whole season. And then, we lost contact with each other because of the war, and then everyone leaving Russia after the Revolution. Borissoff, like many émigrés, went East, and via Manchuria eventually came to the United States. I went west after leaving Russia.

Many, many years later, after a BSO concert I conducted which was broadcast, I got a letter from Borissoff filled with compliments for my conducting. It was then that I recalled all our work together with the quartet. He was a very nice person.

During the summers when classes were over, the conservatory students usually got jobs playing in summer orchestras. We earned our income for the rest of the year by playing in these orchestras, which could only exist because of the fact that the students were free and eager to make some money. The summer repertoire was of course not as variegated as in the winter. It inclined to the popular, to works which were considered accessible to an audience made up primarily of vacationers. In the summer, it was the standard repertoire, and sometimes lighter music, and ballet music. "Swan Lake", for instance, was an important number. In the winter, no regular symphony orchestra would play it, - not that they didn't think it was worthy of them, - but because it was the special province of the ballet orchestra. As a matter of fact, a little before the time I came to Russia, and even while I was there, the ballet was *the* orchestra in St. Petersburg, and the concertmaster of the ballet was *the* important position in music. Both Vieuxtemps and Wieniawski held that position. And Auer came to Petersburg primarily as concertmaster of the ballet. That was his main source of income.

In 1911 I started as a concertmaster during the summers while I was still at the conservatory; I was in an orchestra near Kharkov. In 1913 when I was a graduate student, I played in Rostov on Don, and the following summer, I played at Pavlovsk near St. Petersburg, and I was also concertmaster of the Warsaw Philharmonic in their summer concerts in Riga. The demands on the concertmaster in Riga were considerable. Every week you had to play a new major work which was quite an experience. Everything I had learned the preceding year I would have to play with the orchestra during the summer season.

Speaking of Riga I can't help recalling an amusing incident that happened there with Misha Piastro. He had a facility like nobody and he had a specialty which nobody else could do the way he did it. He was the only violinist I heard who played Wieniawski's *Carnival Russe* with a special sort of trill. The piece, of course, is a theme with variations. In one of the variations there is a descending scale from the high G written in eighth notes. Suk played it in trills, and everyone else did the same. But Piastro, instead of trills, made a tremolo, at the tip of the bow, in a way no one had ever heard. It was like an electric buzz. He did it with a completely stiff arm, b-r-r-r-r-r. No trill could sound like that because it had the effect of a percussion instrument, almost a snare drum. That was Piastro's "specialty".

It happened that Carl Flesch, the well-known teacher and author of textbooks on how to play the violin, heard Piastro play his 'electric buzz'. That was at a summer concert in Riga where Flesch was appearing as a soloist in the Brahms concerto. The conductor of the orchestra, in which Piastro, still a student, was playing, told him, "You should play something for Flesch, he's an established great artist," and Mischa said, "Sure, I will." So he played for Flesch who was very impressed and then Piastro played his special tremolo. And for Flesch that was an eye-opener. Basically, Flesch was a virtuoso violinist whom tricks interested more than anything else. Although he claimed he was doing music, what he really was interested in was how to do those tricks. And Flesch decided to find out for himself how to do that electric buzz because Mischa couldn't explain it to him. He didn't know himself how he did it. And Flesch probably practiced all afternoon to see whether he could imitate Piastro's tremolo and it affected his arm so that when he played the concerto in the evening, he could hardly move his arm. And Mischa would get such a kick out of telling that story.

Flesch, by the way, was a very nice person. But he was one of those virtuosi who achieved success through sheer will power and labor. They were not 'naturals', really, they worked hard. Even Szigetti was not built to be a violinist, but he had so much intelligence and so much perseverance as well as musical background and talent that he was able to make a career as a virtuoso. He was called the violinist's violinist. And he was a very gifted, extraordinary man. So Flesch really achieved his success through sheer perseverance, and, I think he was an excellent teacher. He really made a study of violin playing, as much as it is possible to study such a thing, and those who studied with him spoke very highly of him. I knew him pretty well, not as a teacher, but I met him several times and we spoke. He was a very educated man.

At the conservatory, well, actually after I graduated, - I stayed on for graduate work in harmony and counterpoint, - I studied composition with Glazunov. As everyone knows, he used to love to drink and after a concert he would often get pretty drunk, and sometimes had a hard time finding his way home. Well once, his mother came to me and begged me, "Please, take care of my son, he likes to drink." And after that, when I was with him and we had left the restaurant or tavern where he had been drinking, we would go to the tram stop and, he was so drunk, I would literally have to push him on to the tram, and tell the driver where to let him off.

PROFESSIONAL ACTIVITY IN RUSSIA
AND SCANDINAVIA (1912-1920)

[In addition to Burgin's first concertmastership in the Helsingfors Symphony Orchestra, he served as concert master for the Stockholm Concert Society and the Christiania (now Oslo) Philharmonic and played under the direction of Max Fiedler, Artur Nikitsch, Richard Strauss, Jan Sibelius and others. Sibelius' Violin Concerto was one of the "new" pieces Burgin had re-introduced to Auer (who knew of it but had never played it) and brought to his class. A bit later, when Burgin was already the concertmaster in Helsingfors, he became personally acquainted with Sibelius and worked with him, which led to his becoming an authoritative interpreter of the Violin

Concerto – starting in 1915, he performed it all over Scandinavia, and it became one of his signature concertos later with the BSO.[17] *]*

My first permanent job was in Finland. My chair companion in the orchestra was Anton Sitt. He was a very old man but still played very well. I was only 20 then, in 1912, and I was Sitt's protégé, so to speak. I stayed in Helsingfors until 1916 and then I went to Sweden (Stockholm) for three years, then to Oslo and from Oslo to Boston. I was primarily a concertmaster although I did travel as a soloist in all of those countries. I always had two or three weeks leave as was the custom in Europe when young aspiring concertmasters still wanted to be active. So I played in practically every city in Finland, in Denmark, in Norway, and in all Scandinavia. But my prime activity was chamber music – I always formed a quartet in a city – and orchestra.

In the sense of my musical development from the time I was a boy studying in Berlin and New York, I was inclined to be more cosmopolitan than my colleagues. I sort of went outside Russia in search of things to play. To me there were other composers besides the marvelous Russian composers, Rimsky Korsakov, Tchaikovsky, Scriabin, whom we all loved. And perhaps my cosmopolitan tastes changed my attitude toward foreign countries. I remember that my philosophy, from very early youth, was that when I went to a country, I wanted to be a part of it. I became interested in the language. For example, I learned to speak Norwegian so well that many Norwegians thought I was born there, and I read the whole literature - Hamsun, Thorson, Ibsen – every word they wrote. It was the same thing in Sweden. I tried to assimilate myself with the culture of the country I was living and working in.

When I knew I was going to go to Finland, I found out that Sibelius had written a concerto. It was only then that I found out about it, and I practiced it and brought it to class. Auer was not familiar with it although he knew Tseitlin had studied it, apart from him. In Finland, I played works by composers like Järnafelt, Melatene, Hannikainnen, lots of composers who are not very well known. I was always in contact with these composers and played their works.

So it had always been my attitude when I settled down in a new country to assume that I was going to stay there, hopefully, for some time, and therefore I wanted to learn the language and the literature. I am generally interested in literature, not only Russian, but also German. German literature helped me a great deal to learn the northern Germanic languages. When I went to Finland, I tried to learn not Finnish, but Swedish. There were at that time a considerable number of Swedes still in Finland who did not consider themselves Swedes but Swedish-speaking Finns.

The orchestra I was associated with in Helsinki was the Swedish-Finnish [Helsingfors] Symphony Orchestra, as opposed to another orchestra of equal size in the same city – the Finnish-Finnish [Folk] Symphony, which was conducted by Kajanus. These two orchestras were somewhat at odds with each other between 1912 and 1914 because Kajanus' orchestra was more nationalistically inclined. It rejected the Swedish culture which had been enforced on the Finns and leaned more, in its choice of repertoire, towards ethnic Finnish musical culture. The Swedish-Finnish Orchestra inclined towards Germany.[18]

Poor Sibelius, who was a great composer, didn't care one way or the other, but he had to please both sides. Kajanus, who was closer to Sibelius, usually was the first one to perform new works by the composer. But Schnéevoigt, the conductor of the Helsingfors City Orchestra, who had been born in Finland but educated in Germany, also conducted a great deal of Sibelius. Outside of first performances which Sibelius himself tried to conduct – I say "tried" because he was not very secure as a conductor – Kajanus would usually get the first performance, out of old friendship.

It was a very strange situation. In a city that had at that time a population of about 150,000, the capital of a country of only three million, there were two big symphony orchestras, and each one gave a series of symphony concerts plus other concerts. In other words, there wasn't a day without symphonic music going on in Helsinki. From the point of view of the present time and also from the point of view of the musical situation in Russia at that time, Finland was really way ahead of any other country, musically. And all because of the special political situation that existed there.

It was in Finland that I first met Sibelius but I became considerably more intimate with him only much later (in 1949) when I returned to Helsinki with my wife, Ruth[19], to play and conduct there. I do recall my first contact with Sibelius as a composer-conductor. Before I left Finland, Schnéevoigt's orchestra was offered to Sibelius for the purpose of rehearsing the first two movements of his Fifth Symphony which was not yet completed. Sibelius wanted to find out how the symphony sounded and conducted the rehearsal himself. I must say, my first impression was not very favorable, probably because he was a very inexperienced conductor. Although in conversation he had very set ideas, and one could not argue with him, when he took the baton in his hand, he was completely lost. I later thought that he probably resembled Bruckner a little bit, whom I did not know personally, but who was known to be timid, insecure, and so forth. But Sibelius was aware of his weaknesses and he appreciated the chance to conduct his own work. Not everybody gets an opportunity to have a professional orchestra to try out how his works sound before they're even finished.

From Helsinki I went to Stockholm where I became concertmaster of the Concert Society Symphony Orchestra and also formed the Burgin String Quartet.[20] There I had an opportunity, and the really great experience of playing two weeks under the baton of Richard Strauss. He came to Stockholm as a guest conductor and at six or seven concerts we performed every symphonic work he wrote up to the Alpen Symphony. It was a first rate orchestra. He had the finest musicians of Europe because Sweden was the only country in war-time Europe that offered good food, not *ersatz*. All the best players from Germany, Czechoslovakia, from every country wanted to come to Stockholm so they had a really marvelous orchestra. And Strauss himself was also very happy to come there and eat decently.

Strauss's conducting was superb. He was the only composer in my experience who was really a great conductor. Strangely enough, my feeling was that he had lost interest in many of his own compositions, with the exception of two works, "Domestic Symphony" and "Till Eulenspiegel," which he still liked. He rehearsed those two works very carefully although he conducted all the other symphonic poems, too. He was a very reserved person, not easy to approach, but he was an outstanding conductor.

I had a very interesting experience with him. I was then in my early twenties – it was just two or three years before I came to the States – and pretty cocky, too. I spoke German very well, which was also a great advantage. Strauss didn't hassle me. I played the *Heldenleben* and everything, and although he didn't go out of his way to compliment me, you could see that he was quite happy. He never said a word to me, but when somebody else would not do something quite right, he would speak up.

Well, as I said, I was cocky at that time and much less nervous than I am now or have been since then. So I got up enough courage to go and see him in the green room and ask him one question, hoping to expose him for having written something in the *Heldenleben* that is not clear. There is a little phrase for the violins and the bass clarinet playing an octave lower, which starts from the A sharp over middle C: A sharp, F sharp, inversion of an F sharp major chord, followed by a D major chord, a simple resolution from F sharp major into D major – all very correct. But the inversion where the bass note is F sharp goes down from D to F sharp, which is lower than the G string on the violin. And that seemed strange to me.

So I had the *nerve* to go to the master and ask him, "How do you want us to play this note?" Rather than pointing out the obvious, that we could not play that note, I put it indirectly, "How would you like us to play it?" And this was his answer which certainly put me in my place. He said, "You know, this stupid question is put to me so often that I am sick and tired of answering it. But seeing that you are a young man, very young, I'm going to ask, 'What would you want me to write there, instead of the F sharp? A G natural? Because you can't play the F sharp? If I had done that, you would be right to come to me and say, 'That's a mistake. It's the wrong note.' So you can't play the G. And I cannot write it. But you can't expect me, just because you lack an F sharp, to ruin this beautiful curvy line, to spoil it, just because you can't play the note?"

His answer was very discouraging to so aspiring a musician who had been brought up to honor every little note the composer writes. I said, "I'm sorry to have bothered you," saw that that was the end of it, and left. But his answer bothered me for a long time. For years, I tried to explain it to myself, and I think I know what is behind it. The F sharp, of course, is played by the bass clarinet, and nobody in the violin section plays it. But everybody tries to create the illusion there is an F sharp and moves his hand down from the third position to somewhere below the G string and makes believe that he is playing. And that creates a certain effect, what we call *glissando*. Only in this case it's not a glissando that one intends to execute but one which comes about theoretically because even your face expresses that you have to go below the lowest string. And I think that effect is what he had in mind. I don't blame him for not explaining that to me because explanations in such a case shouldn't be necessary. Still, I will never forget that encounter.

HOW I BECAME CONCERTMASTER OF THE BSO

After three years in Stockholm I went to Oslo and from there to the United States as concertmaster of the BSO. It was Monteux who brought me to America. We did not know each other when I was in Scandinavia, but the conductor with whom I worked in Helsingfors and Stockholm, Schnéevoigt, used to conduct in Holland every summer at Scheveningen – a very big summer resort with great musical activity. Schnéevoigt was the regular conductor there and Monteux was often invited as a guest conductor. In 1920 Monteux, then conductor of the BSO, was looking for someone to take the place of the concertmaster who had just resigned as a result of union strife. I don't know exactly what happened that caused the concertmaster to resign, but I was told something to the effect that he didn't behave quite right in public. He didn't stand up at the conductor's request because the musicians were on strike. In any case, whatever happened between them made it impossible for him to stay there. And so, Monteux was looking for a new concertmaster.

He spoke to Schnéevoigt and Schnéevoigt recommended me. He wrote me a letter saying that although he hated to let me go – because I had been working with him for years, not only in Helsinki, but in Stockholm and Christiana (we had been together all the time) – "I thought this is a rare opportunity and my conscience would have bothered me if I hadn't mentioned you. Now that doesn't mean that you'll get it, but I thought I ought to do my share. And for that purpose you should contact Monteux immediately and play for him."

I received Schnéevoigt's letter in London. That was right after the First World War, in 1920, and it was the first opportunity for Russian citizens to go out to the West. Schnéevoigt also wrote that Monteux was soon going to Paris and suggested that I go to play for him there. Schnéevoigt even helped me get a visa. I had some friends in Paris who had left Russia during the Revolution, and they invited me to come and stay with them. It was an ideal opportunity.

I played for Monteux at his home. He told me that unfortunately his piano playing was very poor and he could only play some of the harmonies once in a while. He asked me what I wanted to play from the standard repertoire – Tchaikovsky, Brahms, Beethoven. I played a section of this and that for about 45 minutes in all. He didn't bother me about orchestral works because he knew I'd been concertmaster for Schnéevoigt for five or six years. Nevertheless, I thought I'd better tell him that I was not too familiar with contemporary music outside of Germany since the conductors whom I knew didn't care much for contemporary music. In Sweden we had had to play twice the nine Beethoven symphonies, and symphonies by Bruckner and Brahms. I told Monteux that I knew very few things in the French repertoire and that I wasn't familiar with modern compositions. He replied very charmingly, "Neither do I know modern music. Nobody can tell what's going to be composed, but I hope I will conduct it and we'll study it together."

Well, Monteux evidently liked my playing and he told me to return to London immediately and sign a contract.[21] The manager of the BSO, Mr. Bremen, was still in London, but had to leave for America the next day by boat. I succeeded in getting a permit to go to London, which was very difficult at that time. I reached Mr. Bremen, signed the contract to go to Boston, and that was how Monteux engaged me.

[Part I of Memoralia ends in the autumn of 1920 when Burgin's career in America with the BSO began – the fulfillment of his boyhood dream. Asked when he arrived in Boston about his tastes in music by Olin Downes, then music critic for the Boston Herald, Burgin replied, "There are for me only two kinds of music…music that is good and music that is bad. I like music of all periods when it is interesting. Perhaps I like some music which is not (pure) music. For example, I am fascinated by much of the later music of Ravel, but I think that it is more color than music. I am fond of some, though by no means all, of Richard Strauss, but I do not care for the Strauss of Zarathustra, Don Quixote, Symphonia Domestica. Those compositions are too programmatic. Each page of music is ultimately associated with a page of some novel or story. Suppose you make a mistake as to which adventure of Don Quixote is being illustrated by the orchestra? Then you are all wrong. Then you have kissed the wrong girl in the dark. That

kind of music is scenic, music for an ideal cinematograph – a kind of moving picture, in a word, for the ear. There is a place for that kind of music, but its place is hardly in a concert hall. The later Strauss is to me wholly a dramatic composer. I do not know his operas over well, but I think of him as primarily a composer for the theater."]

BEFORE THE BOSTON SYMPHONY ORCHESTRA, 1910 – 1920. All photographs from the *Richard Burgin Archive*

Richard Burgin as a Conservatory student, inscribed: "In memory of the summer season," 1910.

Лауреаты С.-Петербургской Консерваторіи.

Пропечатанные крупнымъ шрифтомъ состояли или состоятъ въ преподавательскомъ персоналѣ С.-Петербургской Консерваторіи.

(Съ 1887 до 1902 г. медали были отмѣнены).

ФАМИЛИИ И ИМЕНА	Годъ окончанія и выпускъ	Медали: Большая золотая	Малая золотая	Большая серебряная	Малая серебряная	Премія Михайловскаго Дворца	Рояль жертвуемый г. Шредеромъ	Премія В. В. Шуберта
Выпускъ 1912 года.								
Гершевичъ Роза	1912. 47 в.	X X X X X						
Кондратенко Зинаида	» » »							
Мовшовичъ Мирка	» » »						X	
Боровскій Александръ	» » »							
Сирота Пинхосъ	» » »			X X X X X X				
Фишбергъ Мойше	» » »						X	
Окунь Ита	» » »			X X X X X X X				
Раппопортъ Эмилія	» » »							
Рудникъ Соня	» » »							
Фрейфельдъ Бася	» » »							
Бургинъ Рихардъ	» » »			X				
Идельсонъ Іосифъ	» » »			X X X X X X				
Мильнеръ Сроль	» » »							
Штейнманъ Мордко	» » »							
Ведризова Люція	» » »				X			
Львова Антонина	» » »				X			
Меттеръ Соня	» » »				X			
Патрина Лидія	» » »				X			
Сахарова Ольга	» » »				X X X X X X			
Смирнова Вѣра	» » »							
Якоби Таубе	» » »				X			
Тульчинская Елизавета	» » »				X X X X X			
Шмаевскій Саулъ	» » »							
Шмаргонеръ Марія	» » »		X X					
Курзнеръ Павелъ	» » »							
Добровольская Елена	» » »			X X X				
Лейбова Софія	» » »							
Эйзлеръ Лея	» » »							
Гвирдманъ Илья	» » »			X X X X X X X				
Кустовъ Георгій	» » »							
Меренблюмъ Петръ	» » »							
Хазанкинъ Моисей	» » »							
Ямпольскій Абрамъ	» » »							
Кадлецъ Георгій	» » »						X X	
Кусевицкій Шраге	» » »							
Сарычевъ Владиміръ	» » »							
Быстрицкій Александръ	» » »							
Зильбергъ Яковъ	» » »							X X X

Laureates of the St. Petersburg Conservatory, 1912 Graduates (in Russian). Richard Burgin is listed eleventh (x) as recipient of the Large Silver Medal.

Leopold Auer's class in the summer at Loshchwitz, Germany. Auer is seated with cane in the center middle row. Burgin is first on the left of the back row; Jascha Heifetz is third from the left in the back row.

Left: Leopold Auer, inscribed in Russian: "To Richard Burgin from his old teacher, L. Auer, Petrograd, 29.1. 1915."

Right: Scandinavian composer Christian Sinding, inscribed in German: "To Mr. Richard Burgin with fond memories from Christian Sinding, September, 1920."

Right: Advertisement for *Pirastro Wondertone Strings,* endorsed by Richard Burgin, 1920's.

Burgin (far left), Koussevitzky (center) and the BSO in the 1920's.

Above: Richard Burgin on his professional postcard during his early career as concertmaster and virtuoso in Russia and Scandinavia

Photo of Jean Sibelius inscribed, To my dear friend, the great violinist Richard Burgin, Jean Sibelius. Photo by Goodwin, 1923.

MEMORALIA PART II

"Richard is a free soul. He likes to do big and important things. That he has done such things all his life so far, seems not to be enough for him."

(Ruth Posselt, 1971)

[Part II of Memoralia continues the story of Burgin's career in the United States, albeit non-linearly, indirectly and sometimes, sotto voce. His long tenure with the BSO (as concertmaster from 1920 to 1962; as assistant conductor under Koussevitzky from 1935 to 1943; as associate conductor under Koussevitzky, Munch, and Leinsdorf from 1943 to 1966) forms the implied mise en scene of his narration in this part which focuses on: his experience with and impressions of Pierre Monteux, Serge Koussevitzky and Charles Munch; his role as assistant and associate conductor; the heretofore unpublished and unsung role he played in originating the curriculum of the "Academy" (later, the Berkshire Music Center) at Tanglewood; his thoughts on conductors and conducting in general, on virtuosos, and on composers he worked with and knew well during his tenure.]

THE BOSTON SYMPHONY ORCHESTRA
PIERRE MONTEUX (1920 – 1924)

Monteux was an example of a conductor who had the natural ability to hear with his inner ear. He could not even play piano, but he had this marvelous ability to learn a score and hear it in his head as he learned it, so that when he came to the first rehearsal of a new piece, he knew it so well, we were all amazed at how he would notice the slightest mistake that anybody made despite his never having heard the piece performed before.

Sacre de printemps

The first time I played Stravinsky's *Rite of Spring* was when Monteux did it with the BSO in 1922 shortly after I had become concertmaster. I was simply astounded by that piece, for three weeks I walked around as if I didn't know what had happened in the world, as if a revolution had taken place. I had the feeling that something very important had happened to me but I could not really clarify in what way. I only knew something tremendous had occurred, that life was not the same anymore. Those sounds, those rhythms, they were completely new to me; the poly-tonality, the general drive, everything about it, there was not one measure that didn't stir me, and I felt completely at a loss. I couldn't even say that I disliked or liked it, no. It was something way beyond that; it was as if something phenomenal had happened in the musical world.

We rehearsed *Sacre* very well and were led by a man who knew the piece inside out. That was before we belonged to the union, of course, and time was of no consequence – we had two rehearsals a day lasting 3 ½ hours each – but nobody dared to say even one word because most of us felt that that was a new way of making music. In fact, there was a feeling we could have rehearsed it even longer because everybody sensed that it was a very important thing.

KOUSSEVITZKY (1924 – 1950)

It was 1922 when I first came in contact with Serge Koussevitzky on a person-to-person basis. About twelve years before that happened, when I was a student at the Petersburg Conservatory, my colleagues and I knew of Koussevitzky as a great artist on the double-bass and as a conductor of his own orchestra. We students always looked forward to the concerts which he conducted or which were given by guest conductors of his orchestra. We always looked forward to those concerts because of the excellence of the orchestra which he himself created. It was known as the Koussevitzky Orchestra and was founded in Moscow, but they gave a series of concerts in Petersburg. They always gave interesting programs and at that time, very avant-garde ones. I think I first heard works by Debussy, Stravinsky, and Scriabin at those concerts. They were always Koussevitzky's favorite composers.

I met him in Paris in the late spring of 1922 - I was on vacation for the summer after my second season in Boston. Of course, I stopped in Paris and happened to be present at a concert given under Koussevitzky's leadership of an orchestra composed of French musicians. I saw him after the concert, introduced myself, and was immediately invited to come to his house the very next day – which I did. There was something about Serge Koussevitzky; as soon as you shook hands with him you felt completely at ease; there was some charisma about him that made you feel comfortable.

I enjoyed a conversation with him lasting almost two hours in which I gave him information about musical life in the United States. He asked me to come again a couple of days later, and I did so. When I left Paris, I carried with me a wonderful feeling of having spent a few hours with a person who was warmhearted, who made you feel at ease, who was what we call a grand seigneur. He also told me that he probably would come to Paris the next summer, and that I should be sure to see him again.

In April of 1923, Mr. Monteux told me that he was leaving Boston. It was for purely personal reasons and was not yet officially announced. I expressed my sincere regrets and asked him, naturally, who his successor would be. He said he was not at liberty to tell me the name, but to rest assured because it was somebody I knew and had seen the year before. I drew the proper inferences and when I went to Paris, I just went straight to see Koussevitzky without an invitation. Again, he received me warmly and asked me more questions. I had to go into all kinds of details about the orchestra although he still did not say that he was coming as the next conductor. Only the following day did he finally break down and say, 'Yes, I will be your next conductor.'

From then on, my association with him brought me in contact with him every single day, not only in our professional work, but also in his home. I almost became a member of the family and I became very attached to him as a person. I admired him for certain traits which, to me, were very important. He was a person of great integrity. He was very tolerant – with the exception of one thing. He couldn't stand a lackadaisical attitude towards music. That really rubbed him the wrong way. Otherwise, he was very sympathetic to the problems of the musicians with whom he dealt. I admired him as an artist because of his enthusiasm, his involvement with the work he was doing.

However, unlike Monteux, but similar to many conductors, Koussevitzky lacked the natural ability to hear music with his inner ear, an ability that is necessary for studying scores. He did have the ability to listen to music when it was performed. Despite his outstanding talent, Koussevitzky's musical experience and knowledge lay in his intuition more than in education. His greatness as a conductor came from his ability to project his natural talent despite the obvious shortcomings in his musical education.

When Koussevitzky came to Boston, he needed quite a bit of help, musically, and he made a happy choice in employing Nicolas Slonimsky as his private assistant. Slonimsky, whom I knew very well and was in practically daily contact with at the beginning of Koussevitzky's tenure, was an outstanding musician, in fact, unique. Slonimsky did everything for Koussevitzky that he needed, he prepared and coached Koussevitzky in every detail of the music he would conduct, from reading and analyzing the scores to playing everything for him on the piano. He also acted as Koussevitzky's musical secretary. In a word, Slonimsky was a very important person for Koussevitzky, probably one of the reasons why Koussevitzky did not leave the BSO in discouragement after the first couple of seasons, when he and the orchestra went through a natural, but sometimes very rocky period of adjustment. Koussevitzky liked Slonimsky very much but his second wife, Natalya Ushakova, did not, and since she also had a great influence on Koussevitzky, Slonimsky eventually left.

There is no doubt in my mind that as a team, the orchestra came to work ideally with Koussevitzky. Achieving such teamwork did take a certain amount of time, and during the period of transition when we were getting used to a conductor who differed extremely from his predecessor, all sorts of rumors arose about problems of communication between Koussevitzky and the men in the orchestra.

It is true, as has been widely noted, that sometimes Koussevitzky was hard to understand in English. Not to belabor this point because it has been already exaggerated and has little to do with true communication, I do remember an amusing linguistic miscommunication that happened between me and Koussevitzky. We were rehearsing in the Shed [at Tanglewood] when he suddenly shouted something to me that sounded like "Alt-Horn!" Puzzled, I looked up and said, "Alt-Horn? There is no Alt-Horn in the score." "No, no, I didn't say 'Alt-Horn,' I said "alcohol," said Koussevitzky impatiently, adding in Russian excitedly, "A bee just stung me on the nose."

Aside from such unimportant things, however, the so-called problems of communication between the orchestra and Koussevitzky when he first came to Boston, were, to my mind, quite in the nature of things. They happen in every orchestra. A conductor who comes new to a first rate orchestra needs several years before he gets the orchestra to play the way he would like them to play. The important thing is that Mr. Koussevitzky overcame whatever difficulties he had initially with the orchestra, and comparatively speaking, he overcame them relatively quickly. After a couple years everybody understood and felt what he wanted.

Actually, there was a time for telling Koussevitzky almost anything, only you had to find the right time. And to find the right time, you had to see things from his point of view. For instance, if he had been preparing a new work devotedly, at that moment he himself regarded that work as a great masterpiece. If, after the last rehearsal, he asked you for your impression, he would naturally be irritated if you told him there were some things in it you didn't like. He *had to* believe in the work totally if he was going to be able to give himself up to it completely at the concert. Before the concert, if he asked you about it, all he wanted from you was confirmation. A month or two afterwards, he would recognize the weak points in the composition, perhaps he would even repeat your opinion as his own. But before the performance his faith must not be shaken.

※ ※ ※ ※ ※

There was also talk, as the years wore on, about the rarity of guest conductors during the Koussevitzky regime. I don't know, really, what the reason for that was. Actually, the practice of inviting guest conductors is a comparatively new procedure in the business of music. In my youth, it was a very rare thing, almost unheard of, to engage somebody to conduct somebody else's orchestra because an orchestra and its conductor were considered one unit. So guest conductors were rare birds. But later, and especially here in America, inviting guest conductors somehow became a common practice, a practice that reflected the so-called star system and went against the original idea of the conductor and orchestra as one unit. And when you think of the BSO before Koussevitzky came, before Monteux – who was actually forced to leave Boston for purely personal reasons -, then the regular conductor was Karl Muck and I don't think there were any guest conductors, then. It was naturally considered the orchestra would be at its best with the regular conductor. So, that was probably the basis of Koussevitzky's reputed "dislike" of guest conductors.

Later, because of pressure from the audience, the board of trustees, and maybe the management, Koussevitzky was persuaded gradually to change his way of doing business. The musical justification for the practice of guest conductors is that no conductor can conduct every composition, so it is perfectly all right, once in a while, to invite another conductor who supposedly specializes in compositions which the regular conductor doesn't like or has already done. However, having a constant change of conductors isn't very good for an orchestra. Every conductor has his own little ideas, a great deal of time is wasted in rehearsal to adjust and re-adjust, and it creates a situation where it is no longer important *what* is played but *who* plays it. That, of course, is actually detrimental to the music. So I don't see anything wrong in Koussevitzky's preference for having few guest conductors.

Ultimately, Mr. Koussevitzky's greatest asset was that he could convey his own tremendous enthusiasm about music to the audience. To him, each concert was a new experience. He was just not cynical at all. He still loved the music no matter how often he played the same work

People have called the BSO the most perfect orchestra during Koussevitzky's tenure and although it is very difficult for me to comment on this opinion since I was one of the participants in that "perfect orchestra," I am very suspicious that such an opinion is really wishful thinking simply because it is not quite realistic. An orchestra changes constantly. Hardly a year goes by where out of 100 people, for one reason or other, two or three or more either leave, or die, or are sick. Boston was a little bit more fortunate in this sense, because the turnover was smaller than anywhere else. At one time that may have been because it was not a union orchestra, but later on, we were unionized and the turnover rate was not affected.

Koussevitzky was with the BSO for twenty five years. That's a long period, a whole generation, and naturally, when he got used to all the players and when the players got used to him, a family feeling developed, and no one discharged someone just because he disliked his appearance.

Koussevitzky also had one thing that I think is especially important for conductors to have, - a great deal of imagination and a convincing way of making music and enjoying it. That rubs off on the players no matter how cynical they are. Sooner or later they fall for it. Koussevitzky was sometimes wrong but when he was right he was sublime.

With Koussevitzky there was very little cynicism among the orchestra members and there were reasons for that. Having been originally a bass player himself, and being very independent due to his financial situation, he really tried to take care of the members of the orchestra. He took a personal interest in everybody's well-being. And whenever there were gripes with the management, one could always count on him being on the side of the orchestra. So naturally, the players could only reciprocate this attitude with a sincere desire to please him.

There is one thing that people are apt to overlook when they speak about orchestras, even conductors sometimes don't realize it, and that is that musicians in the orchestra do not perform for the audience. A soloist, when he stands up in front of the auditorium, performs for the audience, but the musicians in the orchestra perform only for the conductor. It couldn't be otherwise because when you have four horns, let's say, and you are playing a Brahms symphony (where Brahms actually uses only two horns except we had four in the BSO), nobody in the audience can say whether it is the first horn that plays something, or the third horn who plays the same subject in a different tonality. Neither could anybody say whether it's the first oboe or the second. People assume that if it's a longer melody, it's probably played by the first-desk player, but the listeners don't see who is playing what. The player, however, is very eager, whether he's second, third or first chair, to play for the conductor so that the conductor gets affected. The conductor is his listener.

Now, when a conductor is aware of the player and when he indicates, maybe just by a twinkle in his eye, that he is aware that he's playing and is pleased, the player thinks, 'That is the man I am playing for,' and he plays his heart out for him. On the other hand, if the conductor doesn't notice, or is not quite aware that the individual player is there, or doesn't look at him, or if he's doing something else, then such a conductor is no conductor to him. A player, a performer, needs an audience, that's what makes a performer. So, Koussevitzky had this awareness of each individual's playing. When he heard somebody play and it appealed to him, he could almost be brought to tears and for a performer that is very, very inspirational. There are great conductors whose faces are completely immobile; they are very well aware of who is playing but they take it all for granted. And they are right; they should take it for granted, on the professional level. Psychologically, however, even professionals who understand that they are expected to play well, still want to be appreciated. And although Koussevitzky could get very angry at individuals in rehearsal, he could also show real appreciation for individual performances. That's part of the reason why I would say that the give and take between the orchestra and the conductor during Koussevitzky's tenure was the best that could be desired.

Koussevitzky was deeply affected by music. He became part of the composition he had to conduct or perform. He absorbed the composition, and perhaps the composition absorbed him. Therefore, he probably felt towards the composition just like he felt towards the orchestra. He identified himself with the orchestra and called it "my orchestra." It was not the Boston Symphony Orchestra, it was his orchestra. I think that he felt that way about music he performed, too. So whether he performed the *Pathetique* or the *Romantic,* the Ninth by Mahler or the Ninth by Beethoven, it was his piece. I think that was one of his strong points and because he carried a great conviction about the performance, he communicated that to the audience.

I might mention an anecdote at this juncture. After Koussevitzky performed a particular work of a contemporary European composer, the composer's compatriots surrounded him and asked him how he liked it. He said, "Well maybe it wasn't exactly what I intended, but it was good. It was very good." I think that says a lot. If it's very good, it really doesn't matter if it's a little different. Perhaps, it should be a little different; otherwise, life would be too monotonous.

THE JOB OF ASSISTANT / ASSOCIATE CONDUCTOR (1927-1966)[22]

[As Robert Sabin noted in Musical America (March 1962) on the occasion of Burgin's retirement as concertmaster: " The world-renowned refinement and intellectual distinction of the Boston Symphony owe much to Mr. Burgin's leadership. [...] Everyone knows of Mr. Burgin's brilliant career as a concertmaster, but many people are not equally aware of his distinguished achievements as a conductor."

In 1924, when Serge Koussevitzky contracted a severe cold just before a performance of a new work, Honegger's Pacific 231, Burgin stepped in to conduct the BSO for the first time. From then till 1934, he became the regular conductor of the Boston Symphony's Young People's Concerts and was a Guest Conductor of the orchestra on an annual basis. When he already had some say in making his own programs, he revealed two noteworthy aspects of his work as a conductor, in general: his personal fondness for the music of Bruckner and Mahler which informed his pioneer efforts to perform their works, decades before they became the staples of orchestra programming they are today; and his profound interest in and enduring commitment to performing contemporary and "new" or undeservedly forgotten music.

Withal, he conducted seven world premieres with the Boston Symphony, works by Toch, Harris, Dukelsky, Menotti, Cowell, Blackwood and Moevs. Burgin also introduced to the United States works by Malipiero, Shaporin, Poot, Krenek, Langendoen and Foss. His numerous Boston and Tanglewood premieres included four works by Hindemith – he also gave the US premiere of the Hindemith Violin Concerto in April 1940 – as well as works by Miaskovsky, Krenek, Vogel, Levant, Lopatnikoff, Mahler, Creston, Revueltas, Haieff, Vaughan Williams, Shostakovitch (the Fifth Symphony which he introduced to Boston in 1939 after Koussevitzky rejected it), Khatchaturian, Ives and others.]

As for my role in the BSO as assistant and associate conductor to Koussevitzky, that was sometimes complicated. Part of the issue was inherent in the position itself. First of all, an assistant or associate conductor is simply a necessity in every major orchestra to fill in for the main conductor at short notice because of scheduling conflicts, sickness, or something like that. One cannot get a guest conductor on five hours notice or sometimes, as happened to me, five minutes notice. Already being on stage as a violinist, I remember being called back to the green room and told to put my violin away and conduct since the conductor suddenly became ill and couldn't do it. That is the position of an associate conductor. Every conductor in other orchestras also had an associate conductor and Koussevitzky, as a matter of fact, suggested that relatively late. He originally intended to conduct all the concerts, but when he found that that was physically a little too taxing, he considered having an assistant conductor and he chose me.

As associate conductor with Koussevitzky and Munch, even when it came to my own programs, I was obviously limited in the selection of works I could conduct since my programs had to fit in, first of all, with their programs and like every associate conductor, I had to get the main conductor's permission, even in the case of works which he didn't have plans to do.[23] So, there were always certain problems involved in making programs. There were also occasionally issues involving personalities, vanities, rivalries, that sort of thing.

I remember, for example, one episode that happened after George Szell had come as a guest conductor [January 1945]. Just before he left, I was informed suddenly that I would be conducting in Boston after Szell's departure. Koussevitzky had decided to make himself absent for three weeks. I thought at the time, maybe he believed the transition from Szell to his appearance would be softened if I conducted in between.

Another example of the complexities of being an associate conductor concerned Koussevitzky's attitude to Soviet music. On one hand, he was always very interested in contemporary music and in new Soviet composers. It took years, however, before he himself would establish musical relations with the Soviet Union. The first time the BSO played a work by a Soviet composer was during the 1928-29 season when I conducted Miaskovsky's Eighth Symphony. Almost ten years later, things hadn't really changed. Koussevitzky at first announced his intention to conduct Shaporin's Symphony in the 1936-37 season, but then, he changed his mind, cancelled it, and gave it to me to introduce to Boston in 1938-39. When asked why he had decided not to conduct it, he claimed there was no political significance in his decision; he simply had not had time to study the score. Actually, he had expressed a liking for Shaporin's work. Yet, I don't know if his not having enough time was the whole reason. And maybe politics wasn't either. At first, he did not want to conduct the Shostakovich Fifth with the BSO, and so I was the first one to conduct it in Boston (in the 1938-39 season). But when Koussevitzky heard me conduct it, and heard the success it had with the audience, that was the end of it for any program of mine, I couldn't touch it anymore until after he retired.

When Koussevitzky was invited to conduct the Shostakovich Fifth with the New York Philharmonic, I happened to be sitting at that concert next to Otto Klemperer who was hearing it for the first time. Klemperer and I were well-acquainted, we had met in Germany, and when he saw me at the concert he remembered me right away. So we sat together and Klemperer listened very intently. His first words about the piece were: "Aber das ist ja Mahler, Gustav Mahler." (But that's Mahler, Gustav Mahler!) And he was right. It is true that Shostakovitch was very influenced by Mahler whom he got to know through Solovetinsky, a music critic, reviewer, and writer about music who knew Mahler's music very well and was a close friend of Shostakovitch's and had a great influence on him.

Speaking of Mahler, it was difficult at first for me to program his music when I conducted the orchestra. I wanted to do the complete Mahler Fourth, but the trustees said no. Mahler (in the early 1940s) was taboo- people considered him long, tedious, and everything else bad. I always liked Mahler very much; so I compromised and asked to do the last two movements of the Fourth. They agreed. Then, after the performance, we got letters asking, why don't we do the whole symphony? So I was allowed to do it later that season. Things had improved greatly in the fifties and sixties – my Mahler programs with the BSO generally had an enthusiastic response from the orchestra and the audience.

THE BERKSHIRE MUSIC CENTER

The BSO is very proud of Tanglewood and they should be. Of course, Koussevitzsky played a very, very important role – he was the initiator of the idea and the guiding spirit behind its creation. But I was the one who persuaded Koussevitzky how the Academy, as they called it then, should be set up.

That happened in August 1939 when a meeting was called at Tanglewood with Koussevitzky, Judd, and anyone else who wanted to participate, to discuss the proposed Academy. Before leaving for the meeting, I jotted down an outline of my ideas for the instructional program and I intended to read it at the meeting. However, at that first meeting, which lasted over two hours, nothing was accomplished. Everybody was talking and nobody was listening. I realized that if this was the kind of meetings we were going to have then nothing would get done.

After supper that evening, I took Koussevitzky aside, made him listen to my plan carefully and asked him to make possible suggestions point by point. I explained every sentence, as if I had to read it to a child. Finally he understood everything and agreed that nothing should be changed in regard to the plan for the Academy. And that's how it was first set up.

The BMC has evolved over time and now (1970s) they have changed the orchestral program that I directed for many years. Some of the works which I originally suggested as a must for study began to get slightly obsolete although they are still played. Anyway, what I stressed when I was in charge of the BMC orchestra, was the importance for each instrumentalist who participated,- because they were students, not professionals,- to have an opportunity actually to perform what professionals considered the difficult part for their instrument of a major work in the repertoire. And I didn't decide on works for the BMC orchestra to perform by using only my own judgment, I asked every instrumentalist in the BSO for their opinions. And I found that they came up with some amazing answers, which I would never have thought of.

For example, I asked a very dear colleague of mine, a horn player, if he could tell me what he considered a particularly difficult part for horn in the orchestral and opera repertoire. I would have thought that he would mention some Strauss piece like *Don Juan* or *Till Eulenspiegel*. But he said, "From the point of view of the difficulty of performing a few measures perfect, on the stage, it would have to be the second (slow) movement of Beethoven's Second Symphony." I was taken aback since there are very few notes to play there. I said, "Well, what actually is so difficult in that?" He said, "You don't realize what the horn player goes through when he sits there for about seven minutes, not playing, and then has to pick up his horn and start on a high B…"

COMPOSERS

I have always looked upon a composer as a kind of enigma. How does it come about that he creates this piece of music? This question arose in my mind especially when I was in close contact with a composer as was often the case when I was conducting his work or when I played under his direction. And it wasn't only the composition that interested me, but the composer's personality, his whole attitude and how he went about communicating, outside of his music, with the musicians whom he needed in order to have his work performed. And in this respect, three great composers made a particularly great impression on me, actually there were four, but the fourth one did not conduct the BSO, so my contact with him was not close: Bartok, Schoenberg, Hindemith and Stravinsky. Bartok was only present at our performance in Boston under Koussevitzky of his Concerto for Orchestra which was commissioned by Koussevitzky for the 50th Anniversary of the BSO. It's a great work and the BSO should be proud that they were the ones who brought it about.

Schoenberg was an unforgettable case in many ways. First of all, I was awe-stricken by the man and also by his work, which was something new. It was something that I worked very hard to understand, it was a new idiom, a new world. Hindemith was the closest of all to me and we became good friends. I had several encounters with Stravinsky because he conducted several times and I also had the great privilege of playing under his direction, *L'Histoire du Soldat*.

SCHOENBERG

It is well known of course that Schoenberg had to leave Germany when the Nazis came to power. In fact, he was lucky to have been able to escape. And everybody I knew in the musical world in the United States felt an obligation to invite him to conduct their orchestra, as did Koussevitzky. That was the least they felt they could do because they themselves did not do anything to perform his work, or very little, except for "Transfigured Night." Koussevitzky was aware that Schoenberg was a personality, that he had done something important in music. Perhaps we did not quite understand what his innovation was but we felt instinctively that something had happened. So Schoenberg was invited to come and conduct the BSO. I was somewhat familiar with Schoenberg though at that time I will admit he was an enigma. Still, I felt that he was also something that only happens once in a lifetime.

I myself had already conducted his *Pierrot Lunnaire*.[24] That was in 1928 in Boston. There was an organization of rather snobbish members of the Boston elite who supported private performances of interesting, worthwhile new works and chamber music. And I talked them into sponsoring a concert for *Pierrot Lunnaire*. I also convinced them it was a piece that was not suitable for playing in a room and it would also be nice to give a wider audience of listeners a chance to hear it. They agreed, and supported the concert financially. We rehearsed that every day for three weeks. But that was several years before Schoenberg came to conduct the BSO.

When Schoenberg came, from the very first rehearsal, there was something about his personality, at least to me, that put one in awe of him. I looked upon him as if he were a person who had come from another world. And when he conducted, he conducted not like a professional conductor but like a composer conducts his own work. Every remark he made was so to the point and nothing was unnecessary, no stories, no affectations, nothing but purely technical remarks about the music. However, his selection of works for his program was a disappointment to me – they were: an arrangement of a Bach piece for organ, *Verklaerte Nacht*, and Opus 5, *Pelias and Melissande.* Still the old type of music but when he did that, his remarks were very interesting. I had no opportunity to speak to him during the rehearsals, I just watched him, took in everything he said. Everything went pretty well, we had our regular four rehearsals and then came the concert.

That first of his concerts took place in Cambridge, in Sanders Theater. We were already warming up when I was told Schoenberg would like to speak with me. I thought that he probably wanted to make some last-minute comments for me to tell my colleagues, to remind them of certain things. I took my violin and went downstairs to the conductor's room. And I started to speak – the conversation was in German – "Is there something you would like me to say?" "No, no," he cut me off, "It has nothing to do with today's program at all. I just heard that you did my *Pierrot Lunnaire* some time ago." "Yes, I did," I replied. "Well, did you find it a difficult piece to put together?" "Yes," I said, "as you know, it is a difficult piece. And it was new to us." "Well, how many rehearsals did you have?" "We had seventeen with the players alone and then we had five more with the singer – we got her from New York." "Well," he said, "that is very nice to hear. But I hope you did not perform that in Symphony Hall?" "No, no, we didn't." "Where did you perform it?" he asked, and I replied, "In the hall of the New England Conservatory, Jordan Hall." "And how large a hall is that?" he asked. I said, "It has a capacity of 1200 seats." "Oh," he sounded disappointed, "that was much too big a hall." And then I made a repartee which I consider to be one of the most stupid of the century, so to speak, probably because I was in such awe of him. I said, "Maestro, es war nur halb voll, it was only half full!" Which in fact was the case.

It was the most idiotic thing to say but he was such a wonderful person, he simply ignored my gaffe and fell in with my unintentional witticism, saying, "Thank goodness!" That immediately put me at ease. So I said, "Maestro, why are you so happy that the hall was only half full?" He then became quite serious: "I'll tell you, and I'm speaking from my own experience. You know, I understand that Boston is considered one of the really musical cities in this country and I have no doubt it is so. But I do doubt that you could find more than 600 people in this city who would enjoy and be interested in listening to a work like *Pierrot Lunnaire.* I say that from my own experience. Therefore, if you had more than that, or if you had a full house, you would have 600 people who would hate this piece. And let me tell you, there's nothing more terrible than to sit next to a person who hates the piece that you're interested in. I myself have been present at concerts of my work where people next to me hated my music, and we almost got into a fight!" Which was actually true.

I realized quickly that what he was really trying to say was that *Pierrot Lunnaire* is a chamber piece and is not ideally suited to a large hall. But his attempt to put me at my ease with his wonderful wit and self-irony was so typical of him. Then, I had the courage to say, "You know, Maestro, allow me to tell you that I was a little bit disappointed that you didn't select for your program a more recent composition than ones you wrote at the time you wrote *Verklärte Nacht.*" And he said, "Well, I don't see why I should carry on my shoulders the responsibility of atoning for all the sins conductors have committed by not playing my music. Just because you people don't play my recent works, why should I be the one to bore my audience with them?" Schoenberg was really a unique person.

HINDEMITH

Hindemith was, quite simply, a great personality. There was hardly anything in music about which he lacked the authority to say something worthwhile. He also believed that it was not worth arguing with someone unless he could answer *your* question, that is unless he could explain 'Why?' rather than simply make a statement about what *he* thought.

Hindemith and I were very often together in musical endeavors. I played under him, conducted his works, and also played his violin concerto in this country for the first time. I gave the first performance in April 1940 and later Ruth took it over and played it all over the United States.

How I ended up giving the first American performance of the Hindemith Violin Concerto came about in a very strange and roundabout way. When Hindemith came to this country, I think it was in 1938 or 1939, and I got to know him, we became very friendly. On the whole, he was not a very easy man to get to know, but he took a liking to me, and I was very happy about it. And we used to argue about many of his works. I played his quartets, the first and second, and I also liked his *Kammermusik No. 4*, which I found terribly difficult and still think is a difficult thing. In fact, I could *never* manage to play it well enough to my satisfaction although I studied it hard. And the only satisfaction I had was to have a pupil who managed to play it very well, and I enjoyed it very much when he played it for me.

Anyway, when I got to know Hindemith a little better, I once said to him, "Paul, I have been practicing your *Kammermusik* No. 4." "Why do you waste your time studying that piece?" he said, which was very strange to me. "It's not worth the time you are spending," he continued. And I said, "I can't understand why you say that. I like it, but I don't understand why you write so difficultly for the violin because you're a violist and a violinist." He repeated, "As I said, I don't see why you bother with it." And we got into an argument, but you can't argue with a composer who evaluates his piece not according to *your* ideas. However, I finally found something that stopped him. I said," You know, Paul, the moment you compose a piece, and the moment it is printed, you lose all jurisdiction because anyone can take it and has the right to express his opinion." Well, that had an effect. He said, "Well, that is true," and there was no more argument. Then he said, "You know, I am going to send you a concerto for violin and orchestra," and added, "wenige Noten aber schön." ("Fewer notes, but beautiful.")

And that's how we left it. Shortly afterwards, I performed his piano quartet with clarinet, violin and 'cello in E flat – I don't know why people don't play it. It's a beautiful work. That came about because the Schott people, his publisher, were trying to promote him in this country. They arranged concerts of his works and wanted to arrange a New York concert. They had already engaged people, but he said, "No, I want to have my friends from Boston come and play it." So Sanroma, the pianist, Polochek, a BSO clarinetist, and I had to prepare the work despite the fact that there were plenty of musicians in New York to play it. But he insisted that he wanted us, and so we did it.

Finally, he had to go back to Germany – he had come here alone, without his wife – probably to settle his affairs because ultimately, he knew he would come to the US if he could. He was not very friendly with the Nazis and they were not very friendly to him. And, his wife was Jewish. So, about two weeks before he was due to leave, I still hadn't heard anything about the new concerto which was supposed to be so beautiful, and with fewer notes – that was very important! For a while I thought that it was one of those nice things that a composer promises you but forgets about and there was nothing to be done. But then, I thought, 'Why does he bother to send it to me? He's published, after all.'

And when I went to say good-bye, I said, "Paul, about that concerto you told me you would send me, why do you bother? I can buy it, your publisher is Schott, right?" He said, "Of course,

Schott is my publisher." (Schott was his publisher all his life for once you get a publisher, you are married to him, no divorce is possible.) He said, "But you can't buy it yet." "Why?" I asked. He replied, "Because it's not yet in print." Then I said, "Listen, could you let me see a manuscript of it, something," because I was so eager. I had loved his music before I even knew him. "Well," he said, "I'm sorry, I haven't got a manuscript because it isn't written down." I thought he was pulling my leg because he had already told me that I could not have the first performance because he had already promised it to a certain violinist and the premiere was set for September 19 [1939] in Holland.

So I said, "How is that possible? It is now May and you tell me it hasn't been printed, it hasn't been composed, there's no manuscript, and yet it's going to be performed on September 19th?!" He said, "I didn't say it's not composed. It is composed, just not written down. I've got it all composed in my head but I haven't written it down yet." Well, such things were new to me. I could not disassociate composing something from writing it down. I still thought that was the same thing. He continued, "Well, you know I'm taking the boat to Europe and I'll be on the boat six days. There's nothing else to do then so I'll write it down, and when it's written down my proofreader will check the manuscript, okay it and then it will be printed and performed."

Hindemith was in fact very akin in his manner of composing, to Bach or Mozart. As we all know, Mozart could write out an opera overture the night before the performance, it was all already composed in his head. He didn't have to change anything. Or Bach was able to dictate the *Art of the Fugue* from memory because he himself did not write it down, also as everyone knows. Hindemith was a unique case and I valued my experience with him highly because I was always so interested in how composers do things, compose and create. As a matter of fact, he finished writing down the last two or three pages of his E Flat Major Symphony in my house in Jamaica Plain, very early one morning, around 5 A.M.

I finally got the violin concerto, but only in February 1940 and only after writing to the Schott representative in London and pestering them. They at first replied that they had not gotten it yet. At last, they sent me a facsimile of the violin part with a letter asking me to inform them immediately when I would perform it because they had a great demand for the concerto and Mr. Hindemith wouldn't allow anybody to have it until I had performed it. And that really made me mad. They sent me one copy of the violin part and expected me to know the concerto without anything else. I wrote back that I could tell them nothing until I received the score both for my self and for the conductor.

Well, finally in February the music arrived and I did perform the Hindemith with the BSO and Koussevitzky, in April, and about a month later I had to have an operation. While I was recuperating, my wife learned the concerto and played it so beautifully that she eventually played it with Hindemith in New Haven, in New York and everywhere, all over the country. It really is a beautiful work, beautiful. And with fewer notes.

I later realized that "Mathis der Maler" was a turning point in Hindemith's work and ushered in a new period in his compositions and attitude to music that perhaps he did not want to acknowledge. The only exception might be something he recommended to me, a work which I love very much, *The Four Temperaments*, a suite for string orchestra and piano – a beautiful piece. I don't know the year it was composed but I think it was written just around the time of "Mathis der Maler." Hindemith also told me that there were some nice things in the third quartet, but everything else he wrote before "Mathis," you couldn't even mention to him. His remark about the violin concerto, "Wenige Noten aber schön," was also very apt. There were too many notes in all his earlier work, but like most composers he gradually got rid of those superfluous barnacles that seem to attach themselves to the main body.

STRAVINSKY

As a conductor, Stravinsky was very insecure. It was a psychological issue with him. He told me when he went on the podium, he had a fear that he would fall down – he had this feeling of falling. He told me that after he conducted his new work, *Jeu de Cartes,* with the BSO (January, 1944). He was marvelous in rehearsals – every word he said was meaningful, nothing was wasted. But in the performance, he simply got lost in his own piece. That is, he made a little technical mistake due to the large number of irregular, asymmetrical measures in the score. That kind of mistake does not faze an experienced orchestra of players whose parts have them playing continuously, without rests. When they notice that the conductor has made a mistake, they keep on playing and the conductor will find his place. But, the players of instruments like the winds in that piece who do not play continuously and have measures to count and cannot watch the conductor all the time during the rests but look for either a cue, or know approximately when to come in and then look at the conductor, they can get confused.

In this performance, when Stravinsky forgot where he was, we violins and cellos just stopped watching him and played on. Our rests were only one or two quarter notes, which didn't keep us from staying in time. But the wind instruments had rests for ten or twelve measures at a stretch and those measures were in all different rhythms. When they finally thought they had to come in, they looked up for their cue, but the beat was not directed at them. Besides, Stravinsky himself was already nervous, wondering where he had made the mistake and turning the pages of the score back and forth. It was a real calamity.

Now, in *Jeu de Cartes,* the movements are called "hands" (deals); there are four of them, and each hand starts in the same way. What had happened was that before the first hand was finished, someone started the second only to hear his neighbor whisper, "No, wait, it's not time yet." Several attempts were made to right the situation. In the meantime, Stravinsky was *completely* at a loss. He heard something was not right and tried to find the place where he thought we were, but we were nowhere. There was nothing to be done but stop playing altogether, and for a moment, we stopped. Then we started a new movement, and it was all right.

But I have never seen a person in such a despondent mood as Stravinsky was after this performance. He asked me to come and talk; he felt more at ease with me because he could speak Russian – not that he couldn't speak other languages, but he felt more at home in Russian. He called me upstairs and began, "Tell me, Richard Moiseyevich, what happened?" Well, I could not tell him straight out that he had made a mistake, so I said the next best thing, "Evidently there was a misunderstanding between the orchestra and you." "No," he replied, "it goes deeper than that. Do you realize this is the same as a situation where Igor Stravinsky has forgotten his own name? It's amnesia. Imagine, Igor Stravinsky, I mean, *the* Igor Stravinsky suddenly doesn't even know his own name. It's not like making a mistake conducting another composer, it's a mistake with your self." It was very difficult to calm him down. "Yes," he said finally, "I know what it is. When I go up on that podium, I get frightened, scared, as if I am going to fall down." It was a typical Russian situation out of Dostoevsky!

MUNCH (1949-1962)

[Despite a personal liking for Charles Munch, Burgin nevertheless did not spare his contempt for Munch's unpredictable and flagrantly unmusical excesses as a conductor. The "lack of balance in the extreme" that characterized many Munch performances in Burgin's view ended up distorting the music – something the concertmaster could not overlook, or easily forgive.

The following opinions and impressions of Munch's personality and conducting were expressed in Burgin's private correspondence with his wife, often at her prompting. They refer to specific incidents and performances that took place during the BSO's transcontinental tour in April-May 1953 and its Far Eastern Tour in 1960.]

I liked Munch at the beginning, and often thought that certain things he did, like giving five hundred dollars for [violinist] Harry Dubbs [after he suffered a serious, ultimately fatal heart attack], and many other things were in themselves admirable. Still, his gestures of generosity were sometimes so out of proportion, so distorted, as his music making was at times, that I could not help feeling, such a person could easily go to the other extreme, and become mean and hurtful especially if he felt insecure.

Munch in these concerts [New Orleans, April 28, 1953] is right in his element, acts like a monkey, yells, jumps and makes grimaces as if he is going to lose his mind and to hell with the music. It's quite a show for the gallery. But what goes on with the music is simply disgusting.

Yesterday [May 1, 1953] a very interesting incident happened. Munch came into the club car where a few of us were gathered just before going to bed. At the concert he had been mad as a hornet. The concert went off poorly. Nobody knew what got into him. When he came into the car, he saw me, sat down opposite me and asked how I felt. Naturally, I asked him how he felt, to which he answered, ' When I do not conduct I always feel well but when I do, then it depends whether the concert is played well – if so, then I am happy, otherwise I am not, and tonight I was not happy.' 'Well,' I said, 'are you sometimes happy?' There was a long pause – 'Yes,' he said, 'sometimes.' – 'In that case,' I said, 'at least there is something to go by.' Everybody around had a laugh. Then suddenly, he turned to me and said, 'You are the associate conductor but more conductor than associate.' I asked, 'What does that mean?' No answer. Suddenly, he invited everybody to have a drink. Scotch and soda. Another one, and so on. He got in a better mood; the conversation was rather pleasant, everybody participated. Suddenly he turned to me and asked, 'Tell me, what do you do to obtain the Koussevitzky sonority from the orchestra?' I looked at him with a blank expression and asked: 'What do you mean by that'? – 'Well,' he said, 'How do you succeed in getting the Koussevitzky sonority?' I looked around at everybody and had a feeling that they all knew what he was talking about, but I hadn't any idea. I answered, '*Sonority* is an expression I never use when I conduct the orchestra. I confine myself to purely technical terms and don't know what *Koussevitzky Sonority* means.' 'Well,' he said, 'That is what W.S. Smith wrote after the concert you conducted.' And that was what had been eating him.

* * * * *

Yesterday [May 5, 1953] we played before a capacity audience, an attendance of over 6000 people. The concert started off with Munch calling me into his room before going on the stage to tell me that I should not be surprised if he conducted like an old rag. He was obviously nervous and said it to get some sympathy. He added that he had not wanted to conduct tonight's concert and agreed to do it only because Judd [the manager] insisted. Of course, he got all my sympathy and I reassured him everything would be all right. Well, he started off conducting in such an indecisive manner, that after the ninth measure of Barber's Overture, the second violins did not know where they were. The thing threatened to fall apart. However, the orchestra knows that piece so well that somehow we held together. Then, Munch pulled himself together and went to the other extreme. With each successive piece he got more into his element, became more and more wild, gesticulating, jumping, and yelling. Each crescendo was reinforced by a violent accelerando – the *pp* was inaudible. In *ff* the trumpets blasted away and the percussion had a wonderful time. In short, it was a real show. The people went wild. – The success unprecedented, the musicians bewildered. In sum, a real Munch performance. We played a couple of loud encores. And that brought the house down.

Yesterday [May 15, 1953], Munch called me to his room, just a few minutes before the concert was supposed to begin. I found Stagliano [James Stagliano, first horn] in his room. When I asked him whether he wanted to see me, he said he did and continued: "As I just said to Stagliano I wanted to tell you that I have been informed the local critic, Cassidy, is out to kill me; I am somewhat nervous tonight." "Well," I said, "Do you think that the attitude of a stupid critic can affect our playing tonight? Don't worry, this orchestra can play well, and therefore you can be at ease."

When we went out, Stagliano turned to me and said, "What a crazy fellow he is, to call me in and ask me to play well. That's one way to make a fellow nervous. This man doesn't know what it takes to perform in public on an instrument. A rank amateur."

Well, we played well. He had a great success, in spite of the fact that in the second part of the program, when he felt that the audience was with him, he threw all restraint to the devil and became musically so unbalanced that we probably gave the most distorted performance of the Brahms 1st Symphony I ever witnessed.

THE BSO TOUR OF THE FAR EAST
(May-June, 1960)

(Excerpts from letters to Ruth Posselt)

In Formosa
Yesterday we had our first concert. A miserable performance. The program had a lukewarm reception. The Beethoven Symphony was way above them. Only the encores were received with enthusiasm. It seems the audience (which consisted of half Americo-Europeans and half Formosans) was unable to concentrate for any length of time on serious music.

Matsuyama, Japan
I conducted the 2nd concert today. Both cities had audiences which were exposed to hearing live symphony orchestras on average of once every two years. Naturally, music like Kirschner and

even Mahler was way beyond them. Of course, Tchaikovsky they liked, but best of all they liked encore pieces.

Japan

The last week was very hard on us. Let me give you a rough idea about the routine associated with our tour. You get up in the morning, around 7 (in my case 5, with an hour walk through the streets of the town) to have breakfast. 7:30 you wait for the bus to take you to the station. You arrive at the station and wait a barren hour before you board the train. No porters. You carry your suitcases on and off the bus, the train, into the hotel. Train ride between 4-7 hours. Officials meet you at the platform. Flowers. Snapshots. Introductions. Again bus. Hotel. You wait in line to register. Unpack, eat something, you wait for the bus to take you to the hall. Change. Anthems. Same program. Lukewarm reception. Big applause at the end of the programs. One encore, bigger applause, second encore, still bigger applause. Presentation of flowers. Change again. Bus back to the hotel. Look for a place to get a little to eat. Hotel restaurant closes at 10 p.m. To bed, mostly Japanese style. Don't sleep too well. Next day the same procedure. It's the monotony that gets you. As Alfred [Alfred Krips, Burgin's stand partner] says, 'there is nothing to look forward to. All that is left for excitement is Munch.'

Tokyo

Yesterday I conducted a concert which had quite a big success. After our two encores and an extra bow, I motioned to the orchestra to leave the stage and call a halt to the applause. But the audience kept on applauding a long time after the orchestra left the stage.

Manila

The concert I conducted had a big success. Many of the men (like Gomberg, Stagliano, George [Zazofsky], Alfred [Krips] and others) kept congratulating me on the performance. This in spite of the fact that in the hall (a huge place, with a capacity of 5-6 thousand seats, packed) it was so hot and humid that the orchestra had to play without their coats.

CONCERTMASTER AND ASSOCIATE CONDUCTOR OF THE BSO, 1920–1962. All photographs from the *Richard Burgin Archive*

Newlyweds Richard Burgin and Ruth Posselt, July 14, 1940.

Charlotte Martinu shows Richard Burgin a small bird as her husband, Bohuslav (on left), and Gregor Piatigorsky (on right), look on. Summer, 1941 (?)

Igor Stravinsky, inscribed in Russian: "To the dear, highly esteemed musician and violinist, Richard Moiseyevich Burgin from I. Stravinsky, with fond memories, Boston, April, 1940. *Photo by Harcourt-Harris, New York.*

Paul Hindemeth playing the rebec.

Serge Koussevitzky and Richard Burgin, 1940's.

Burgin and his young daughter, Diana, summer, 1949.

Ruth Posselt (4th from left) and Richard Burgin (3rd from right) welcomed in Warsaw, Poland, June, 1949.

DR. SERGE KOUSSEVITZKY

The distinguished conductor of the Boston Symphony opened the 12th annual Berkshire Music Festival at Tanglewood, and at the same time observed his 75th birthday. Here he cuts the birthday cake.

Posselt and Burgin rehearsing the Bach Double Concerto with the BSO in Symphony Hall, 1949.

Left: Koussevitzky and Burgin, holding his son, at the maestro's birthday party, Tanglewood, 1949.

Burgin rehearsing the student orchestra at Tanglewood.

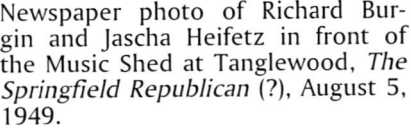

Newspaper photo of Richard Burgin and Jascha Heifetz in front of the Music Shed at Tanglewood, *The Springfield Republican* (?), August 5, 1949.

Newspaper photo of Posselt and Burgin as guest performers at a Tanglewood Benefit concert, summer, 1954. *The Berkshire Eagle.*

Charles Munch conducting the BSO in Leningrad Philharmonic Hall, September 8, 1956. Burgin is seated to the right of the conductor. *AP Wirefoto, The Boston Daily Globe.*

Burgin conducting, 1958. *Whitestone Photo, New York.*

Richard Burgin and Soviet violinist, Leonid Kogan.

Concertmaster Richard Burgin and Associate Concertmaster Alfred Krips.

Right: Burgin rehearsing the chorus for Mahler's Symphony No. 2, 1962.

Charles Munch and Richard Burgin greeted by geishas upon arrival in Tokyo, Japan, BSO Tour of the Far East, 1960. *AP Wirefoto. The Boston Globe (?)*

Joseph Silverstein, Erich Leinsdorf, Richard Burgin at Tanglewood. *The Berkshire Eagle*, July 2, 1962.

Charles Munch (center) and Richard Burgin (right) at Munch's retirement luncheon, Tanglewood, 1962.

THOUGHTS ON MUSICIANS AND MUSIC

CONDUCTING AND CONDUCTORS

After all, the conductor is an element in musical performance that is basically unmusical, in the sense that he is the only person that does not produce sound or create sound but nevertheless is needed to get some sound out of an orchestra.

* * * * *

One finds a certain timidity in composer-conductors. Many composers feel awkward on the podium. They can be very objective during rehearsals and know exactly what they want, but in concert they become too personally involved. Ravel was the classic example. He once managed to conduct 'La Valse' in four – all the way through. Richard Strauss, on the other hand, was really first-rate – when he was interested. When he conducted in Stockholm (1917), he did some Mozart and Wagner, but mostly he did his own works. He loved "Till Eulenspiegel" and the "Sinfonia Domestica" but other than those, he just beat time. Schoenberg would pester the players in his orchestra a great deal, but he was an extremely interesting conductor; each gesture had a point to it. Prokofiev was quite good, particularly with his own works. Stravinsky was wonderful in rehearsal; he could tell you precisely what he wanted, but in a concert anything could happen.

* * * * *

Some conductors have very good memories, and Erich Leinsdorf was one of them. The most remarkable memory I ever encountered was that of Guido Cantelli. He knew literally every part. But even such people are not entirely infallible. Toscanini, you know, once had a memory slip and had to stop and go back to the beginning. I remember that even Monteux, whose memory was second to none, got completely lost, once. The concert was with the BSO in Paris, in 1952 I think. In a certain section of the William Schuman Symphony, the entire brass section entered a whole measure too late, and continued to play until the end of the section ahead of the rest of us, with Monteux merrily conducting as if nothing happened. I strongly suspect he was not aware of it. He conducted from memory. Igor Markevitch, who also had an excellent memory, said once that he believed that it would be impossible to write one page from memory exactly as it appears in the score. And furthermore, the same would probably be true for the composer if he were asked to do it a few weeks after it was written. I prefer to have the score in front of me. For me, it's basically a matter of feeling secure but I also can't forget that in my youth, playing or conducting by memory was considered an affectation, and not in good taste.

* * * * *

I once asked Henri Temianka which he found easier, playing the violin or conducting. He said, "Let me think a minute." "No you don't have to think," I answered. "I'll make it easy for you. Right now it is six in the evening. If I were to ask you to conduct the accompaniment to the Beethoven violin concerto tonight, would you accept?" "Of course," he said without a moment's hesitation. "Now," I insisted, "if I were to ask you to *play* the violin concerto tonight, would you accept?" "Of course not," he said indignantly. "Well, there is your answer." I said.

VIRTUOSI

I know many virtuosos and I do not envy them. They tell me what it's like to play the same few pieces over and over and know they have to go here and then be there. Not for me. I like the orchestra.

* * * * *

Violinists and other soloists are not themselves wholly responsible for their success – it does not depend on their playing alone. They need managers and managers generally do not accept two stars, or two possible stars. Each manager ideally wants one star as well as other, lesser known artists; they sell their artists in packages and they are not going to compete with themselves. So, no matter who comes to him, if the manager already has his star, he is satisfied with that one.

There are other elements that enter into career success; first of all, age. Somehow a child prodigy affects the audience much more than an older serious musician no matter what the child plays. We cannot help that. We are amazed at the *ability*. When a child performs, the audience does not really listen to the piece of music the child performs, it listens to the way the piece is projected by a very young person. Actually, that is the only way people do listen to performances – though I don't say there aren't exceptions. Only, when a performer has reached a certain age, when he is an adult, listeners will take into consideration other aspects, not only technical mastery – that would be taken for granted – but also the ability to present a piece of music that satisfies them, rightly or wrongly. And so they begin listening to the playing itself.

※ ※ ※ ※ ※

I was very, very impressed with Menuhin and I remember distinctly how he played the first time I heard him. He played the Beethoven Concerto and he was only about 16 or 17 years old, which is a very young age for a violinist to play such a serious and big work. I also had some reservations about his playing, but since Mr. Menuhin is still [in 1974] a great artist, I don't think it's proper for me to dwell on my reservations. I may have been quite wrong.

※ ※ ※ ※ ※

Some people have compared Toscha Seidel with Heifetz who studied at the St. Petersburg Conservatory around the same time. Toscha was there at the same time as I and was a year older. But Toscha was not of the same musical caliber as Heifetz even though he may have impressed audiences very much – he was very outgoing in his manners and in his playing. Even while he was still a student, however, most of the older students who looked at things more deeply, and more professionally, did not quite believe that he would last that long as a virtuoso or even develop beyond what he had already achieved.

※ ※ ※ ※ ※

It is strange but virtuosi of genius sometimes feel insecure. Even Heifetz was not an exception. I remember once at our house,- I was then married and Ruth was there – at a party, after a concert, Heifetz came up to us, and started the conversation by saying, "Have you heard this Oistrakh?' "Of course," Ruth said "And what do you think of him," he asked with a scowl. Ruth said, "I think he is really extraordinary, a great artist." Heifetz said, "Oh, I don't like his playing at all."

Then, he continued on another point that obviously annoyed him, "And I don't like all these contemporary concertos. Now I suppose you like the Bartok, the Hindemith and the Alban Berg." "Oh," Ruth said, "Very much, I've played them all." "Well, I am going to send you all my copies because I don't think one of them is worth ten cents." Then, he added, "You wait till you hear a performance of a modern composer I'm going to broadcast." So Ruth and I said, "We'd love to hear that."

It turned out to be the Korngold Concerto. We happened to be on the road when that was broadcast, but we had a radio and we listened. Of course, he played that as well as anyone could, but my first response to Ruth was, "Isn't this terrible, how he can compare that with concertos by Prokofieff and Hindemith? What are we going to tell him? We've got to tell him something. He'll be very hurt."

MUSIC EDITING

One of the problems with edited versions of works for the violin, is that there is no definitive type of fingering that can be considered better or worse than another; neither is there a definitive type of bowing. In a broader sense, editing a piece of music could be considered a certain kind of crime. When you edit something that a composer has written, you are actually saying not only that the composer didn't make clear in his music how he wants his piece to be played, but also that *you* do know what he wants. There might be some value in editing if the editor has been in personal contact with the composer, but in most cases, he is not. Nevertheless, I always told my students if a piece is edited by somebody, they should take this into consideration and should have a certain amount of respect for whoever has edited it. Because, we must assume that the fellow who edited it was hired by the publisher and probably paid for it and therefore, we must assume that the editor had a reputation worth paying for. To say, *a priori*, a certain edition is no good is wrong. One should see what the editor says but keep in mind that is not always what the composer wrote. A good editor should distinguish what the composer indicated (or might have indicated) and what he is indicating. The editor may think he has improved it, but it also is possible that he didn't improve it. There's also the question of ability – the editor's and the player's. Maybe the editor isn't quite as good as the player, and maybe, on the contrary, he is much better, and his way of doing things is not within the player's capacity.

I once had a conversation with my good friend Joseph Gingold who edited quite a number of pieces. I asked him, "Joe, you have edited so many things and of course, I've seen most of them, so tell me, does the publisher tell you what type of player you are editing for, and does he provide you with any guidelines?" "Well," he said, "as a rule they leave me pretty much alone, but sometimes, they do give some general guidance." "What kind of guidance?" "Well, if it is a piece they want to sell and they know it is rather difficult, they may suggest that if there is any possibility of simplifying it somewhat, then to include simpler alternatives. They don't force me to do anything unmusical, but I do occasionally have to take into consideration that maybe my edition will be used by a young student who is not quite capable of overcoming certain problems and difficulties and who doesn't know yet that he has the right to change things for himself, as we all do, and so for such players I give simpler alternatives." In other words, editors, even if they are excellent and experienced musicians, can not always rely wholly on their own judgment, they sometimes have to give in to the commercial aspect of editing.

Therefore, I am very enthusiastic about the publication nowadays of unedited Ur-texts. In my few contacts with composers, I've been amazed how lenient they are. If you grasp the essence of what they want, they will allow you to do almost anything and the last thing they're concerned with is what fingering or bowing you use. Once you start playing, they feel you understand what it's all about. So I think it behooves us to develop a certain arrogance, if you wish, and have a little more faith in our convictions about our understanding of a work of art before we attempt to project it with our instrument because otherwise, we can only imitate and that will be a cliché, it won't be the real thing, no matter how well we imitate.

TEACHING

[Burgin's remarks on teaching, for the most part spoken to Professor Dann in their previously mentioned 1974 interview when Burgin was 81, were based on the accumulated experience and wisdom of teaching, both violin and conducting, for over fifty years. Burgin himself could not say when, exactly, he began teaching. Raphael Bronstein, who had been Burgin's fellow student in Auer's class at the Conservatory, recalled in his memoir of Burgin going to him at that time for help in playing Bach: "Auer always demanded his pupils play Bach after their first few lessons, but I had had no experience with that...I was asked to play the g minor Sonata and asked Richard for his help. He generously gave me my first true picture of Bach, with an analytical approach which has continued to influence my understanding of the composer's greatness throughout my life."[25]

Once Burgin came to the United States, he quickly established himself as one of the two most prominent violin teachers in Boston, the other being the Bohemian (Czech) virtuoso, Emanuel Ondricek (the teacher of Ruth Posselt). In addition to private pupils, including several of his BSO colleagues who took private lessons from him over the years, Burgin also held teaching positions at various institutions in the Boston area. In 1924 he joined the faculty of the New England Conservatory of Music where he remained until his retirement from the BSO, eventually becoming head of the string department and director of the orchestra there. He also taught at Wellesley College, Boston University, and the Berkshire Music Center at Tanglewood (from 1940 to 1963). From 1963 until the end of his life, teaching became his professional focus. In addition to his work as Professor of Music at Florida State University (1963-1972), during the summers Burgin served as master teacher, director, and/or conductor in various seminars, workshops, and string congresses in the United States and Canada: the National Youth Orchestra of Canada (1965); Co-director of Stetson Festival Institute at Daytona Beach and Director of the Institute Orchestra (1966); Director and Conductor of the orchestra of the Annual AFM Congress of Strings (Eastern Section) 1967-1970 ; 1968, May 26-31, Director, 5th annual Conducting Symposium for Young Experienced Conductors at FSU School of Music (1968); Director of string program and coaching staff at Stetson University's Summer Institute (1972); co-director of International Conducting Symposium at Jacksonville University (1975); Master teacher at New College Music Festival, Sarasota Fl (1976-1980); and Leader of the String and String Conductors Workshops at Artsperience, Canadore College, North Bay, Ontario (1978)]

Teaching has advanced. It is better than it was. I am a great believer in the future. There have always been talented students, but today one can teach more in depth. Today [1977] you teach by explanation, not imitation. Yet, too much analysis can also ruin the performance of music.

I have been a teacher ever since I can remember and I have some very particular ideas on the education of a musician. I am critical of what they call general education and the broad range of subject requirements for music students in most colleges. There is a prevalent feeling among music majors at universities that they cannot study what they really want – they don't have the time. Therefore, I often argued at FSU faculty meetings about the so-called curriculum, if music students have to study a science, why can't they study acoustics?

Our conception of teaching violin is of necessity split between teaching the ability of playing the instrument, and the musical value of the music one plays. We must not forget that the violin is an instrument that requires a very early age to begin practice. It's a very delicate instrument and usually those who are successful at playing it, whether as a soloist or in any other capacity, those who are really outstanding musicians, they all started very, very young, from maybe four to eight years old, seldom later. There are exceptions, and very successful ones, and they are very proud of the fact that they did not start so early, they even brag about it, and rightly so. But ninety nine percent of successful violinists started very early.

At the age of five or six all one can do is develop the ability, the physiological aspect of handling and mastering an instrument, and that is completely natural because a child can not comprehend anything else about violin playing. And so, teachers focus on that.

With a gifted child, you can make extraordinary progress. But then comes a turning point, usually around the age of twelve or thirteen, which has a big effect on the future, and teachers really cannot do anything about that. That's probably the point when, as Auer used to say, some get better and others get worse.

I personally am opposed to the idea that technique, mastery of the instrument, is all-important. It is conceivable that one can master the violin to such a point that technical mastery itself becomes ideal and can even give great satisfaction to the listener. But it is still the application of one's mastery towards expressing what one feels in the music that is decisive. Artistry still has to be related to musical thought, the musical composition itself and other intangibles that go beyond just playing the notes beautifully, in time and in tune. There is something – it's very hard to put your finger on what it is – there is something beyond technical mastery, and everybody will agree there is. The very fact that some compositions can last for so many years and still be enjoyed and others can not, proves that there is quite a difference between a work of one composer or another or even between two different works by the same composer, both technically irreproachable. The instrumentalist has to develop with the music he performs. If he only stays at the height of technical efficiency and ability, then sooner or later, he will not satisfy a great number of people, no matter how well he plays.

Talent, I think, is determined by the ear, not in the sense of pitch only, but by sensitivity to beauty of sound. I think that a genius like Heifetz did not just have an ear for music, or perfect pitch, he had an ear sensitive to the quality of sound, an ear sensitive to resonance. And he would never be satisfied until he reached the point that satisfied his ear. The tragedy is that the moment such a musician satisfies his ear, his ear gets better, and so he's never happy, really. It's the tragedy of genius, the moment he comes close to his ideal, it eludes him and he has to work harder.

My personal experience and private conversations with talents of this caliber is that they are never really quite happy. No matter how well a great artist performs his or her part, I have seldom encountered one that is totally happy. Well, they are happy that they had a success, that they were appreciated, but in terms of inner happiness, they never think that they have really achieved all they wanted. There's always something that they would like to have done still better. On the other hand, I've found with lesser talents, that very often they are quite satisfied and happy even if they come not quite to what they hoped to, but very close. That has been my experience: that the great artists never stop working, really are always unhappy and in great need of focusing on something else, to get away from what their real aim is.

* * * * *

There is one thing which has been somewhat neglected in our teaching of single voice instruments, that is, every orchestral instrument. Our music has harmonic progressions or implied harmonic progressions, it has polyphony and counterpoint. And the moment you have polyphony and counterpoint, or even polyrhythms, an instrumentalist on a single voice instrument cannot be considered a soloist in the literal sense of the word because one voice cannot perform the music alone. The moment one player can't play alone he has to play with at least one more person, and that means there's bound to be a certain give and take in the performance of music.

Unfortunately, that is something that has not been sufficiently impressed upon all the young talents who often achieve great virtuosity in the mastering of their instruments. They are sometimes not even aware that others are also participating and that unless they play music which is written only for their instrument – and that is perhaps no more than one and a half percent of the whole music literature – they are not performing solo. They may be performing a very important part, but they are not performing that part alone. It is probably better nowadays [1970's] because of the technical means that are available for listening to get the general idea of a piece, like recordings and so forth.

That was not the case in my early youth because we did not have those means of acquainting ourselves with the entire work – we could hear it only when we had the opportunity to attend a live performance. So we had to prepare by ear, train our ears so that when we'd look at the score, we could at least imagine what was going on.

I once conducted an informal survey among my colleagues, not so long ago. I remember speaking to an excellent young viola player who is also a teacher and I asked him, "When did you first get interested in playing the Bartok Concerto for Viola?" He said it was when he was still young. "Well," I continued, "was it suggested by your teacher or did you hear it and want to play it or did you hear of it, or how did it happen?" He replied that he happened to have heard it on a tape, performed by a well-known artist. "And what was your reaction?" I asked. He said, "I thought I'd like to study it and try my ability on it." "And what did you do then?" "Well, I got the music," he said, "and I spoke to my teacher and told him I'd like to study it." I said, "When you bought the music, what did you do first?" "Well," he said, "I took my part and found the passages that I thought would be difficult and started to practice them."

That one case seemed to me characteristic. And it is similar to an actor who wants to learn the role of the lead in a play getting a copy of just his lines and learning them irrespective of whether they are part of a dialog or what their context is, or what brings his lines about. That would be inconceivable. But it happens all the time with players of single voice instruments in music. If you want to understand a piece of music, especially a complicated work, even listening to a recording of the whole piece several times isn't enough, you really need to find out how the composition is constructed and that means – studying the score. And that is somewhat neglected in musical education, even now.

By not having a serious look at the score to begin with, the instrumentalist is liable to waste an enormous amount of time because he is likely to discover that what he thought was so extremely important to bring out, turns out to be of very little consequence as far as the totality of the composition is concerned. What the soloist thought was so important in his part may not even fit in at all well with the work as a whole even to the point where, when a major work is performed of symphonic proportions, the player of the so-called solo part, the star performer, is not at all concerned with what is going on and he can actually be in contradiction sometimes with all the other people on stage. Correcting this sort of soloist's tunnel vision is somewhat neglected by teachers.

Now I know that many teachers say that a student can listen to a recording and find out about the whole work that way, but that is a dangerous approach because he will be listening to preconceived opinions and he has to accept them because he hasn't formed an opinion of his own. I think it would be much better if he would, to the best of his ability, study what the score says and then compare it with an experienced performer (or group) to see to what degree he was on the right track or wrong track. He might even decide that the recording is wrong and he is right! I wouldn't mind that either.

Styles of playing certain works have become standardized to such a degree, even "mistakes" have been standardized, that one sometimes wishes one's students would, regardless of the standard, have their own ideas and articulate them. If they do so successfully the result would probably be much more convincing than just imitating their favorite. I think there's a Latin proverb to the effect that when two people say the same thing, it is not necessarily the same. So, imitation at best is still a copy, not the *same* thing. Of course, the really gifted players realize that and get out of it and they do project their own originality. However, the great majority of so-called "talented players" certainly play beautifully, for the most part, but in their "beautiful playing," there is nothing of their own at all. In fact, their way of projecting what is a good imitation may be an imitation not necessarily of one, but of two or three different players.

I suppose my criticism in this case is to a certain extent a criticism of teaching, in cases where teachers do not encourage originality in their students. Of course, I can understand that approach because encouraging originality goes against the very nature of teaching whenever teaching means inculcating in the student the teacher's experience and the teacher's feeling.

And that is why I think that fingering a piece for an advanced student is completely wrong, not because the fingering is wrong – it is probably correct – but because it really trains a gifted young musician to be an eternal student. The teacher who does that fails to convey to students some very important things if not about music, then about life: namely, that as a rule, pupils are younger than teachers, that besides the works the pupil is playing now, he may be playing newer works ten years from now and then, still newer works. The main fact about an advanced student is that he is at the point of development where he does not need the teacher anymore. That should be the teacher's aim, his hope; just like a father wants his child to grow up to the point where he won't need a father anymore. And vice versa: the student's aim should be to get rid of his teacher as soon as he possibly can without doing himself any harm, and stand on his own feet. And the mutual striving to separate from each other will make a really wonderful student-teacher relationship.

For five years I was at the New School in Sarasota Florida where Joe Silverstein had a master class and invited me to come. In one of those classes, after students had played and he commented, one of the younger students, very gifted, asked me a question. Because I 'd had such a long career and remembered artists who achieved great fame who they knew about but had never heard, they asked me, if I thought that the general quality of playing and studying now had deteriorated or improved or was about the same as it was in my time, three generations ago? And I thought about it and said that I honestly thought it had improved. It's amazing what has been accomplished nowadays (mid-1970's). I don't know whether the improvement is due to better teaching, but the general way of making music, the methods of communication available has led to improvement because nowadays, we can listen to each other more – then, you had to go to a concert to hear a piece, now you can listen to it in several different performances, without leaving the house. Music has become much more accessible.

To give an example of how slowly and imperfectly one sometimes came to know certain things back in my youth, I recall that when I first got acquainted with the Kreutzer Sonata by Beethoven, I knew it as a piece for two violins because my teacher then was

Lotto who played *everything* on the violin, including all accompaniments. And you didn't miss much from his violin accompaniment. But because I had no way of easily hearing it otherwise, I really thought that it was a piece for two violins because that's how I played it with Lotto when I was a boy. I never suspected there was a piano part in that piece.

The first time I heard the Kreutzer Sonata played as it is written was two or three years later, in the summer, out of town. I happened to come into a house where a violinist and pianist were practicing after I heard the music, recognized it but could not believe a violinist and pianist were playing it! It impressed me enormously because I was crazy about that piece. Even for two violins, I was crazy about it. It was a *new* world.

* * * * *

I believe that the best way to approach the study of a work that is new for you is not to listen to a recording of it, but to study the score in its entirety, just the way an actor has to get acquainted with the whole play before he learns his lines. The actor has to know at least who is talking to him. He may be the star of the show but he still needs others to communicate with – without the rest of the play, he is nothing. He can not always have soliloquies, be Hamlet all the time, philosophizing to himself. When you are playing with others you not only have to react, you have to know who you are reacting to.

And in addition, it is worth reading the score even if you are not capable of always hearing the music simultaneously. You can still see how one part relates to another. Because if you rely on only listening to another person playing, on a recording, then when you play it more or less that way, you are actually imitating. That's the danger of it. It isn't how *you* conceive it but you take it for granted that this fellow on the record is famous, he is an excellent violinist and therefore, you think, 'I can't go wrong if I do it as well as he does, and maybe I'll do it even better. However, what he does is still not what your conception is – that's the danger.

This is especially true with works that have been played so much that a tradition of performance has developed and all that is left is to change the performance with exaggerations. Of course, there is a great deal of freedom in interpretation, in anything, and in art, more than anywhere else. But there is always a point beyond which, if you take too much liberty, you lose the work's sense of proportion. And when someone hears a too-free interpretation, it's as Goethe says, "Man merkt die Absicht und man ist verstimmt" ("One realizes the intention and one is put off.") That is the danger of being over-supplied with material, that it may take away the initiative of working it out by one self. I don't say that anybody should take his own conception as the *only* one. You should compare it with others and you may even change your opinion some times and other times you may think you do it better, or different, in any case.

That's why I'm inclined to think there is no such thing as a "definitive" performance. One of my BSO colleagues once told me that Leinsdorf came to a rehearsal of Tchaikovsky's Fifth Symphony, a work every orchestra knows and hardly rehearses, just runs through, and said before beginning, "Gentlemen, now, I think we're going to prepare a definitive performance of the Tchaikovsky Fifth Symphony." My colleague's reaction to me in telling this, was quizzical, "Is there such a thing as a definitive performance of the Tchaikovsky Fifth?"

MUSINGS ON THIS AND THAT

The players in an orchestra are like actors in a play. Each has his role and, in the final analysis, it is the actors who actually create the performance. But the director sets the pace, the tone, the emphasis of the play. From him the performers derive their characteristic style.

* * * * *

Not even the notes that are printed should be considered the holy Bible. There are lots of misprints in printed scores, but many composers could care less once they have gotten rid of that composition. It is gone, it is not *theirs* anymore. Otherwise, their creative ability will stop. They have more important things to think about, they always look forward to the next piece, like writers to the next book. The last piece is gone.

* * * * *

Amateurs are very sensitive to criticism whereas professionals and serious students react positively to it.

* * * * *

The Dean once asked me why all my students got A's and I answered: "Either they get A's or they stop studying with me."

* * * * *

Time by the calendar is of little significance to me. Time is rather the framework within which music is performed.

* * * * *

I can remember a time when people would walk out on a Stravinsky work, but now he is widely accepted; an example is 'Rite of Spring.' It is not that the public itself has changed, it has merely changed its attitude and come to appreciate what was there all the time.

* * * * *

I imagine, as in everything else, you gain more and more confidence the more you play a work. And of course, as in everything else, there comes a point of diminishing returns, and when you reach that point, you stop playing that piece, as a rule.

* * * * *

Art is the last illusion of mankind, just as it's been said, tradition is the last bad performance.

* * * * *

When conducting any piece, one must operate on the assumption that the composer knew what he wanted and put it down on paper.

* * * * *

There is no such thing as performing for zero. You have to have a listener. You are communicating and you have to have somebody feel that this communication has found its target, whether favorably or not, that's almost beside the point, since an unfavorable response at least means you are listened to.

* * * * *

The sign of an artist is not how freely one plays but how freely one plays in time.

* * * * *

I can't think of anything more satisfying than to feel that one has played really well. Real great music played sensitively is bound to impress an audience that is the least bit intelligent.

* * * * *

I feel that my function in the orchestra as concertmaster was to protect the weakest link; the strong links didn't need me.

* * * * *

I wonder why departures in life should be considered as occasions for congratulations. Let's have them when you're still present, not when you have shortened your future.

* * * * *

No art form moves faster or goes as far in experimentation and change as does music. Musical concepts are like idioms that grow or burst forth from traditional music. Perhaps the electronic innovations, new instruments and "no music" of today [1967] may now be fads, but continued experimentation in this area will bring about lasting principles, whether related to performance, instrumentation or composition.

* * * * *

Not every contemporary composer is a great composer. Neither is all modern, nor all classical music, for that matter, good music. In Beethoven's time there were many popular composers who are long forgotten.

* * * * *

America has made enormous cultural strides. 50 years ago there was no such thing as an American composer.

* * * * *

Being a professional [classical] musician is a very difficult way of making a living because in this country, there is a demand for such music from only a very small segment of the musical population.

* * * * *

Music should be concerned first of all with performing great compositions and not with projecting "stars." That is the last thing we should worry about. It is really not so important who conducts an orchestra, it is important how the orchestra plays WHAT. That is the essence of music, to my way of thinking.

* * * * *

The world we live in is often at odds with itself, its inhabitants cramped and distorted by fear. Fear is at the basis of human misery. Fear of hunger, of cold, of one's neighbors, even of one's self. Fear fosters greed and greed makes our great industrialists put their own interests even above the survival of mankind. Yet, I continue to have faith that the earth's inhabitants can somehow pull themselves out of their predicament. We must never give up hope. That is the most important thing of all – hope! Without that we are lost!

AFTER THE BSO, 1966 – 1977.

All photographs from the *Richard Burgin Archive*

> **Daytona Beach Festivals, Inc.**
>
> presents the inaugural
>
> **florida international music festival**
>
> featuring the
>
> **LONDON SYMPHONY ORCHESTRA**
>
> *Colin Davis, Music Director*
>
> Guest Artists:
> Richard Burgin, Guest Conductor
> Aaron Copland, Guest Conductor
> Janos Starker, 'cello
> John Ogdon, piano
> Jaime Laredo, violin
> Barry Tuckwell, horn
> Gervase de Peyer, clarinet
>
> at
> PEABODY AUDITORIUM, DAYTONA BEACH, FLORIDA
>
> July 28 through Aug. 21, 1966

Flyer for the Florida International Music Festival, 1966, where Richard Burgin guest-conducted the London Symphony Orchestra.

Professors Edward Kilenyi and Richard Burgin of Florida State University, October, 1967.

The Florestan Quartet at Florida State University. Left to right: Ruth Posselt, Richard Burgin, Harry Dunscombe, Robert Sedore.

Richard Burgin at his home in Tallahassee, Florida, in front of his memoralia-laden piano.

Burgin conducting a rehearsal of string-players at the Congress of Strings, 1967.

Burgin playing his imaginary violin while teaching, 1970.

Burgin (left) at the conferring of an honorary degree on Gregor Piatigorsky (center) at Florida State University, 1970.

Burgin rehearses the student orchestra for a Benefit performance at Florida State University School of Music. Photograph in the *Tallahassee Democrat*, April 20, 1972.

Above: Richard Burgin with his students at the International Conducting Symposium, Jacksonville, Florida, May, 1975.

Left: Burgin teaching a master class at the New School, Sarasota, Florida, summer, 1977.

IMPRESSIONS AND MEMORIES OF RICHARD BURGIN[26]

Leonard Bernstein, composer, conductor, pianist

I have only just returned from Europe to learn of Richard's death, I am strangely shocked: he was somehow immortal in my mind.

Malcolm Brannen, Retired concert violinist and Professor of Music

There are so many wonderful teaching moments that I had with him. I remember how he illustrated how to correct an intonation problem. He made me play it 5 times correctly before I could go on (a tried and true method), but with an added twist. If I played the passage 3 times correctly but goofed on the 4th try, I now owed him 5 more correctly for that goof plus 2 additionally from the first attempt. Within a minute of my futile efforts I owed him well over a hundred! Point well made.

Sarah Caldwell, Director of the Opera Company of Boston

The death of Richard Burgin marks the passing of a giant among musicians. [...] His enthusiasm for music of all periods and styles was a constant revelation of the musical insights he had and a source of continual wonderment to his colleagues, students and friends.

Not long before his last illness he and I had been discussing the second violin concerto of Schnittke: his interest and enthusiasm was surely as great as it had been for the second violin concerto of his fellow student Prokofiev, which concerto, in fact, he brought back to Koussevitzky in manuscript form.

Richard played with the Opera Co. of Boston in repertoire as diverse as Berlioz's "Damnation of Faust," and Lukas Foss' "The Jumping Frog of Calaveras County" (with which he toured with the Opera Co. to the Kennedy Center and to Denver); from Donizetti's "Don Pasquale" to Puccini's "Tosca" with Magda Olivero which christened our new theater; in Humperdinck's "Hansel and Gretel," and in the American premiere of Sir Michael Tippett's "The Ice Break," in which his long violin solo at the end of the second act was a reminder that great art never dies.

Ronald Carbone, Assistant Principle Violist, American Ballet Orchestra

My first memory of Richard Burgin is of course my audition for him at NEC at the beginning of my first semester in Boston in September, 1966. He was very polite and asked me what I had to play. I was happy to offer him quite a lot but he only asked for one piece. I began to play as well as I could even though I was horribly nervous. He stopped me after a page or two and thanked me. He sat me down and proceeded to give me a list of composers and etudes to begin remedial work. I had hoped to impress him, I only left depressed. He really was kind, but made it clear that certain areas of technique and musical education had to be fixed or filled in. He was quite right. I also remember him looking out of the window while I was playing as he had figured me out after just a few lines of the Bruch D minor concerto. The lessons did go well and soon I was preparing for my first jury at the end of the second semester. It was very important as continuing with my scholarship was at stake. I had to play a solo Bach suite and the Prokofiev five pieces. Until that time, Richard Burgin had never complimented me although he had gotten enthusiastic and often discouraged, as had I. But at my rehearsal with the pianist right before my jury he jumped up after I finished the Prokofiev and said happily to the pianist, "He plays these wonderfully, don't you think!" I was completely amazed and really overwhelmed with gratitude. Lessons were a joy from then on for all of my years with him, even when he was frustrated with my not just occasional slowness.

All great teachers and performers like Richard Burgin give their students wonderful information and training but few also give the tools and encouragement for independent growth and personal insight. By example and instruction he gave us all a gift that continues to grow and give us joy with the passing years.

Jerome D. Cohen, former Music Assistant to John Williams

Richard Burgin was my conducting teacher from 1957-1963. Each and every lesson with him was a revelation, for we concerned ourselves not only with technique, but with musicianship, philosophy and ethics. It is safe to say that Richard Burgin was one of the two people who had the greatest influence on my musical development. Once in a lesson, Mr. Burgin said, "We must operate on the assumption that the composer knew what he wanted and put it on paper." That really stuck with me, and was always an approach I tried to use when preparing scores. His imagination and musical curiosity also rubbed off on me.

Harry Ellis Dickson, former associate conductor, Boston Pops and violinist, BSO

[...] Even in non-musical things he was a brilliant man, one of the ranking bridge players in Massachusetts, and an enthusiastic follower of politics.

I remember once going to dinner at his house when Heifetz was there – the adulation that even Heifetz had for Burgin was touching. When Heifetz played the Sibelius concerto for the first time he went to Burgin to be coached, for Burgin had played it with Sibelius; Heifetz looked up to Burgin almost like a father. When we went to the Soviet Union in 1956, we found out that all the Russian string players felt that way about him.

Within the orchestra he was often the go-between between Koussevitzky and the players. Koussevitzky would talk to Burgin and then Richard would go to people and warn them, "The old man is looking at you." When Richard was asked about his role in cementing relationships in the orchestra, he always said, "I feel that my function in the orchestra is to protect the weakest link; the strong links don't need me."

Joseph Gingold, former concertmaster, Cleveland Orchestra and Professor of Violin, Indiana University

Richard Burgin was a superb musician, a great concertmaster, whose tenure of 42 years was a model of leadership to all of us who occupied similar positions in American orchestras. He was also a completely selfless man.

He was among the first to play the Sibelius concerto: it was his insistence that interested Jascha Heifetz in the work, and with Heifetz it really caught fire. He did the same with the Second Prokofiev Concerto. Prokofiev was a fellow student of his and gave Richard Burgin the American performance rights, but Burgin gave them to Heifetz and told him, "You go ahead and play it," and it became a great success.

His enthusiasm never waned. Just over a year and a half ago we were both on the faculty of the Sarasota College summer festival. The chamber orchestra was composed of students and faculty members, and I had the privilege of playing with him in this orchestra. And I tell you, he played like a young man of 20 – he just gave all for the music. He had an encyclopedic mind and total recall of things that happened more than 60 years ago. Altogether he was a wonderful human being, and I will miss him greatly. So will all of us who love music.

Lois Elfenbein Gosa , violinist in the Jacksonville Symphony.

When I think of my teacher Richard Burgin; I can't help but think of his delight in "solving situations". His eyes would light up with a brilliant fingering for a passage. His focus on music was powerful. Time was never wasted. It was not enough to fix a note that had been played incorrectly; one had to know why it had happened. Such lessons in life are timeless. Since Richard Burgin also performed with the Jacksonville Symphony Orchestra, I can say I often saw him practicing. I remember his respect for the music; his integrity. Integrity.

Nathan Gottschalk, former Professor of Music, State University of New York at Albany

As a long time student of Richard Burgin I want to pay homage to the memory of a great man who had a profound influence on my musical life. I have never met a musician who exuded such musical integrity with every measure of his impeccable and exquisite musicianship. This quality is one of the many legacies that he instilled in his students. His firmness as a teacher was always tempered and balanced with his gentleness and warmth as a human being.

I recall what a stickler he was for playing perfectly in tune. There was an incident when I was being corrected for faulty intonation. In despair I asked him when one learns how to play perfectly in tune. Without batting an eye he responded "Never."

Seiji Ozawa, Music Director Emeritus of the Boston Symphony Orchestra

The death [of Richard Burgin] is a great loss to the world of music. I have great memories of his performances in Japan during the 1960 BSO Tour there and fond recollections of him from the summer of 1961 when I was a student at Tanglewood.

Willis Page, conductor and former music director of the Jacksonville Symphony Orchestra

I learned so much from Richard, and I regret that I didn't seek out his vast knowledge more frequently. He was so willing to impart his brilliance in such a humble way, that it was inspiring not only to me but to all who would listen. Richard was one of the greatest, in music, in performance, in conducting, in wisdom and knowledge and as a person. He had the humility of greatness, most of all he had integrity.

On another occasion he gave me a lecture on playing in time. He concluded his remarks with the conviction that I have repeated hundreds of times: "The sign of an artist is not how freely one plays but how freely one plays in time."

Charles Rex, concert violinist and former Associate Concertmaster of the New York Philharmonic

Richard Burgin was able to give his students not just a spectacular education into the technical aspects of playing the incredibly difficult instrument we call a violin, but he was able to give his pupils an extraordinarily unique perspective into the music itself. At the time I studied with him, Mr. Burgin was what might be best described as one of the proverbial "grand old men" of music. I remember as a student hearing him perform in his late seventies, this as part of an ensemble doing a Rossini quartet. This was not just good playing for his age. This was great playing by any standard. All of us students were simply staring at each other in amazement at what we were hearing. His speed, his accuracy, his bow arm with a particular emphasis on his *spiccato*, was nothing short of astounding. And yet, for all his technical prowess and his ability to teach it, the thing that stands out above all else was the unique insight he was able to bring to the music he taught. It is daunting to remember that Mr. Burgin was a toddler when Tchaikovsky died, he was five years old when Brahms died, and he was a teenager when Brahms' great friend Joseph Joachim, the man for whom Brahms turned to for advice on his Violin Concerto, also passed away. Thus to Richard Burgin, the works of these great composers were contemporary compositions. One can imagine the impact of studying works like the Brahms or Tchaikovsky Violin Concerti with a man who was in a position, if not actually to meet the composers, to have met and known men who more than likely knew Brahms and Tchaikovsky intimately as well as any number of the greatest Russian composers of the 19th century. This gave a freshness and vitality to the music that would have been extraordinarily difficult to match with any other teacher. Richard Burgin's love of music never waned during his long life. I often remember passing by his studio at Florida State University, sometimes late in the evening, only to hear Mr. Burgin himself practicing a piece that he surely had performed countless times but that he would be teaching to one of his pupils in the near future. He was one of the most selfless and devoted men to the cause of music and his students that I have ever met, and I consider myself extremely fortunate to have had the opportunity to study for so many years with such an extraordinary man and musician.

Joseph Silverstein, former concertmaster of the BSO and conductor of the Utah Symphony

The dedication with which he persisted in programming difficult and unfamiliar music when he conducted the BSO instead of seeking the easy triumphs he would have received with popular programs is a good example of his selflessness.

We often speak of that remarkable bow technique, which he used so brilliantly in the Bach Brandenburg Concerti.

I have watched Richard coach a string quartet of middle-aged amateurs who had little hope of performing the work that was the subject of their efforts. He coached them as if they were about to perform in the musical capitals of the world.

Who could imagine the early years of the Berkshire Music Center without his wise and patient guidance?

At the New College Music Festival in Sarasota, Fla. where we taught together, I spoke to Richard about a baroque-style bow that I had with me. This ageless wonder couldn't wait to try it out in the hope that he would once again add to his vast musical experience.

In the Koussevitzky era he acted as the diplomatic liaison between the orchestra and the temperamental maestro and was instrumental in the birth of the BSO pension fund [and the unionization of the orchestra].

The strongest feature of his musicianship was his absolute reverence for the intentions of the composer. He used his superb intellect in searching every page of music for some additional insight into the thoughts of the creator. His belief that the performer must serve the music, not use it was absolute, and he had only pity for musicians who didn't live by this dictum.

My favorite example of his incredibly quick wit gives further insight into the warm reverence with which we all remember him. Once, during one of many card games, Charles Munch suddenly asked, "Richard, why does the orchestra sound so well when you conduct?" without a second's hesitation came the reply, "That is because I am not playing."

Robert Taylor, former music critic for *The Boston Globe*

It may be pertinent to point out that it was Richard Burgin whose incalculable musical contribution made Serge Koussevitzky possible. Koussevitzky was a prodigious musician, but he was in certain respects a throwback to the 19th century ideal of the virtuoso conductor, a tsar of the podium. One rather doubts that in America – particularly in an orchestra subject to labor upheavals – the conductor autocrat could adapt without a Richard Burgin. Mr. Burgin had a calming effect. He shared Koussevitzky's cosmopolitan cultural background, and was a consummate musician who saved many a rehearsal when the superb beat of the conductor went awry. Was it the rehearsal with Menuhin (the lost Schumann concerto) or with Heifetz (first Prokofiev) that Richard Burgin retrieved? No matter. The point is that, as the 42 years attest, he was without ego. He put the music ahead of himself.

George Zazofsky, former Assistant Concertmaster, BSO

Richard was an iconoclast, shedding ancient ideas for contemporary truths. He often said, "Tradition is the last bad performance."

Despite his enormous intellect (background), he retained a kind of childlike curiosity about people and the world around him, always thirsting for new ideas, new music, and new friendships. On one occasion, he spoke about pains in his right shoulder (bursitis). A few days later, he confronted me with, "You know, George, I was looking through the library shelves and stumbled on a book about Freud and some of his ideas. I believe some of my shoulder problem may be related to psychogenic factors."

On the many tours here and abroad, Richard's wardrobe trunk was bulging with new scores from all over the world.

At one point in our friendship, Richard expressed his feeling that the modern bow was rather poor in its design, even including the ones fashioned by the master bowmaker Francois Tourte. Richard spent years in redesigning the frog of his bow. During this period we performed Strauss's "Ein Heldenleben" with its protracted difficult violin solo. I was stunned when I noticed Richard using his experimental frog during the performance. One would normally expect a long period of at-home practice before playing with it in concert, especially "Heldenleben." But this was also typical of Burgin.

I believe that were Richard cast alone in the desert he would find a wild weed and through his love for all things living, he would eventually transform it into an exquisite orchid.

Richard truly belonged to the world, and everyone who crossed paths with him was enriched as a result.

ENDNOTES

Notes for Introduction

1. Dr. Dann graciously made a copy of these invaluable tapes available to me after Burgin's death.

2 Published by Slavica, 1989. A second, corrected edition forms the other part of this double-book.

3 Words of Ruth Posselt spoken to the author on May 1, 1981. The only traces of Burgin's first wife that I have found are mentions of her name, Henrietta Borsh-Burgin, on three or four concert programs, dating from 1913-1916, and the recently discovered information that Henrietta Borsh served as Jascha Heifetz's accompanist in Scandinavia in 1916. The couple was married in 1913 and divorced about 4 years later. The versified story of their romance in *Richard Burgin, A Life in Verse*, is entirely fictional.

4 Unpublished letter from George Szell to Richard Burgin. *Richard Burgin Archive*

5 Quoted in *Time* magazine, January, 1957.

6 Much of the fan mail Burgin received also concerned his Mahler performances. He particularly valued this note from Dr. Hugo Leichentritt: "On Saturday night I did not find the occasion to tell you personally how much impressed I was by your magnificent performance of Mahler's fifth Symphony. This was a performance of the first rank, remarkable alike for its technical excellence and its artistic quality, its intellectual mastery of the complicated score. It was an exciting experience, and I congratulate you sincerely on this achievement." (Dr. Hugo Leichtentritt, unpublished letter to Richard Burgin, Nov. 20, 1948. *Richard Burgin Archive*)

7 "Modest Wizard," *Newsweek*, April 30, 1962

8 For more on Ruth Posselt, see my *Performing Life. The Story of Ruth Posselt, American Violinist*. Troy, New York, The Troy Bookmakers, 2016. Distributed by University of Massachusetts Press.

9 There may be some readers who remember the popular ventriloquist, Edgar Bergen and his puppet, Charlie McCarthy.

10 This and many other opinions and descriptions of Burgin's teaching that I provide and quote subsequently were originally given to Lisa Ellen Robertson and are quoted or paraphrased by her in her doctoral dissertation, *Richard Burgin, Artist and Master Teacher*, FSU School of Music, 1998.

11 Readers may find this story of one of Burgin's students reminiscent of Burgin's own experience, recalled in *Memoralia* Part I, as a student in Auer's Quartet class more than half a century earlier.

12 Manuscript: *Basic Left Hand Techniques of the Violin and Viola – Thoughts for the String Teacher* by John Wilcox, Youngstown State University.

Notes for Memoralia Part I

13 Burgin thoroughly enjoyed the irony of coming from a family which, as far as anyone knew had produced no musicians before him in either his maternal or paternal lines. He explained his genetically un-preordained vocation with the quip, "After all, one has to start somewhere."

14 Gary Graffman, *I Really should Be Practicing*, Avon Books, 1981, p.10; 35

15 Burgin's personal file at the St. Petersburg Conservatory contains all of the documents issued to him every six months that certify his student status and give him the right as a Jew to live in St. Petersburg in rental apartments. Each time he rented an apartment he had to register with the local police station.

16 From 1916 to 1918, Burgin was assistant teacher to Auer in Stockholm and Oslo.

17 On the occasion of Burgin's 25th anniversary as concertmaster, *The Boston Globe* wrote: "No one, not Heifetz himself, has ever played the violin concerto of Sibelius in this town, who understood it as well or made it say as grandly that which it alone knows how to say."

18 The two orchestras merged into the Helsingfors City Orchestra under Schneevoigt's direction in 1915.

19 Ruth Posselt (1911-2007), American virtuoso violinist.

20 According to Ernst Törnquist, who played second violin in the Burgin String Quartet, the group was respected, well-liked and active in introducing audiences to contemporary Scandinavian composers' chamber works, notably those by Wilhelm Stenhammar.

21 Burgin omits a detail from the story of his audition for Monteux. When he finished playing, Monteux praised him, saying, 'You're one of the few violinists who doesn't play sharp.' And then, he offered him a 3 year contract. In reply, Burgin surprisingly, but characteristically, said, 'Maestro, do you mind if we make it for one year?' Monteux, naturally, was somewhat taken aback and asked, 'Do you mind if I ask, why?' Burgin explained, 'I'll tell you. It might turn out that you don't like me. If that happened, I wouldn't want to stay. But if we make the agreement for one year, then you won't have to continue with me if we don't get along, and if, as I hope, we become friends, and enjoy working with each other, then we can always renew the agreement on a longer-term basis.' And Monteux thought that was a wonderful idea.

Notes for Memoralia Part II

22 In addition to conducting the BSO, Burgin served as music director of numerous regional, semiprofessional and student orchestras in New England, Canada and the US, and later at Florida State University, where he founded and directed the Faculty Chamber Orchestra. In 1958, at the invitation of Pablo Casals, he conducted a week of concerts of the Puerto Rico Symphony. After his retirement from the BSO, he was a guest conductor with the London Symphony Orchestra, the Atlanta, Dallas, Orlando, and Jacksonville Symphonies, the New York Naumberg Symphony, Boston Philharmonic, Zimbler Sinfonietta, etc., and from 1973 to 1975, the tireless Burgin was on the staff at the Conducting Symposium presented by Jacksonville University's College of Fine Arts in association with the Jacksonville Symphony and its director, Willis Page. In recognition of his expertise, wisdom and experience as a conductor, Mr. Burgin served for many years as a judge in the prestigious Dmitri Mitropoulos Conducting Competition.

23 A complete list of Burgin's programs with the BSO appears at the end of this book.

24 Concert of Modern Music under the auspices of The Chamber Music Club and of the Flute Players' Club, Jordan Hall, Monday, April 23rd 1928. The program also included the Stravinsky *Octet* and Hindemith's *Six Songs from Das Marienleben* and Gruenberg, *The Daniel Jazz*.

25 Raphael Bronstein, "Richard Burgin Remembered." Quoted by Lisa Robertson in in her doctoral dissertation, *Richard Burgin, Artist and Master Teacher*, FSU School of Music, 1998.

26 The comments of Bernstein, Caldwell, Cohen, Dickson, Gingold, Gottschalk, Ozawa, Silverstein, Taylor and Zazofsky are quoted from "Colleagues pay tribute to a musical giant," Boston Sunday Globe, 10 May 1981; Mr. Page's remarks date from 1975; and those of Brannen, Carbone, Gosa and Rex were made via email to the compiler [DLB] in 2010.

PRINT SOURCES OF RICHARD BURGIN'S WORDS AND WORDS ABOUT RICHARD BURGIN

McLaren Harris, "Professor Burgin Chats on Music," *The Boston Sunday Herald*, 6 November 1966.

"Colleagues pay tribute to a musical giant," *Boston Sunday Globe*, 10 May 1981.

"Modest Wizard," *Newsweek*, 30 April 1962.

Robert Taylor, "A seeker of truth," *The Boston Globe*, 4 June 1981.

Sabine Ehlers, "Music is His World," *The Tampa Tribune*, 1 October 1971.

Robert Sabin, "Richard Burgin: Veteran in Two Careers," *Musical America*, March 1962.

Moses Smith, *Koussevitzky*, New York, 1947.

"Olive Crown," *The Boston Globe*, 1945.

"First Chair," *Good Listening*, September 1953.

"Concertmaster," *Time*, 21 January 1957.

"Music a 'Fast-Moving Art," *Florida Flambeau*, 3 April 1967.

"FSU Orchestra Is Formed," *The Tallahassee Democrat*, October 1967.

"Where Are They Now? Richard Burgin," *VSA Journal*, Spring 1976.

Mary Nic Shenk, "Music festivals: Where virtuosos teach and play," *St. Petersburg Times*, 12 June 1977.

Henri Temianka, *Facing the Music. An Irreverent Close-up of the Real Concert World*. New York: David McKay Company, Inc., 1973.

Malcolm Brannen, "The Art of Editing-Musical Ownership," *American String Teacher* May 2005.

DISCOGRAPHY – COMMERCIAL RECORDINGS

A. WITH RICHARD BURGIN AS VIOLINIST

1. Albinoni: Trio sonata for 2 Violins & Continuo w. Ruth Posselt, Cambridge Society for Early Music	Kapp 9024
2. Bach, J.S. : Brandenberg Concerti 1,2,4,5 with Boston Symphony Orchestra, Charles Munch, conductor	RCA LM-2182, 2198
3. Busoni: Violin Sonata No. 2	Circle L51-104
4. Dall'Abaco: Sonata for 2 violins & Continuo, Op. 3 No. 1, w. Ruth Posselt, Cambridge Society for Early Music	Kapp 9024
5. Mozart: Horn Quintet in E-flat, K. 407 with James Stagliano, horn; Joseph De Pasquale, viola; Jean Cauhape, viola; Samuel Mayes, 'cello	Boston B-201
6. Strauss: Don Quixote with Gregor Piatigorsky, 'cello, Joseph De Pasquale, viola, Boston Symphony Orchestra, Charles Munch, conductor	RCA LM-1781
7. Strauss: Ein Heldenleben (Feb. 16, 1957) with Boston Symphony Orchestra, Charles Munch, conductor	(CD) WHRA-6017
8. Tchaikovsky: Quartet in E-flat minor, No. 3, Op. 30 (first recording) with Leo Panasevich, 2nd violin, Joseph De Pasquale, viola, Samuel Mayes, 'cello	Boston B-206

B. WITH RICHARD BURGIN AS CONDUCTOR

1. Bach Family Set, with Boston University Chorus and soloists. *Record 1*: Georg Christoph Bach: Siehe, wie fein; Johann Christoph Bach: Es erhub sich; Johann Nicolaus Bach: Finale from "Jesaisher wein und Bierrufer". *Record 2*: Johann Bernhard Bach: Ouverture in D. *Record 3*: C.P.E. Bach: Sinfonia; W.F. Bach: Harpsichord Concerto in E-flat, Daniel Pinkham, hpsi. *Record 4*: J.C. Bach: 3 Pieces from "Amadis".	Boston BUA-1; B-402 BST 1008; B-403 BST 1006; B-404 BST-1007; B-405 BST-1403

2. Bach: Music of Jubilee, with the Boston (New England) Brass Ensemble, and the Columbia Symphony Orchestra	Col. ML-4435
3. Barber: Violin Concerto (Apr. 13, 1962) with Ruth Posselt, violin, and the Boston Symphony Orchestra	(CD) WHRA-6016
4. Bloch: Baal Shem, with Ruth Posselt, violin, and the Florida State Faculty Chamber Orchestra (Oct. 17, 1967)	(CD) WHRA-6016
5. Britten: Serenade for Tenor, Horn and Strings, with David Lloyd, tenor, James Stagliano, horn and String Orchestra of Boston Symphony Members	Boston B-205
6. Corelli-Barbirolli: Concerto Grosso, conducting the 12th International Congress of Strings, 1970	Cap. Custom SAAB 4110/13
7. Gabrielli & Frescobaldi: Music for Organ and Brass with E. Power Biggs, organ, and the Boston (New England) Brass Ensemble	Col. ML-5443 Col. MS-6117
8. Hindemith: Concerto for Organ, Strings and Tympani with E. Power Biggs, organ; Roman Szulc, tympani; Joseph De Pasquale, viola; Samuel Mayes, 'cello, and the Columbia Symphony Orchestra	Col. ML-5199
9. Khachaturian: Violin Concerto (Oct. 28, 1955) with Ruth Posselt, violin and the Boston Symphony Orchestra	WHRA-6016
10. Mozart: Divertimento in D, K. 136 conducting the 12th International Congress of Strings, 1970	SAAB 4110/13
11. Poulenc: Concerto for Organ, Strings and Tympani with E. Power Biggs, organ; Roman Szulc, tympani; Joseph de Pasquale, viola; Samuel Mayes, 'cello and the Columbia Symphony Orchestra	Col. ML – 4329
12. Tchaikovsky: Violin Concerto with Ruth Posselt, violin and the Springfield (MA) Symphony (May 7, 1944)	(CD) WHRA-6016

PRIVATE RECORDINGS (CD's in the Richard Burgin Archive. For inquiries: Diana.Burgin@umb.edu.)

1. Bach: Violin Concerto No. 1, Richard Burgin, violin and conductor, with the Boston Symphony Orchestra	10/22/66
2. Bach: Brandenburg Concerto No. 2, Richard Burgin conducting the Florida State Faculty Chamber Orchestra	10/17/67
3. Beethoven: Quartet in C, Op. 18, No. 4; Florida State University Quartet with Posselt, 1st vln, Burgin, 2nd vln, Sedore, vla, Dunscombe, cl	10/19/65
4. Beethoven: Septet (Exc.); Quartet, Op. 130 (incomplete); Florestan Quartet with Posselt, 1st vln, Burgin, 2nd vln, Sedore, vla, Dunscombe, cl.	12/2/70
5. Brahms: Clarinet Quintet; Florestan Quartet with Harry Schmidt, clarinet.	11/23/71
6. Brahms: Piano Quartet in G, Op. 25; Florida State University Quartet with Edward Kilenyi, piano.	11/24/64
7. Borodin: Quartet in D minor; Florestan Quartet.	3/13/70
8. Dvorak: Piano Quintet in A, Op. 81; Florestan Quartet with Mary Harris, piano	3/13/70
9. Haydn: Quartet in D, Op.64, No. 5; Florida State University Quartet	11/24/64
10. Haydn: Quartet in E-flat, Op. 22, No. 2; Florestan Quartet	11/23/71
11. Hindemith: Quartet No. 3, Op. 22; Florestan Quartet	3/13/70
12. Honegger: King David. Richard Burgin conducting the Florida State School of Music Orchestra with Harry Dunscombe, narrator; Brenda Boozer, soprano; Karen Poliboro, contralto; Walter Richards, tenor; Louise Van Dyck Sedore, Witch of Endor	5/26/69
13. Mahler: Symphony No. 2. Richard Burgin conducting the Dallas Civic Symphony, (soloists unidentified).	ca. 1969

14. Rimsky-Korsakov: Scheherazade, Richard Burgin, violin solo with the Boston Symphony Orchestra, Serge Koussevitzky, conductor	3/18/44 12/3/46
15. Stravinsky: Concerto in D; Histoire du Soldat; Apollon Musagete; Richard Burgin conducting The Zimbler Sinfonietta in an All-Stravinsky Program	1957

PROGRAMS CONDUCTED BY RICHARD BURGIN AND THE BOSTON SYMPHONY ORCHESTRA, 1927-1967

*Starred works have been digitally remastered from live radio broadcasts on CD. Many are in the Richard Burgin Archive; for inquiries: Diana.Burgin@umb.edu.

fp = first performance

1. December 2-3, 1927
Cherubini, Overture to Ali Baba
Brahms, Concerto in D (Spalding)
Shreker, Prelude to a Drama
Liszt, "Mazeppa" Symphonic Poem No. 6

2. Nov 30/Dec 1 1928
Miaskovsky, 8th Symphony
Beethoven, Piano Concerto No. 5
Strauss, Salome's Dance from "Salome"

3. Nov 29-30, 1929
Rimsky-Korsakov, Suite from Le Coq d'Or
Borodin, Symphony No. 2 in B minor
Saint-Saens, Violin Concerto (Thibaud)
Wetzler, Symphonic Dance in Basque Style

4. Dec 12 1930
Krenek, Little Symphony
Mozart, Piano Concerto K. 488
Sibelius, Symphony No. 1 in E minor

5. Dec 4, 1931
Vogel, Two Etudes, fp
Toch, Little Theater Suite, fp
Berezowsky, Violin Concerto
Chausson, Symphony in B flat major

6. Jan 13-14, 1933
Vaughn Williams, Pastoral Symphony, fp
Mozart, Concerto for violin in D major K 216
Chausson, Poeme for violin and orchestra
Stravinsky, suite from "Petrouchka"

7. Nov 24/25 1933
Vaughn Williams, A London Symphony
Tchaikovsky, Violin Concerto (Toscha Seidel)
Moussorgsky, A Night on Bald Mountain

8. Jan 12-13, 1934 (in place of Arnold Schoenberg)
Schoenberg's Transcription of Bach's Prelude and Fugue in E flat
Schoenberg, Verklaerte Nacht

9. Dec 7-8, 1934
Hindemith, Mathis der Maler, fp
Malipiero, Concerto for Violin, fp
Dvorak, Symphony No. 5

10. Dec 21-22, 1934
Corelli Concerto Grosso
Hill, Symphony No. 1
Toch, Big Ben, fp
Saint Saens, Symphony No. 3

11. Apr 12-13, 1935
D.S. Smith, Epic Poem
Roussel, Symphony in G minor
Rachmaninoff, Piano Concerto in c minor
Rimsky-Korsakov, Introduction and Wedding March

12. Nov 8-9, 1935
Shostakovitch, Symphony No. 1, fp in America
Prokofiev, Concerto for Violin, Op. 19 (Heifetz)
Respighi, Fountains of Rome
Ravel, Alborada del Gracioso

13. Feb 28-29, 1936
Weber, Overture to Euryanthe
Beethoven, Piano Concerto No. 5
Harris, Symphony No. 2, fp
Wetzler, Symphonic Dance in Basque Style

14. Feb. 25, 1936
Rameau, Ballet Suite
Berlioz, Excerpts from "Faust"
Roussel, Symphony No. 3, Op 42
Saint Saens, Concerto for Violoncello No. 1
Ravel, La Valse

15. Apr. 28, 1936
Svendsen, The Carnival in Paris, Op. 9
Grieg, Concerto for piano
16. Nov 27-28 1936
Bach, Toccata in C for Organ
Hindemith, Mathis der Maler
Kalinnikov, Symphony in G

17. Feb 26-27, 1937
Weber, Overture to Oberon
Mozart, Serenade in D major
Shaporin, Symphony in C minor, fp in America

18. Nov 26-27, 1937
Bach Brandenburg Concerto No. 6
Poot, Symphony, fp
Chausson, Symphony in B flat, Op. 20

19. Nov. 2, 1938 Meeting of Friends A Chamber orchestra led by RB performed Mozart's Symphony in A major, K. 201

20. Nov 4-5, 1938
Haydn, Symphony in D, No. 86

Krenek, Piano Concerto No. 2, fp
Loeffler, A Pagan Poem, Op. 14

21. Jan 20-21 1939
Shostakovich, Symphony No. 5, fp in Boston
Bach, Toccata and Fugue in D minor
Langendoen, Improvisations for Orchestra, fp in US
Liszt, Les Preludes, Symphonic Poem No. 3

22. Apr 14-15, 1939
Smetana, Overture to The Bartered Bride
D.S. Smith, Symphony No. 4, Op. 78 (conducted by the composer), fp
Wagner, Prelude to Parsifal
Wagner, Bacchanale from Tannhauser
Wagner, Daybreak and Siegfried's Rhine Journey from Gotterdammerung

23. Nov 3-4, 1939
Toch, Pinocchio, a Merry Overture, fp at these concerts
Hanson, Symphony No. 3 (conducted by the composer)
Haydn, Concerto for Violoncello in D
Strauss, "Don Juan"

24. On Nov 16, 1939 Ruth Posselt performs the Hill Concerto in Sanders Theatre (RB conducting)

25. Jan 26-27 1940
Poot, Ouverture Joyeuse, fp at these concerts
Schumann, Concerto for piano (Hofmann)
Brahms, Symphony No. 3

26. Jan 29-30 1940
Mozart, Overture to Marriage of Figaro
Brahms Concerto for violin in D major
Prokofiev, Classical Symphony
Strauss, Don Juan
Fernandez, "Batuque," fp in US

27. Jan 27-28 1941
Bach, Suite in B minor for Flute and Strings
Mendelssohn, Symphony No. 4 in A major
Ravel, Ma Mere L'Oye, Five Children's Pieces
Tchaikovsky, Romeo and Juliet Overture Fantasia

28. Jan 31, Feb 1 1941
Handel, Fireworks Music, fp at these concerts
Bosmans, Concertstück for Violin and Orchestra, fp (Soloist: Ruth Posselt)
Piston, Concerto for Violin and Orchestra, fp in Boston (Soloist: Ruth Posselt)
Brahms, Quartet for Piano and Strings in G minor, arr. Schoenberg, fp

29. Mar 21-22 1941
Bach, Prelude and Fugue in C major transcribed for winds by S. Koussevitzky
Chausson, Symphony in B flat
Stravinsky, Concerto in D for Violin
Stravinsky, Orchestra Suite from Petrouchka

30. Dec 18 19-20, 1941
Walton, Overture "Portsmouth Point"
Beethoven, Piano Concerto No. 5
Strauss, Symphonia Domestica

31. Jan 15 16-17, 1942 RB conducting (in place of Bruno Walter)
Tchaikovsky, Andante funebre e doloroso from the String Quartet No. 3 e flat
    minor Played in memory of Natalie Koussevitzky, died January 11, 1942
Brahms, Piano Concerto No. 1

32. Brahms, Quartet for Piano and Strings in g minor (Arr. by Schoenberg)

33. Jan 23-24, 1942
Vivaldi, Concerto for violin and String Orchestra
Hindemith, Symphony in E flat, fp
Schumann, Concerto for Violoncello and Orchestra in a minor
Smetana, Vltava

34. Jan 26-27, 1942
Vivaldi, Concerto for violin and string orchestra in a minor
Beethoven, Concerto for Piano No. 4 (Arrau)
Dvorak, Symphony No. 5 (New World)

35. Jan 30-31, 1942
Piston, Sinfonietta, fp at these concerts
Copland, Suite from "Billy the Kid," fp
Mahler, Symphony No. 4 (3rd and 4th movements), fp

36. Feb 20-21, 1942
Gliere, Symphony No. 3 in B minor "Ilya Muromets," fp in Boston
Chadwick, "Melpomene" Dramatic Overture
Liszt, "Todtentanz" Paraphrase on the *Dies Irae* for Piano and orchestra

37. Feb 27-28 1942
Haydn, Symphony No. 104
Mozart, Recitative and Aria (Dove sono) from Act III of Marriage of Figaro
Weber, Recitative and Aria (Leise, leise) from Freischutz
Sibelius, Symphony No. 1

38. Mar 2-3 1942
Levant, Overture 1912, fp in Boston
Levant, Dirge, fp in Boston
Lalo, Concerto for violoncello in d minor
Sibelius, Symphony No. 1 in e minor

39. Nov 6-7 1942
Lopatnikoff, Sinfonietta, Op 27, fp in Boston
Bizet, *Agnus Dei* from Music to L'Arlésienne
Wagner, *Träume* Song with Orchestra
Schubert, "Die Allmacht," Song with Orchestra
Mahler, Symphony No. 1

40. Nov 30-Dec 1 1942
Bach, Suite in B minor for flute

Lopatnikoff, Sinfonietta, Op. 27
Mahler, Symphony No. 1

41. Jan 14 15-16, 1943
Reznicek, Overture to *Donna Diana*
Strauss, "Don Quixote" Op. 35
Saint-Saens, Piano Concerto No. 4

42 Jan 22-23, 1943
Hindemith, Nobilissima Visione Concert Suite from the Ballet "St. Francis"
Robert Russell Bennet, Sights and Sounds, fp
Tchaikovsky, Romeo and Juliet Overture
Loeffler, A Pagan Poem, Op. 14

43. Jan 25-26, 1943
Respighi, Old Dances and Airs for Lute
Mozart, Piano Concerto in C K. 467
Strauss, Don Quixote

44. Mar 18, 19-20, 1943
Haydn, Symphony No. 95
*Dukelsky, Violin Concerto in G minor, fp Soloist: Ruth Posselt
Mahler, Symphony No. 3 (First Part), fp in Boston

45. July 18-19; Aug 29-30, 1943
Schoenberg, Verklaerte Nacht
CPE Bach, Largo mesto from Concerto No. 3
Beethoven, String Quartet in A minor, Op. 132, fp in Boston

46. Nov 26-27 1943
Beethoven, Symphony No. 2 in D
Bach, Prelude and Fugue in E flat for organ
Gardner Read, Symphony No. 2 (conducted by the composer)
Gershwin, Porgy and Bess, fp at these concerts

47. Nov 29-30 1943
Brahms, Academic Festival Overture
Beethoven, Symphony No. 2
Schoenberg, Verklärte Nacht (arr. for orchestra)
Gershwin, Porgy and Bess

48. Dec 3-4, 1943
Mahler, "Das Lied von der Erde"
Hanson, Symphony No. 4 (conducted by the composer)
Brahms, Academic Festival Overture

49. Feb 28-29 1944
Mozart, *Eine kleine Nachtmusik*
Brahms, Symphony No. 3
Mussorgsky, Prelude to Khovantschina
Mussorgsky-Ravel, Pictures at an Exhibition

50. Sept 3-4 1944
Purcell, Suite from *Dido and Aeneas*
Hindemith, Theme with Variations According to the Four Temperaments, fp
Shostakovitch, Two Preludes for String Orchestra, Op. 11
Tchaikovsky, Serenade for Strings Op. 48

51. Oct 27-28 1944
Mozart, Overture to *Der Schauspieldirektor*
*Bach, Organ Toccata in C major
Paganini, Concerto for Violin in D, No. 1 (Francescatti)
Hindemith, Theme and Variations – The Four Temperaments (Lukas Foss)
Ravel, Alborada del Gracioso

52. Nov 3-4 1944
Beethoven, Overture to Goethe's *Egmont*
Beethoven, Symphony No. 7
Shostakovitch, Symphony No. 6

53. Feb 2-3 1945
*Brahms, Variations on a Theme by Haydn
*Chopin, Concerto No. 2 in f minor for piano (Malcuzynski)
Strauss, "Don Quixote"

54. Mar. 23-24 1945
Mahler, Symphony No. 4
Tchaikovsky, Recitative and Air from *The Maid of Orleans*
Creston, Symphony No. 2, fp in Boston

55. Nov 2-3, 1945
Beethoven, Overture to *Creatures of Prometheus*
Menotti, Piano Concert in F, fp (Firkusny)
*Morton Gould, "Spirituals" for String Choir and Orchestra
*Tchaikovsky, Symphony No. 2

56. Dec 28-29 1945
Bartok, Concerto for Violin (Menuhin), fp in Boston
*Brahms, Academic Festival Overture
*Milhaud, *Saudades do Brazil,* fp at these concerts
Mendelssohn, Concerto in e minor

57. Oct 29, 1946
Handel, Concerto grosso in d minor
Prokofieff, Suite from ballet, *Shut*
Haieff, Divertimento, fp in Boston
Sibelius, Symphony No. 1 in e minor

58. Nov 1-2, 1946
Handel, Concerto grosso, op. 6, no. 10
Revueltas, *Cuanahuac,* fp in Boston
Prokofieff, Suite from *Shut*
Sibelius, Symphony No. 1

59. Nov 22-23, 1946
Haydn, Symphony No. 95

*Stravinsky, Symphony in Three Movements
Ravel, Le Tombeau de Couperin Suite
Strauss, Death and Transfiguration

60. Dec 20-21, 1946
Milhaud, Suite Provencale (composer conducts)
Milhaud, Symphony No. 2 (composer conducts)
De Falla, Suite from El Amor Brujo
De Falla, Nights in the Gardens of Spain (Luise Vosgerchian, piano)
De Falla, Three Dances from Ballet

61. Oct. 14, 1947
Prokofieff, Classical Symphony
Strauss, Don Juan
Ravel, Ma Mere L'Oye
Beethoven, Symphony No. 5

62. Oct. 17-18, 1947
William Schuman, Symphony No. 3
Strauss, Don Juan
Ravel, Ma mere L'Oye
Sibelius, Symphony No. 5

63. Oct 23, 1947
Mendelssohn, Symphony No. 4
Hanson, Serenade for Flute, Harp and Strings
Ravel, Ma mere L'Oye
Beethoven, Symphony No. 5

64. Oct 24-25, 1947
Cowell, Short Symphony, fp
Brahms, Violin concerto (Ginette Neveu)
Hindemith, Symphonia Serena, fp in Boston

65. Oct 29-30, 1948
Brahms, Symphony No. 3

Poulenc, Concerto for organ and string orchestra, fp these concerts
Hindemith, Symphonic Metamorphosis of Themes by Von Weber

66. Nov 19-20, 1948
Bizet, Symphony in C major
Mahler, Symphony No. 5 in C sharp minor

67. Nov. 21, 1948
Poulenc, Concerto for organ
Mahler, Symphony No. 5

68. Jan 4, 1949
Weber, Overture to *Euryanthe*
Brahms, Symphony No. 3
Bruckner, Adagio from String Quartet
Rimsky-Korsakov, Suite from *Tsar Saltan*

69. Dec 16-17 1949
Berlioz, Overture to Béatrice et Bénédict
Brahms, Variations on a Theme by Haydn
Wagenaar, Symphony No. 4 (conducted by the composer)
Schubert, Symphony No. 2

70. Jan 17, 1950
Berlioz, Overture to Beatrice et Benedict
*Schubert, Symphony No. 2 in B flat
Brahms, Variations on a Theme by Haydn
Shostakovitch, Symphony No. 1

71. Jan 20-21, 1950
Couperin, Overture and Allegro from Suite "La Sultane"
Vaughan Williams, Concerto in C for 2 Pianos, fp in Boston
Bartok, Suite from "The Miraculous Mandarin," fp in Boston
Shostakovitch, Symphony No. 1

72. Feb 28, 1950
Haydn, Symphony No. 88
Paganini, Concerto for Violin No. 1 (Ossy Renady)
Tchaikovsky, Symphony No. 6

73. Mar. 24-25, 1950
Rossini, Overture to "L'Italiana in Algeri"
Strauss, "Don Quixote"
Bartok, Concerto for Orchestra

74. Apr 11, 1950 (Same program as above)

75. Apr 14-15, 1950
Bach, Passacaglia and fugue in c minor
Harris, Kentucky Spring (composer conducting)
Mahler, Das Lied von der Erde (Soloists: Jennie Tourel, David Garen)

76. Feb 20, 1951
Beethoven, Overture to Egmont
Mendelssohn, Symphony No. 4
Brahms, Quartet for Piano and Strings (arr. by Schoenberg)

77. Feb. 23-24 1951
Beethoven, Overture to Egmont
Hindemith, Symphonic Dances
Brahms, Quartet for Piano and Strings (arr. by Schoenberg)

78. Mar 20, 1951
*Haydn, Symphony No. 104
Roussel, Symphony No. 3 in G minor
*Beethoven, Symphony No. 7

79. Mar 29-30, 1951
Haydn, Sinfonie concertante for violin, cello, oboe, bassoon
Mahler, Symphony No. 5 in C# minor

80. Apr. 1, 1951
Beethoven, Overture to Egmont
Chopin, Concerto No. 2 (Joseph Battista)
Brahms, Quartet for Piano and Strings (arr. Schoenberg)

81. Fri, Aug 10, 1951 Tanglewood on Parade: RB conducted Bloch's "Nigun" and Arbos' "Tango Espagnole" with Ruth Posselt as violin soloist

82. Nov 2-3, 1951
Weber, Overture to Der Freischutz
Foss, Piano Concerto No. 2, fp in America
Brahms, Symphony No. 4

83. Nov 4, 1951
Beethoven, Overture to Leonore
Honegger, Symphony No. 5
Tchaikovsky, Symphony No. 6

84. Nov 9-10, 1951
Mendelssohn, Overture to A Midsummer Night's Dream
Haydn, Violoncello Concerto in D (Piatigorsky)
Strauss, "Don Quixote"

85. Feb 19,24, 1952
Beethoven, Overture to Egmont
Beethoven Piano Concerto No. 5 (Byron Janis)
Tchaikovsky, Symphony No. 5

86. Feb 22-23, 1952
Beethoven, Suite from "Creatures of Prometheus" Ballet
Mahler, Symphony No. 9

87. Mar. 18, 1952
*Haydn, Symphony No. 95
Mahler, Symphony No. 9

88. Apr 4-5, 1952
Handel, Concerto grosso in d minor
*Prokofieff, Suite from the Ballet "Chout"
Tchaikovsky, Symphony No. 5

89. Oct. 24-25, 1952
*Hindemith, Concerto for organ and chamber orchestra, fp at these concerts
*Vaughan Williams, Fantasia on a Theme by Thomas Tallis
*Mahler, "Songs of a Wayfarer" (Eunice Alberts)
Shostakovitch, Symphony No. 5

90. Jan 27, 1953
Weber, Overture to Oberon
Schumann, Concerto for Violoncello
Shostakovitch, Symphony No. 5

91. Mar 17, 1953
Mussorgsky, Night on Bald Mountain
Beethoven, Symphony No. 5
Sibelius, Symphony No. 1

92. Dec 11-12, 1953
(same program as below except in place of Beethoven, *Ruth Posselt played Lalo's Symphonie Espagnole with Munch conducting. Performed in memory of Jacques Thibaud)

93. Dec 13, 15 1953
Stravinsky, Danses Concertantes
Beethoven, Piano Concerto No. 2 (Johannasen)
*Mahler, Adagio from Symphony No. 10
Tchaikovsky, Italian Capriccio

94. Jan 19, 1954 Ruth Posselt played the Lalo in Providence, RB conducting

95. Mar 19-20, 1954
Rossini, Overture to La Gazza Ladra

Read, "Temptation of St. Anthony" (conducted by the composer)
Mahler, Symphony No. 4 in G major

96. Mar 23, 1954
Haydn, Symphony No. 88
Mendelssohn, Violin Concerto (Norman Carol)
Sibelius, Symphony No. 2

97. Aug 1, 1954
Schuman, American Festival Overture
Vaughan Williams, Fantasia on a Theme by Thomas Tallis
Khatchaturian, Concerto for Violin, fp at these concerts (Ruth Posselt, soloist)
Sibelius, Symphony No. 2

98. Oct 29-30, 1954
*Bach, Passacaglia and Fugue in c minor
Harris, Symphony No. 7 (conducted by composer), fp in Boston
*Hindemith, Sinfonietta in E
*Mussorgsky-Ravel, Pictures at an Exhibition

99. Nov 2, 1954
Bach, Hindemith, Mussorgsky as above + Vaughan Williams, Fantasia)

100. Dec 14 Providence (same as above?)

101. Feb 20, 22, 1955
Bach, Suite No. 3
Mendelssohn, Symphony No. 4
Brahms, Symphony No. 2

102. Mar 15, 1955
Mendelssohn, Symphony No. 4
de Falla, Suite from "El Amor Brujo"
Brahms, Symphony No. 2

103. Apr 1-2, 1955
C.P.E. Bach, Concerto in D for Stringed Instruments

*Bartok, Concerto for Orchestra
*Prokofiev, Third Concerto for Piano (Graffman)
*Strauss, Dance of the 7 Veils from "Salome"

104. Oct 28-29, Nov 1 1955
*Mozart, Eine kleine Nachtmusik
*Khatchaturian, Concerto for Violin (Soloist: Ruth Posselt)
*Mahler, Symphony No. 1

105. Jul 29, 1956
Prokofiev, Ballet Suite from Romeo and Juliet
Hindemith, Concerto for Violin (Soloist: Ruth Posselt)
Mahler, Symphony No. 1

106. Dec 18, 1956
Cherubini, Overture to Anacreon
Saint Saens, Violin Concerto No. 3 (Soloist: Joseph Silverstein)
*Brahms, Symphony No. 1

107. Dec 28-29, 1956
Vaughan Williams, Fantasia
*Beethoven, Symphony No. 5
Shostakovich, Symphony No. 5

108. Jan 4-5, 1957
Bach, Chorale Prelude and Chorale (arr. By Munch)
Honegger, Rugby, Mouvement Symphonique
Debussy, Rondes de printemps
Ravel, Pavane pour une Infante défunte
Ravel, Alborada del gracioso
Mahler, Symphony No. 4

109-114. Jan 8 1957 RB conducted in New London, CT; Jan 10 in Newark NJ; Jan 11 in Brooklyn (soloist, Ruth Posselt, Bruch violin concerto); Carnegie Hall Jan 9, 12

115. Oct 25-26, 29 (T), 1958
*Liadov, 3 Pieces for Orchestra
*Mozart, Sinfonia Concertante for violin and viola (Soloists: Ruth Posselt & Joe de Pasquale)
*Hindemith, Die Harmonie der Welt, fp in Boston

116. Jan 21, 1958 – Providence, RB conducting, RP soloist (Dvorak violin concerto)

117. Feb 28, Mar 1, 4, 1958
*Shostakovitch, Symphony No. 1
*Schoenberg, Five Pieces for Orchestra, fp at these concerts
*Berg, 3 excerpts from "Wozzeck" (soprano)
*Prokofiev, Scythian Suite, Ala and Lolli

118. Apr 18-19, 22, 1958
*Gluck, Overture to Iphigenia
*Blackwood, Symphony No. 1, fp
Brahms, Symphony No. 2

119. Apr 25-26, 1958
*Haydn, Symphony 102
Stravinsky, Divertimento "Le baiser de la Fée"
*Beethoven, Symphony No. 5

120. Aug 7, 1958 Tanglewood on Parade, RB conducted Copland's Piano Concerto with the composer as soloist

121. Oct 23, 25, 1958
Read, Prelude and Toccata, fp at these concerts
Riegger, Study in Sonority, fp at these concerts
Bloch, Schelomo (S. Mayes)
Prokofiev, Symphony no. 5

122. Dec 23, 30, 16, 1958
Vaughan Williams, Fantasia

Bloch, Schelomo (Mayes)
Prokofiev, Symphony No. 5

123. Mar 3, 1959
Schumann, Overture to "Manfred"
Schumann, Piano concerto (Istomin)
Saint-Saens, Symphony No. 3 (with organ)

124. Mar 20-21, 24 1959
*Beethoven, String quartet in A minor, Op 132, fp at these concerts
*Schubert, Symphony No. 4
*Strauss, Till Eulenspiegel

125. Dec. 24, 26, 29 (Providence), 1959
Bruckner, Symphony No. 5
Mussorgsky-Ravel, Pictures at an Exhibition

126. Feb 5-6, 1960
*Mozart, Symphony No. 39
Kirchner, Toccata for strings, solo winds and percussion (conducted by composer)
*Dvorak, Concerto for violoncello (Piatigorsky)

127. Feb 26-27, 1960
*Hindemith, Konzertmusik for string and brass instruments
*Mahler, Symphony in C minor, No. 2 (Nancy Carr, Eunice Alberts)

128. Feb 28, 1960
*Beethoven, Symphony No. 2
Tchaikovsky, Symphony No. 5

129. Mar 1, 1960
Hindemith, Konzertmusik for string and brass instruments
*Harris, Symphony No. 3
*Tchaikovsky, Symphony No. 5
Tour of the Far East May-June 1960

130. 5/11 Matsuyama
Kirchner, Toccata
Mahler, Adagio from Symphony No. 10
Tchaikovsky, Symphony No. 5

131. 5/21/60 Nagaoka

132. 6/1 Manilla

133. 6/8/60

134. 6/13 Melbourne

135. Nov 4-5, 8 1960
*Beethoven, Symphony No. 1
*Bartok, Suite from Miraculous Mandarin
Walton, Belshazzar's Feast (Donald Gramm)

136. Apr. 14-15, 1961
Haydn, Symphony No. 88
*Mahler, Das Lied von der Erde (Eunice Alberts, David Lloyd)

137. Aug 11, 1961 (Diana Burgin sings in Festival Chorus)
Haydn, Symphony No. 88
*Mahler, Symphony No. 2 (Nancy Carr, Eunice Alberts)

138. Oct 27-28, 1961
*Bartok, Four Orchestral Pieces, fp Boston
*Hartmann, Karl, Symphony No. 6, fp Boston
*Shostakovitch, Symphony No. 5

139. Nov. 24-25, 26, 1961
*Mussorgsky, Prelude to "Khovanshchina"
*Kirchner, Sinfonia, fp Boston
Rachmaninoff, Piano Concerto No. 2 (Graffman)
Sibelius, Symphony No. 5

140. Jan 19-20, 26 (Brooklyn), 27 (Carnegie Hall), 30, 1962
*Stravinsky, Zvezdoliki Cantata for male chorus and orchestra
*Mahler, Symphony No. 3 (Chorus Pro Musica, Florence Kopleff)

141. Apr 13-14, 1962
*Shostakovitch, Symphony No. 9
*Barber, Concerto for violin (Soloist, Ruth Posselt)
*Schoenberg, Variations for orchestra, op. 31, fp at these concerts
*Tchaikovsky, Ouverture Solennelle "1812", Op. 49

142. Oct 30 (T), 1962
Sibelius, Symphony No. 2 in D
Blacher, Variations on a Theme by Paganini, fp
Strauss, "Death and Transfiguration" Op. 24

143. Nov 2-3, 5(M), 1962
*Copland, Preamble for a Solemn Occasion, fp in Boston
*Ives, Symphony No. 2, fp in Boston
*Blacher, Variations on a Theme by Paganini
*Strauss, Death and Transfiguration

144. Dec 7-8, 1962
*Stravinsky, "Le Baiser de la Fée" Allegorical Ballet
*Mahler, Symphony No. 4 in G (soprano voice)

145. Dec 16 (M), 18, 1962
*Fine, Notturno for Strings and Harp, fp
*Messiaen, L'Ascension, Four Symphonic Meditations
Prokofiev, Suite from ballet "Chout"
Hindemith, "Die Harmonie der Welt"

146. Aug 16, 1963 (Tanglewood)
*Stravinsky, Le Baiser de la Fée
*Prokofiev, Piano Concerto No. 5 (Lorin Hollander, piano)
*Sibelius, Symphony No. 2

147. Nov 1-2, 3 (Providence), 1963
*Berlioz, Overture "Le Corsair"
Hindemith, Symphonia Serena
*Tchaikovsky, Symphony No. 6 in B minor

148. Nov 5 (T), 1963
Beethoven, Symphony No. 2
Tchaikovsky, Symphony No. 6

149. Nov 8,9,10; Dec. 17, 1963
Haydn, Symphony in C major, No. 97
*Schumann, Piano Concerto (Darre)
*Sibelius, Symphony No. 5

150. Aug 7, 1964 (Tanglewood)
*Tchaikovsky, Symphony No. 6
Schuller, 7 Studies on Themes of Paul Klee
Debussy, La Mer

151. Oct 9-10, Dec 20, 22 1964
*Schubert, Symphony No. 4 in C minor
*Carter, Variations for Orchestra, fp
Mussorgsky, Pictures at an Exhibition

152-153. Concerts on Dec 3 in Brooklyn and Dec 13 in Providence

154. Nov 5-6, 9 (T), 11, 1965
*Schoenberg, Chamber Symphony, Op. 98
*Debussy, La Mer
*Scriabin, Le Divin Poème, Symphony No. 3, C minor

155-56. Concerts in Providence: Dec 2, 1965; Feb 17, 1966

157. Oct 21-22, 25, 27, Nov 17, 1966
*Bach, Violin Concerto No. 1 in A minor (Soloist: Richard Burgin)

*Hindemith: Symphonia serena
Shostakovitch, Symphony No. 5

158. Feb 14, 16 (Providence), 1967
Weber, Overture to Oberon
Shostakovitch, Symphony No. 5
*Rachmaninov, Piano Concerto No. 2 (Gina Bachauer)

To read
RICHARD BURGIN
A LIFE IN VERSE
turn the book over and begin again

turn the book over and begin again
THE MEMOIRS OF RICHARD BURGIN
MEMORALIA
To read

RICHARD BURGIN
a life in verse

Revised edition of the original from
SLAVICA PUBLISHERS, INC. 1989

Diana Lewis Burgin

TABLE OF CONTENTS

- vi | List of Illustrations
- vii | Foreword
- x | Annotations
- 1 | Chapter One: Childhood
- 29 | Chapter Two: Boyhood
- 55 | Chapter Three: Youth
- 79 | Chapter Four: First Love
- 109 | Chapter Five: The Finnish Connection
- 139 | Chapter Six: The Scandinavian Separation
- 167 | Chapter Seven: In the New World
- 197 | Chapter Eight: Double Concerto
- 229 | Glossary of Names
- 239 | Source Materials

LIST OF ILLUSTRATIONS

1. Josef Joachim's letter, October, 1902
2. Lily, Richard, and Bernard Burgin, ca. 1899
3. Richard as a boy in Berlin
4. Richard Burgin in 1908
5. The Fauré Program, 1910
6. Richard Burgin in 1912
7. The Burgins in 1911
8. Program of 1913 Burgin / Borsh Benefit Concert
9. The Burgin String Quartet, 1918
10. Richard Burgin upon arrival in the USA, 1920
11. Richard Burgin in the 1930s
12. Ruth Posselt, 1929
13. Ruth Posselt and Richard Burgin, 1941
14. Unfinished proof of a family photo, ca.1945

FOREWORD

In the beginning of January, 1981, my father, Richard Moiseyevich Burgin, former concertmaster and associate conductor of the Boston Symphony Orchestra, suffered a speech-destroying stroke while playing bridge near his home in St. Petersburg, Florida. A Russian Jew born in Warsaw in 1892 and educated at the St. Petersburg Conservatory of Music (from which he graduated in 1912, a Silver Laureate in the Silver Age), Richard Moiseyevich was cosmopolitan, assimilated, somewhat of a polyglot, but withal, a native speaker of Russian. Through his unspoken, and probably uncalculating, influence, I was lured to study that language and literature, and ultimately, became a Slavist. In this manner of speaking, my life came out of his.

Richard Moiseyevich was a fine raconteur and himself the subject of countless stories, the majority of which discoursed on his absentmindedness, or bemusement. He would always insist to me, however, that he "never forgot anything important." I wonder. In any case, he lived his long life almost wholly within the oral tradition: rarely recorded as a soloist or conductor; seldom wrote a letter; scribbled only in his stock books; and left behind a dozen or so empty diaries.

There was no small irony in his end. Not only did his stroke deprive him of speech, it occurred precisely one day after I had bought a tape recorder and he had agreed, with secret pleasure (or so I thought), to let me record his "memoirs." His death (on April 29, 1981) realized the metaphor and double entendre of his life – he became absent/minded, eluded recording, eluded me.

In the months following his stroke, I plunged into researching his life, trying to remember it. I was most interested, for obvious reasons, in recovering what, in my literary-historical fashion, I called his Petersburg period. In the process of research Burgin began to acquire the aura of a Petersburg hero (the model of which is, of course, Pushkin's *Eugene Onegin*), if not a superfluous, then, a super-fluid man, supremely ever-flowing...away from me.

By October of 1982 I had gathered a file drawer full of strikingly heterogeneous information about Richard Burgin, yet I still had no idea in what form to inform anyone about his life. Nevertheless, one evening that fall, I sat down to write. My first several pages of biographical prose sounded at best, bad, at worst, sad, in a word, not at all as Richard Burgin had sounded to me.

'But how did he sound?' I asked myself in near despair. 'Well,' I mused, 'often, he sounded...avuncular, like an uncle full of, full of...what? "Most honest principles?" [*Moi diadia samykh chestnykh pravil*?]" How hard that first line of *Eugene Onegin* is to translate! "My uncle full of honest morals, /When he fell seriously ill,"... "*Moi diadia...,*" My dada?... no! Too childish, too sentimental. Better: "My father," ... My father full of..." "My father full of marvelous stories, at eighty seven had a stroke, and left untold the joys and worries he'd lived, of which he rarely spoke."'

I seemed to have caught the sound and rhythm of Burgin in the Onegin stanza (14 lines, iambic tetrameter, with fem/MASC rhymes: (aBaBccDDeFFeGG). What resulted is the present work. It cannot be called a biography of Richard Burgin; rather it is an imaginative work, based in part on Burgin's life and reminiscences up to 1943 and in part, on my reading of it and them.

My *Life in Verse* is related to Pushkin's *Novel in Verse* in a number of ways, some obvious and others subtler. As the dedicatory stanza suggests, *Richard Burgin* like *Eugene Onegin,* is a heterogeneous narrative poem in eight chapters, each provided with an epigraph (or two, or three). Its chapters, unlike Pushkin's, however, have titles. The first three are deliberately borrowed from Tolstoy's autobiographical trilogy (*Childhood, Boyhood, Youth*) and the fourth, *First Love,* comes from Turgenev's novella. After Burgin leaves Russia, halfway through the poem, the titles of the chapters of his *Life* no longer have resonance in Russian literature, although some of the events narrated do.

The respective plots of *Eugene Onegin* and *Richard Burgin* diverge for the most part although there are points of contact and deliberate reversal. Where the plot of Pushkin's novel ostensibly revolves around the fictional life, character, unhappy love and ultimate defeat of the Petersburg dandy, Eugene Onegin, the contents of my *Life* concern the character, profession, loves, real and imagined life of the Russian-American violinist and conductor, Richard Burgin.

Both *Richard Burgin* and *Eugene Onegin* develop in counterpoint to their external narratives, through the relationship between the poet and her/his Muse, the meta-literary, inner story of how the work came to be written. And so, my "serious burlesque" plays upon certain stylistic aspects of *Eugene Onegin*: digressiveness, the influence of Byron, "multivoicedness," the poet's "life in verse," his/her mid-life crisis and anxieties of authorship.

But I have no pretensions to being Pushkin, or even a second Pushkin. In the end, what is Pushkin to me, or I to Pushkin? Pushkin is the "father of Russian literature" and I am a daughter of the realm, so to speak, a reader of his novel and a writer of my *Life*. That *Life* began with a dying father at a loss for words, and ends with a birthing daughter who has found them. The ways in which *Richard Burgin* echoes, parallels, polemicizes with and reverses its parent text, *Eugene Onegin,* reveal its play upon genre, gender and generation.

> Diana Lewis Burgin
> Cambridge, Massachusetts June 1988
> Second, revised edition, November 2016

ANNOTATIONS

All but the universally known of the several real-life and fictional personages referred to in the text are starred (*). Information about them can be found in the alphabetically arranged Glossary of Names at the end. Other items requiring annotation are footnoted and explained at the bottom of the page on which they occur.

The majority of Burgin's recollections, thoughts and anecdotes which appear in the text as direct quotations represent more-or-less literal "versiphrases" of his own words as spoken during an interview with Professor Elias Dann of Florida State University in 1974. Professor Dann graciously sent me copies of the tapes of this interview shortly after my father's death.

From early childhood to the end of his eighty-seven years, Richard Burgin's life was marked by those qualities of warmth, humor, curiosity, imagination, generosity and kindness that stand as hallmarks of a cultured, civilized man, an unforgettable figure who will always remain one of the giants in the history of the Boston Symphony Orchestra.

>   —Steven Ledbetter, *BSO Newsletter,*
>   Summer, 1981.

> *Art is an endless access to revelatory states of mind, a vast extension of living experience and a way of communing with the dead. An intimacy with truth, through which, however much instruction is provided and absorbed, each of us must pass alone.*
>
> —Shirley Hazzard

Not heeding savage Death's intrusion,
With live communion in view,
I wished to narrate an illusion
Of life, far worthier of you,
More worthy of your silent passion,
Your fatherly bequest to me,
Expressed in true poetic fashion
With beautiful simplicity.
But that's beyond me. With compassion
Accept these strophes Oneginesque,
Half-anecdotal, half-scholastic,
Purely factual, fantastic,
The fruits of serious burlesque,
Long sweats and sudden inspirations,
The jetsam of my middle years,
A conscious cynic's observations,
And true believer's heartfelt tears.

CHAPTER ONE: CHILDHOOD

And the echo stayed inside the violin...

–Annensky

I.
'My father, full of marvelous stories,
At eighty-seven had a stroke,
And left untold the joys and worries
He'd lived, of which he rarely spoke.
His reticence evoked adorement,
But oh, my goodness, what a torment
To realize I would never know
The life he played *pianissimo*.
What unbelievable frustration –
To guess at what was left unsaid,
To learn the relatives were dead
Who might provide some inspiration,
To muse and question in remorse:
'How could I fail to ask my source!'

II.
Thus railed a Slavist and professor
When starting her biography,
By Fantasy's mirage possessor
Of papa's Russian legacy.
Friends of Nastasiya and Myshkin!*
With thumping heart I take the risk in
Now offering my *Life* to you –
Its hero is a Russian Jew
Named Burgin, my beloved father;
In Petersburg, he spent his youth,
A period I've tried to sleuth
Or re-imagine, as you'll gather;
I wanted to be scholarly,
But facts, alas, eluded me.

III.
His dad, of cheerful disposition,
A music-loving artisan
Named Moses, labored on commission
In Warsaw for his growing clan.
Although Moiséy was enterprising,
It really is not too surprising
That with so many mouths to feed,
His family often was in need.
In nineteen five the situation
Became, it seems, uniquely bad,
And Moses, facing ruin, had
To look for work in emigration...
But here, I guess I've jumped the gun,
So back to Moishe's first-born son!

IV.
For he, by family tradition,
Was fated for the rabbinate,
And taking on the boy's tuition,
His grandpa tried to inculcate
In him a love for Talmud, Torah,
The meaning of the diaspóra...
In vain. To things rabbinical
The boy was often cynical.
Perhaps he sensed the sharp division
Between his grandpa's Judaism
And his dear mother's atheism,
Which made him chary of religion;
Or maybe he already felt
Another calling in himself.

V.
Of this he gave an indication –
At least according to his niece,
Whose anecdotal information
Was from her mother, now deceased –
When at a concert (so she told her),
A general tapped his father's shoulder
And said, 'Your boy beats time so true,
You'd think he was conducting, too!'
Indeed, the child had caught the rhythm
And waved his arms, completely charmed;
His father gazed at him, disarmed,
But glad he'd brought the child with him,
For when he saw the aforesaid,
He thought, 'My Lord! He's talented!'

VI.
O wondrous tales of *Wunderkinder*!
I love your truth apocryphal!
Not only do your lies not hinder
My faith in the exceptional,
They bolster it. Exaggeration
Itself becomes an explanation
Of giftedness, my mind may doubt,
But which at heart I know about.
And on a note less introspective,
The lives of Jewish soloists,
The Heifetzes and Zimbalists,
From an historical perspective,
Provide a useful way to gauge
The spirit of the Silver Age.

VII.

A frantic time when oh-so-teeny
Prodigies were all the rage,
And hoping for a Paganini,
Their parents pushed them on the stage,
As if enacting a libretto
Entitled, 'Fiddler from the Ghetto.'
The drama reached a fever pitch
At Heifetz's appearance, which
Made *such* a furious sensation
That it aroused concupiscence
In parents of the audience,
Who ringing with the huge ovation,
Rushed home afire to see if maybe
They could not make another baby. [1]

---

[1] The source of this anecdote was Mischa Piastro, violinist, colleague and close friend of Richard Burgin at the Petersburg Conservatory. Piastro told it to Burgin after returning from Berlin where he had the 'misfortune' of making his debut the season after Heifetz's.

VIII.
But I digress. Once he'd detected
The certain signs of talent in
His son, our good Moisey collected
Some funds to buy a violin,
And then set out to find a teacher
To guide his gifted little creature.
At last he found one, first of three,
A fiddler named Winetzky. He
Was in the Warsaw Philharmonic,
And also taught. But practicing
For him exceeded everything –
A kind of life-enhancing tonic –
For when his other work was done,
He'd simply practice, just for fun!

IX.
So, Richard started taking lessons.
He liked his teacher and progressed
So fast that after several sessions,
Winetzky made a strange request:
'*Pan*[2] Burgin, it does seem a pity,
Although we live in one big city,
I can't teach Richard every day.
But I have figured out a way
For him to practice more intensely.
I wonder if you would agree
To let him come and live with me.
His playing would improve immensely,
For pupils need a teacher more
When doing homework than before.'

---

2   *Pan* = Mister (Polish)

X.
Moisey agreed, and it transpired
That he consulted with his spouse,
And they, with great ambitions fired,
Sent Richard to Winetzky's house.
His six months there of education
Instructed him in aspiration,
In practicing with metronome,
And feeling home away from home.
....
....
....
....
....
....

XI.
But very likely he was lucky
In learning how to practice young;
I wish I'd seen him – eager, plucky,
Left elbow in, right arm out-flung,
Lips pursed in zealous concentration,
Perfecting the coordination
Between his left-hand fingerings
And right-arm strokes upon the strings;
Eyes scrunched in pure exasperation
When having got the bowing right
He'd hear a somewhat more than slight
Mistake he'd made in intonation;
The reddening callous on his chin
From practicing the violin.

XII.

Three years he studied with Winetzky,
And when he had a little time,
He started reading Dostoevsky....
(Here truth is sacrificed to rhyme –
Though not entirely, for reading
Became for him a game exceeding
The other kinds of sports and toys
That usually interest little boys.)
But books were not his only leisure
Amusement and activity;
He showed a real proclivity
For playing cards, an utter pleasure
Alike for father and for son,
Particularly when they won.

XIII.

O Burgins! Not for lust or fashion
Are you distinguished as a *rod!* [3]
Your rumpled look bespeaks the passion
Of scores exceeded, bids o'ershot
At bridge. What sets your hearts a-thumping?
Why, dealing, bidding, slamming, trumping!
And north, or south, or east, or west,
A long suit makes you look the best.
But now this "whistful" peroration
Has played its hand and worn me out;
Besides, I've more to tell about
My hero's early education.
Phase two began when suddenly,
Winetzky went to Germany.

---

[3] *Rod* is the Russian word for "clan." It is pronounced, "*rawt*".

XIV.
Yet his replacement was not fated
To fill the pedagogic gap;
A stern man, whom Moisey "just hated" –
Because one day he saw him slap
His son for faulty intonation –
He soon gave in his resignation.
I quote: "If someone hit a child,
That simply drove my father wild!
You know, he once approached a stranger,
An unknown man about to beat
His son, for playing in the street.
'Hey you!' he shouted, 'you're in danger
If you so much as lay a hand…,'
And gave the man a reprimand."[4]

XV.
The final member of the triad
Of Richard's teachers, no doubt you'll
Have heard of: Lotto,* much admired
Exponent of the Massart school.
A naturally gifted virtuoso
Whose mental health was only so-so,
He toured through Europe, won renown,
But then, his mental health broke down.
He quit his career concertizing,
Returned to Warsaw where he taught.
His method, Burgin later thought,
"Would seem to us today, surprising."
(His words were taped by Mr. Dann;*
I'll versify them if I can.)

---

[4] Richard Burgin, Dann Tapes

XVI.
I quote in full since Truth's my motto,
But since my Muse works in reverse,
I must his memories of Lotto
Rephrase somewhat to fit her verse
While trying to retain their flavor,
Each crumb of which I really savor,
Especially since the speaker's dead,
And I'm deprived of leavened bread.
I know the rises and reactions
Of living conversation's yeast
Are missing from my re-baked feast,
But that's the curse of all redactions,
Of trying to revive the word
That from a dead man's lips I heard.

XVII.
"Ja! Lotto was the strangest teacher!
At least, we'd call him strange today.
He was an artist, not a preacher
And rarely told you how to play.
Instead of any explanation
He'd give a perfect demonstration
Of what he wanted – then you would
Just imitate him, if you could.
So, often I would practice pieces
Which were way too hard for me.
There only were two books, you see,
He called them *Etudes* and *Caprices* –
That's Kreutzer and then, Paganini…
He knew of nothing in between!

XVIII.

"There was another thing, however,
About his teaching that I'd say
Was even stranger. He would never
Have more than one pupil a day:
That morning you would have a lesson,
Eat lunch, then have a second lesson,
And just before the evening meal,
You'd give a concert as if for real.
For that he had a whole procedure –
You'd enter from another room,
The *green room*, bow, begin to tune;
You'd play, and he accompanied your
Performance on his violin,
His wife, "the public," listened in.

XIX.

"I admired Lotto, loved him dearly,
Both for his attitude to me,
And as an artist for his really
Phenomenal ability."

....
....
....
....
....
....
....
....
....
....

XX.
The virtuosic expectations
Of Maestro Lotto's tutelage
Filled Richard with high aspirations
For a career on the stage.
Moisey was pleased with his ambition,
Yet knew he was in no position
To help his son financially,
However gifted he might be.
So, Moses had one grave misgiving
About the future of his son:
'His talent may be next to none,
But no one else will earn his living!'
Thus passes carefree childhood
With worries over livelihood.

XXI.
And there was reason to be worried.
In Russia, chances for a Jew,
No matter how he slaved or scurried
To get ahead, were very few.
To work or play away from home a
Musician needed a diploma,
And only Rubenstein's* would do,
From Petersburg or Moscow U.
Yet, musically, youthful Russia,
Aspiring and full of pride,
Seemed a poor relative beside
The age's ruling empress, Prussia,
And reigning king of violin,
Joachim, held court in Berlin.

XXII.

But Petersburg's Professor Auer
Had just begun to win a name
As *the* important teaching power
Behind the throne of Elman's* fame.
And Petersburg's conservatory
Not only gave a chance for glory,
It also granted *the* degree
That guaranteed security.
This fact compelled consideration,
For talents, on the average,
Seem less prodigious as they age –
Unknown the middle-aged sensation,
And last year's wonder held in awe
Becomes this year's *already saw*.

XXIII.

Sic transit Gloria mundi. True, but
How much we want it all the same!
So much, there's nothing we can do but
(And who will say that we're to blame?)
Take up the quest of Kavalerov,*
Delight in envy and despair of
Achieving that old-fashioned goal:
Expense of mind in waste of soul.
Thus, parodying literary
Examples of superfluousness
We spurn mere moderate success
For failure, extra-ordinary.
Yet all of us have learned in school –
Exceptions always prove the rule.

XXIV.
Psychologists have said it's female
To want and yet to fear success,
But Russian novels show that *the* male
Loves losing, too. Hence, the excess
Of self-destructive Karamazovs,*
Pechorins,* Silvios,* Bazarovs,*
Who'd rather leave the task undone
Than risk not being number one;
Who far prefer the laceration
Of being a superfluous man*
Than just another also-ran
Content to thrive in moderation;
Who finally, if they can't be best,
Would die than live like all the rest.

XXV.
To be or not. That IS the question;
And sometimes being is a bore.
It is so vexing, the suggestion:
'You *have* what *is*, there ain't no more!'
So, when you feel you'll never make it,
You may be tempted to forsake it
While making sure the world out there
Will understand *you do not care*.
It's not success we fear, but failing
To win attention; here's the proof:
If others worry, you're aloof,
But if they don't, you end up wailing
In gross self-pity, 'Why oh why
Is *my* lot but to do and die?'

XXVI.
Some say that talent is a blessing
While others deem it more a curse,
But one thing's sure, if it's depressing
To have none, some is even worse.
Is sanguine not to sanguinary
As Mozart to his foe, Salieri,*
The poisoner poisoned by his fate
Of being good but second-rate?
Recipient of modifiers,
A sufferer of the somewhat-too's
Not-bads, and almost-got-it blues,
He's damned by endless qualifiers
To minuses in front of A's
For being, "good in many ways."

XXVII.
Enough! I'll finish this digression
Or I'll run out of things to say
And worse, reveal my own obsession
With fame and give myself away.
So, to my tale I turn directly,
Which, if I can recall correctly,
I left with Moses in a stew
Considering what he should do
About young Richard's education.
He weighed the options carefully,
And then, consulted endlessly
From fear of some miscalculation.
Whichever course he chose to take,
His son's whole future seemed at stake.

XXVIII.
At last he took him to audition
In Petersburg for Auer, who
Accepted him without condition
And offered him a stipend too.
Of course, good Moses was delighted,
And Richard – terribly excited.
He felt he'd passed his first big test,
And things would turn out for the best.
Yet, once back home, upon more sober
Reflection, Moses wasn't sure –
Berlin still had its old allure,
And when he went there in October
Of nineteen two, just on a whim
He took his son along with him.

XXIX,
'Perhaps,' he thought, 'our luck will hold and
Joachim, though a famous man,
Will deign to hear my ten-year-old and
Agree to help him if he can.
It's worth a try,' concluded Moses,
'For man decides, but Chance disposes.'
(Adhering to this principle,
He reconciled fate with will.)
In this case, Burgin's intuition
Proved amply justified. Indeed,
Joachim readily agreed
To give the youngster an audition.
That hearing in Charlottenburg
Surpassed the one in Petersburg.

XXX.

Of this there's written confirmation:
A letter which Joachim wrote,[5]
Containing an evaluation
Of Richard's talent. Let me quote:
He certifies "...the boy possesses
A genuine gift," and then expresses
His "real surprise at the aplomb
With which the child played Vieuxtemps.
He merits serious instruction,
And with a talent such as this,
Steps should be taken to resist
That most exploitative seduction
Of forcing him upon the stage
Before he's musically of age."

XXXI.

Joachim said he would be willing
To teach the youngster, privately.
For Moses, this was simply thrilling,
But money worried him, and he
Replied, "Professor, I'm so sorry,
There's no way I can pay." "Don't worry,"
Joachim soothed his visitor.
"I'll see he's well-provided-for.
I'll get some funds and ask my distant
Relations living in Berlin
If they can take young Richard in,
And he will work with my assistant,
Markees, and every month, you see,
I'll have him come and play for me."

---

[5] Dated October 4, 1902. Original in German.

Josef Joachim's letter evaluating
nine-year-old Richard's talent.

XXXII.
So, it was settled, and my Richard
Left home before the age of ten
To start a life in earnest which had
Been just a wild dream till then.
But since his years away from Poland
Contain another story, whole and
Complete within itself, I too,
Shall put it off till chapter two,
And finish One with speculations
On what my prodigy was like
When he was just a little tyke:
What might have been his expectations?
How did he act? How did he look?
What *was* the childhood he forsook?

XXXIII.
I've seen one early childhood picture
Of Richard, Lily and Bernard
(His siblings). It betrays a mixture
Of youth and fatherly regard:
His hand upon his brother's shoulder
And look of worry make him older,
But his paternal mien can't hide,
In fact, reveals, the child inside.
O first-born child! Your emulation
Of parents satisfies a wish
To be grown up, a childish
Desire for grown-ups' adulation.
How innocent and worldly-wise
The *puer senex's* disguise!

From left to right: Lily, Richard, and Bernard Burgin, ca. 1899

XXXIV.
I know this since I played at mother
From five or six years old, I guess,
And helped bring up my younger brother,
To my great pride and his distress.
But there's a crucial differential
Between the parenting potential
Of him and me. I gave it up
As child's play when I grew up,
Whereas my hero's urge paternal
Was not a role, but an innate
Proclivity, the sort of trait
That Dostoevsky called *eternal*,
For he would father all his life -
His siblings, children, friends and wife.

XXXV.
And thus, when I have seemed alone in
The world, I have most strongly felt
There *muss ein lieber Vater wohnen*[6]
Somewhere above the *Sternenzelt*.
At least, I've wished to feel most strongly,
Since Beethoven could not have wrongly
Made music of an *Ode to Joy*
That even death cannot destroy.
"O *Freude!* Soul of all creation!
O Tochter aus Elysium!
From whence, o daughter, have you come?"
Are you not Death's transfiguration
Who rose when Mother Ceres wise
Effected there a compromise?

---

6   Words in italics are from the Ode to Joy in the last movement of Beethoven's Ninth Symphony.

XXXVI.
Alas! I see that what I've written
Till now about my soloist
Contains a flaw, and I am smitten
With guilt, sincerely feminist.
I've spoken of young Richard's father,
But seem to have ignored his mother.
I find this gap intolerable
But think it may be fillable.
The problem is that very little
About his mother's known to me.
It seems her friends and family
Regarded Ronia as a riddle
Because she rarely ever said
The half of what was in her head.

XXXVII.
Perhaps she was a *gentle creature**
In talk subdued, in silence strong.
For Moses, her outstanding feature
Was *not* to speak when he was wrong,
And in her silent disapproval
He often heard a stern reproval.
With talk, he was the opposite
And could not get enough of it.
And theirs was not a happy marriage:
By blood[7] and passion they were tied,
But in all other ways they vied.
The good old saw I shan't disparage:
It's true that opposites attract,
Yet joined, they seldom interact.

---

7 Richard's parents, Moishe/Moshe Burgin and Rachel/Ronia Krizowska, were first cousins.

XXXVIII.
And thus, we have these loving cousins
Whose marriage was a battleground.
She was a loner, he liked dozens
Of people always milling 'round;
About belief she could be caustic,
He half believed, a mild agnostic;
Her politics were radical,
And his far more canonical;
Moisey was clearly more dogmatic –
At heart, he felt the urge to teach –
While Ronia never stooped to preach
And seemed to be more charismatic.
Her children spoke of her with awe
And took her silent word as law.

XXXIX.
But still, they somehow worked together
In forming Richard's character.
It's hard to say with sureness whether
He took more after him or her:
For Ronia he had great compassion,
And yet he shared his father's passion
For music, cards, and company.
He loved his parents equally,
And when at times he felt suspended
Between their views, unconsciously
He strove for peace and harmony,
On which his happiness depended.
He sought to please with diligence
Both members of his audience.

XL.
By nature proud, an over-reacher,
He often thought himself to blame
Where others might rebuke their teacher,
And in this way, he overcame
The urge for childish rebellion,
Aspired to saint and scorned the hellion,
Repressed his wants, his feelings hid,
And overdid what he was bid.
Of course, no child could have voted
At *that* time in the long debate
Between his parents on his fate.
About their choice, he later noted,
"It was a toss-up in a way,
But either way, I had no say."

XLI,
So, was his childhood good and happy?
Or did it bring him pain and grief?
The question is both moot and sappy –
All I can say is: It was brief.
And has my *Childhood* been inspired?
Or has it grievously misfired?
I do not know, but good or bad,
Too short or long, too gay or sad,
I can't be blamed. My Muse parental
Has called the shots. I had no choice
But try to give her wishes voice;
Like Richard's, mine were incidental.
In what would finally be heard
I was not seen to have a word.

XLII.
We're dutiful, we sons and daughters
Of conscience's modality.
Our childish "wills" with adult "oughtas"
We still before maturity,
But early on, we learn repression
Can be a form of self-expression:
That inner voice that says, 'Don't shirk,'
Awakens real desire – for work,
And work is the most gratifying
Of pleasures. Though one must forego
Some others for it, still I know
No *jouissance* less self-denying:
It isn't like 'the birds and bees'
Where often, one may just not please.

XLIII.
Excessive work may be neurotic
Like nymphomania, drugs or booze,
But it can also be erotic
In self-fulfillment or –abuse.
The urge to work – so strong, seductive,
The stimulus to be productive,
Will get you up and out of bed
And powerfully turn your head
Away from everything. Forgotten
Are food, drink, friends, and pet bow-wow –
Aroused, one has to do it now,
And well-conceived or misbegotten,
One does not care because the fun
Is in the doing, not the done.

XLIV.
And there's the rub. Post-work depression
Is similar to little death;
Hence, the last gasp of this digression,
But now, I'm running out of breath,
And suffering from rhyme occlusion,
That forces an abrupt conclusion.
Of Chapter One there'll be no more;
Besides, I have a date at four,
It's nearly three, the dog needs walking,
I've yet to wash or comb my hair
And still must finish *The Corsair*,
About which we shall all be talking
Tonight, at Janet's. So, adieu!
We'll meet again in Chapter Two.

Richard as a boy in Berlin

CHAPTER TWO: BOYHOOD

–Ach, Berlin!
–Oh, yarn!

I.

My yarn continues in the city
Where Richard spent his boyhood years,
Berlin, which then was sitting pretty
At music's center. Its two ears,
The Petersburgian Polaris
And westerly Venusian Paris,
Were stars of secondary size
In European music's skies.
In France, the new impressionism
Refracted the Teutonic beam,
While Russia sparkled in the gleam
Of German post-Wagnerianism.
Effulgence of Berlin shone bright
In rival and reflected light.

II.

The concerts of the Philharmonic
Were under Nikisch's baton,
A master of technique symphonic
And post-romantic paragon.
The *Oper* thrived on strong sensations
Of fatal feminine vocations:
The "Queen of Spades" malicious play,
The heady dance of "Salome."
The Kaiser thought the last so vampish,
He pitied Strauss and cried, "Mein Gott!
I like this fellow quite a lot,
But this, I fear, will do him damage!"
"The damage," later noted Strauss,
"Provided for my Garmisch house."[8]

---

8 Harold Schoenberg, *Lives of the Great Composers*

III.
When Strauss, the age's Great Composer,
Had reached the apex of his fame,
My Richard, still in *Lederhosen*,
Knew little of him but his name.
Yet, sensitive to all vibrations
That echoed in his generation's
Development in old Berlin,
Unwittingly he took Strauss in
Although at ten, he'd not suspected
That he would meet the man one day
And under his direction play
The poem that his life reflected.
Ein Heldenleben's solo *Streich*[9]
Shall vibrate through my hero's life.

IV.
Nor had he any expectation
That half a century later, he
Would lead *Death and Transfiguration*[10]
With the Boston Symphony;
Or that his daughter'd try to capture
His life through that remembered rapture,
Or turn to articles on Strauss
To coax Berlin's *Zeitgeist heraus*,
Or ponder tomes in Harvard College
Music Library, sigh and think,
'Perhaps I've found some sort of link
In Maitland[11] with Joachim, knowledge
That can in part evoke those times
If only I can find the rhymes.'

---

9   *Streich*= string (German).
10 *Death and Transfiguration* was conducted by Richard Burgin with the Boston Symphony Orchestra several times. The performance recalled here took place in November 1962.
11 Maitland is a biographer of Josef Joachim.

V.

No, Richard's thoughts were more mundane and
Appropriate to a ten-year-old
Confronted by a strange terrain and
Adjustment to a new household.
At first, it all seemed quite bewildering,
But once he got to know the children
Of his new "family" in Berlin,
He felt at home and fit right in.
He quickly learned *die deutsche Sprache*,
Im Hause spieland [12] spent his days
And started lessons with Markees.
Each month or so he'd see Joachim,
Who checked his progress carefully
And treated him most fatherly.

VI.

Joachim, when my Richard knew him,
Was past the age of seventy,
But had begun (as critics view him)
An archetypal prodigy.
He had debuted when he was seven,
And as a youngster of eleven,
He "captivated" Mendelssohn
And went to England where he won
What proved a lasting reputation.
The sounds of Beethoven and Brahms
Contained for Josef special charms –
Renowned for his interpretation
Of their concerti, he composed
Cadenzas every fiddler knows.

---

12 *Die deutsche Sprache/Im Hause spieland* = The German language,/ at home playing...

VII.

In 'sixty-nine appointed rector
Of Berlin's High School *für Musik*,[13]
Joachim was a great respector
Of tonal art above technique.
His study of articulation
And difficulties of notation
In Bach – when to or not to slur –
In pedagogy made a stir.
To florid style antipathetic,
He challenged the Romantic taste
For showiness, with programs based
More on a Classical aesthetic;
And finally, (how could I forget?!),
He led a world-renowned quartet.

VIII.

Joachim has received his share of
Research and praise, but as regards
His playing, scholars aren't aware of
One side of it: his love of cards.
Burgin once recalled with laughter,
"He'd listen to me play, and after,
He'd say, *'Talant hast du recht viel!*
Nun, willst einmal'n Kartenspiel?'[14]
And playing with me gave him pleasure,
You know, since I was very good
At cards. From earliest childhood
It was my favorite form of leisure...
Ja! He was wonderful to me,
Just liked me and played cards with me."

---

13 *Für Musik* = for Music
14 *Talent hast du recht viel! / Nun, willst einmal'n Kartenspiel?* = You're really very talented. Now how about a game of cards?

IX.
Markees had none of these attractions
As we from Burgin's memories cull:
"I had begun to have reactions
To teachers, and I found him dull.
He was, I guess, a bit scholastic,
And so, to make my wrist elastic,
He had me practice every day
A Bach sonata the strangest way:
For several months that seemed unending
I had to hold my right-hand close
To a chair, you see, be forced
To play just with my wrist, and bending
My fingers, crossing strings, you know,
Dee-da, dee-da – with just the bow.

X.
"But later, I appreciated
What this Markees had tried to do,
And also, to be educated,
I think one needs some strictness, too.
A certain discipline in study
Is very good for anybody.
It was his strictness probably
That gave me flexibility…
Outside of Bach, obligatory,
The things I studied were, of course,
Etudes and scales to reinforce
Technique, the standard repertory,
And also, I remember, Spohr –
Concerto Two, in *re minor*.

XI.
"That was a different world from Lotto,
A new approach entirely.
Like many French musicians, Lotto
Would think of sound pictorially.
For him there always was a story
Connected with the auditory,
And whether it was *La Légende*,[15]
Or Sarasate, or Vieuxtemps,
The sound evoked associations;
Accompanying figures dealt
With what the hero saw or felt
In some specific situations;
There was a plot to be resolved,
You had to *live* it, be involved."

XII.
In hearing Burgin's commentary
About his training in Berlin,
I'm struck by two quite adversary
Approaches to the violin:
First there's Lotto, passion, pictures;
Then Markees, restraint and strictures;
From strokes, exultant *en plein air*
To arm held rigid by a chair,
As if (forgive my strange allusion)
A boyish Nastenka*-like flirt
Were safety-pinned to grandma's skirt
To check the childlike effusion
Of untamed virtuosity
With disciplined sobriety.

---

15 *La Légende,* a virtuoso showpiece by Wieniawski.

XIII.
Ideally, they are in conjunction.
In any field of life or art
It's quite impossible to function
With heartless mind or mindless heart.
Unfortunately, that's the trouble,
Since every person has a double,
And raging schizophrenia
Results in neurasthenia.
How often it becomes exhausting
To find the perfect equipoise
Of being-doing, quiet-noise,
Oblomovitizing* and Fausting,
And that's because the middle way
Appears discouragingly gray.

XIV.
Untrammeled feeling can be banal
And in its flabby excess – crass;
But too much discipline is anal
And in its rigor, lacking brass.
To play Bach as the first Romantic
Will always make the purists frantic,
But striking up a J. Strauss waltz,
Demands a little bit of schmaltz.
To find the manner for the master
Is every great performer's goal:
Tchaikovsky thrives on Russian soul,
Too soulful Mozart spells disaster,
And Brahms requires seriousness,
But Paganini – playfulness.

XV.

At times a fiery bravura
Performance surely fits the bill,
But trying to create a furor
At other times, can be quite ill-
Advised. I'd like in this connection
To quote a similar reflection
That Burgin made about the part
The soloist should play in art:
"You cannot always be a Hamlet
And only speak soliloquies,
Give personal philosophies,
Or by yourself perform the gamut;
You also have to interact
With other players, and *react*."

XVI.

I'm sure he meant his words sincerely
And do not doubt that they are true.
Yet, as a boy, I bet, he dearly
Desired to be a Hamlet, too.
He had been dealt at life's beginning
Two hands – one losing, the other winning,
A choice – to be or not to be
A genuine child prodigy.
For having Richard learn to diddle
Orchestral *tutti* parts, and strive
For second violin, at five,
Was *not,* why Moses bought a fiddle.
His dream was purely singular –
A secret wish upon a star.

XVII.

Stars! Program booklets wax about them,
From glossy pics their faces grin,
And playbills, posters, papers hail them,
Regardless of what town you're in.
Berlin, Warszawa, New York City –
All audiences' favorite ditty
Is "Twinkle, twinkle, child star,
How we do wonder what you are!"
The child star, however, flashes
But once, in youth; then it's too late
To use its light to navigate,
Against the rocks of age one smashes;
And Richard was already ten,
Which meant decision-time again!

XVIII.

Though he himself had little notion
Of what eventually he'd do,
The time had come to put in motion
Arrangements for the boy's debut.
Warszawa's orchestra provided
Its sponsorship; it was decided
The *Wunderkind's* debut would be:
December seventh, nineteen three.
I've often wondered, was he nervous?
And asked my mother if she knew –
She was a "child wonder" too –
She answered, "Children are impervious
To nerves, they think it's all a game
Until… they're conscious of their fame."

XIX.

Perhaps. But still, I have the feeling
When Richard's big first night arrived,
He must have found it hard concealing
The butterflies he felt inside.
Did he remember Lotto's lessons –
Those just-like-real performance sessions –
When dressed in velvet, collar'd in lace,
With curls encircling his face,
He walked on stage, tuned up, and waited,
His violin beneath his chin,
For his performance to begin?
And at the end, was he elated
To hear words redolent of bliss –
So sweet, so fleeting – *Bravo! Bis!*

XX.

A Russian newspaper in Warsaw,
Zapádny golos ("Western Voice"),
Reported he "produced a furor;"
That surely made his heart rejoice
And gave the management a reason
To schedule for the following season
My *virtuóza-skripach*á[16]
With Warsaw's *Filarmonija*.
But my young Richard's evolution
To a performing prodigy
Had just begun when suddenly,
In nineteen five, the Revolution
Brought family crisis in its wake
And undercut his first big break.

---

16 *Virtuoza-skripacha* = accusative case of "virtuoso violinist" (Russian)

XXI.

Moisey's decision to leave Poland
Was economic (see *One, III*);
Amid upheavals it was *no* land
For business opportunity.
With less incoming than outgoing
And with his child production showing
No sign of slowing even at six,
Moisey was really in a fix.
In nineteen five his brother Leo[17]
Had left and settled in New York;
He wrote to say that he'd found work,
And Moishe mused, 'Perhaps you'll be, oh
America, deliverance
And offer me a second chance.'

XXII.

So, when the Polish situation
Became unalterably grim,
Moisey resolved on emigration:
He'd take his oldest son with him
But leave at home his several, other
Children and, of course, their mother,
And if his gains should top his loss,
He hoped to bring them all across.
Thus Moishe, having expectations,
Could fight his slough of deep despond.
But Richard? How did he respond?
With joy? Or had he reservations?
Did he, in fact, prefer to roam
Around the world or stay at home?

---

17 Leo (Leib) Burgin, one of Moishe's three brothers, active in the Polish Workers' Movement.

XXIII.

The only memories I'm aware of
Him having of his German years
Were fond: He was "well-taken-care-of,"
Enjoyed the friendship of his peers,
Fit in the family that he stayed with,
And "loved" Joachim, who he played with.
"It was a happy time," he'd tell,
"And with my music I did well."
So probably he felt a spasm
Of sorrow when he had to leave;
Yet only briefly would he grieve
Since he possessed enthusiasm,
And future dreams so filled his mind
That he could leave the past behind.

XXIV.

What future dreams? For me this poses
A puzzle, and my readership
Might also query, why did Moses
Take Richard on the new world trip?
I'm forced to guess the explanation:
Had he a hidden motivation
To spurn the European fame
Already spreading Richard's name?
Had he perhaps become ambitious
To scale the lofty new world heights,
See Richard's name in New York lights,
And hoped the moment was propitious
To launch abroad sensationally
A European prodigy?

XXV.
If so, I think the great sensation
That Richard made was not the kind,
By any stretched imagination,
That could have entered Moishe's mind.

....
....
....
....
....
....
....
....
....
....

2

New York, New York!
(Popular Song)

XXVI.[18]
I love you, Peter Minuit's purchase,
I love your steel and glass attire:
It seems the vault of heaven perches
Atop your tallest Empire spire.
I love your thrust and aspiration,
The grandeur of Grand Central Station,
The tawdry glamour of Times Square
Where gawking tourists stop and stare;
The dazzling cost of your *per diems*,
The glittering stores where in a thrice
One spends ten times your purchase price;
I love the wealth of your museums,
Your theaters, shows, but most of all,
I love in you Carnegie Hall.

XXVII.
My visits there have been infrequent,
Yet I'm among its devotees
Because it conjures up both piquant
And poignant family memories.
I think I'll save my own for later,
But one of Richard's forms the greater
Proportion of this chapter's end.
But first, however, I intend
To give, by way of preparation,
Some facts about the New York scene
When Richard came there as a teen,
Flesh out with details my narration
And build up to his memory
Through strict sequentiality.

---

18 Stanza XXVI parodies the rhythm and diction of Pushkin's well-known paen to the city of St. Petersburg in the *Invocation* to *The Bronze Horseman*, which begins, "I love you, Peter's creation, I love your stern, harmonious look..."

XXVIII.
The concert life in New York City
When Richard went to visit there
Was, judging by my sources, pretty
Much the same as anywhere.
The trustees of the Philharmonic
Society engaged Safonov
To keep the orchestra in time
From nineteen six to nineteen nine;
The Russian Orchestra of local
Repute premiered Rachmaninov,
Scriabine and Rimsky-Korsakov;
And Germans topped the bill in vocal
Performance with their very fine
Liederkranz Gesangverein.

XXIX.
Musicians came from many nations –
Germans, Slavs and Wandering Jews –
The widely-recognized sensations
And hopefuls making their debuts.
The city was a cultural Babel,
But super-talents still were able
To harmonize some rare delights
For musical cosmopolites.
It was a town to test the mettle,
To challenge, realize, or destroy
The dreams of any striving boy,
And Richard, though in finest fettle
When he arrived, was struck with awe
By what he heard and what he saw.

XXX.
The rapid, roaring, groaning gliss of
The subway deafened Richard's ears,
But kindly welcome words from Krisoff
Defused his nerves and calmed his fears.
(This Krisoff was my hero's other
American uncle, Ronia's brother.
My new arrivals lived with him
At one five seven six Madison.)
Once Richard had unpacked and rested,
Reset his inner metronome
And got in time with his new home,
Of all his qualms, he was divested.
He learned some English, felt much freer,
And set about his new career.

XXXI.
The Music School that was connected
With Liederkranz Society
Auditioned Richard and selected
The boy to play as prodigy.
His solos earned him commendation
As well as some remuneration,
And then, a Mr. Filchscheimer,
Who was a wealthy amateur
Of chamber music and was looking
For a fourth, gave him the job.
He'd play quartets and then hobnob,
Earn cash, experience and…good cooking!
He noted, "It was quite a deal –
Five dollars an evening and a meal!

XXXII.
"Those meals there simply were delicious!"
I taste his praises with my eyes.
They whet digressive bits nutritious
To please my palate, epic-wise.
O tempting, titillating dinners,
How you beguile us fleshly sinners!
Bedevil us with eggs and steak,
Diavolos and chocolate cake!
From soup to nuts we love all courses:
In *haute, midi or basse cuisine*
De l'Amerique, la France, ou Chine,
We eat *comme les chevaux* (like horses).
Yet, even when I'm full, *j'ai faim*
For any sort of *pôts de crème*.

XXXIII.
For certain things we all have passions:
Pushkin for feet and Keats for dreams,
Gogol for noses, Byron – fashions,
Swinburne – whips, and Burgin – creams.
Frappées, glacées, anglaises, françaises,
Aux chocolates, vanilles, ou fraises,
All flavors and varieties
My gustatory organs tease.
A cream is dining's culmination
And at its best if saved for last,
But when I'm rushed and must eat fast,
Without a moment's hesitation,
I'll pass the preparatory fare
And quickly have a cream éclair.

XXXIV.
Yes! Cream can make me feel euphoric.
Its marvels are past arguing:
I cite its meaning metaphoric –
The choicest part of anything.
The best of crops or social stations,
Among the highest approbations,
For what can be one's goal supreme
If not the judgment "cream of cream"?
And on a more material level –
I'm fond of such antitheses –
Cream soda, sauces, puffs and cheese
Are goods in which I also revel.
Indeed, for me, good-better-best
Is creamy-creamier-creamiest.

XXXV.
However, though I've hardly sated
My appetite for sweet, rich cream,
I'll end before I am berated
And lose my readers' high esteem.
To those who deem my taste egregious
And scream, 'Enough!' I say 'Who needs-yuz?'
For those who think my diet extreme,
I recommend a bream regime;
On those who judge my dreams unseemly
Or teem with rage that I blaspheme
An epic theme with anatheme,
I wish digressiveness supremely
Beseeming all their watery ilk –
A steady stream of non-fat milk!

XXXVI.
Let's see, where was I?   Yes, preparing
The climax of this second part
By telling how the boy was faring
Professionally in his art.
Besides recitals, Liederkranzing,
Quartets and gigs, he did freelancing
In Arnold Volpe's Orchestra*
And also played the cinema.
Although his state of mind was sunny,
Some little clouds began to form
From pressure to exceed the norm
And constant worries over money.
This darkening sky, alas, portends
A music storm of means and ends.

XXXVII.
The outburst came in nineteen seven,
A gloomy year in Richard's life
When what had seemed a new-world heaven
Was drowned by hellish storm and strife.
The sprinkles started with a panning
And ended in a downpour, banning
The youngster from the concert stage
For working while still underage.
In March, he gave a big recital,
That drew a small (if friendly) house
But made the New York critics grouse.
That hurt, but taught him something vital,
The moral of the concert hall:
In every life, some rain must fall.

XXXVIII.
This was an adage he'd remember,
Perhaps remember to forget,
When in the deluge of November
His whole career was upset.
But I distinctly do remember
The day I learned of that November...
The library. Oh, my eyes were sore
From scanning microfilms of yore,
My strength was sapped, I felt like napping,
About to mutter, 'Nevermore
Will I peruse forgotten lore,'
When suddenly came Katherine's[19] tapping:
'Diana, look!' I bent, stared hard,
And read, "BOY VIOLINIST BARRED.

XXXIX.
"RICHARD BURGIN NOT ALLOWED TO
PLAY WITH VOLPE ORCHESTRA."
(The headlines fit my verse, but how to
Convey the rest without *faux pas*?
It seems I can't make journalism
Conform to my poeticism,
So with the effort I'll make done
And paraphrase the *New York Sun*.)[20]
In brief, before the concert started,
Maestro Volpe was informed
That if the Burgin boy performed,
There'd be no concert. He departed
When asked to leave, but once outside,
He heard the concert start, and cried.

---

19 Professor Katherine T. O'Connor, friend and colleague of the author, who was reading microfilms with her in the New York Public Library.
20 *The New York Sun*, November 22, 1907, carried the article on the front page.

XL.

The reasons for the Gerry's[21] hounding
My Richard from the concert stage
Would really not have been astounding
Had they to do with just his age.
But there was something superseding
That fact, and strangely, it was reading,
Or more specifically, a book
Which from the library he took
To read at home and had forgotten.
When it became long overdue,
They claimed he stole it. (Wouldn't you
Agree with me that that was rotten?
Had Widener[22] gotten on my trail
For late returns, I'd be in jail.)

XLI.

In any case, he was arrested,
And then in Children's Court arraigned.
He "pleaded guilty as suggested
By counsel," under oath explained,
In answer to the accusation
That "ignorant of regulations
In this new land," he "never knew
The library book was overdue."
Then Morris made his peroration
As the eternal suppliant:
'Your Honor, I've spent every cent
I had on Richard's education.
Now he's the sole support, you see,
Of his entire family.'

---

21 The Children's Society
22 Widener Library at Harvard University where the Author received her PhD in Slavic Languages and Literatures.

XLII.

The judge paroled the boy that morning,
But ruled, 'Tonight, you can't appear
At Volpe's concert. Heed my warning,
Or else the Gerry will interfere.'
The story came in several versions –
Which ones are true, and which perversions?
The *Sun* was most detailed, by far;
The *Times* in its details, bizarre:
"One less musician than expected
Appeared last night…and we were told
That Bergmann [*sic!*], fifteen years old,
Was banned because his father objected
To his young son's appearance here
And asked the Gerry to interfere."[23]

XLIII.

I find this last account revealing
Despite the "Bergmann" oversight,[24]
Because inside, I have the feeling
The way it sees Moisey is right.
He knew his son and thus, suspected
That hoping he'd be undetected,
The boy would likely disobey
Judge Wyatt, and attempt to play.
'Is better I should burst his bubble,'
He thought, 'and call this Gerry in
Myself, than have the court step in
And make for us still more the trouble.
As if I do not got enough
Of all this court and legal stuff!'

---

23 Burgin was born on October 10, 1892.
24 The name of the banned player, according to the *New York Times* account (November 22, 1907) was "Adolph Bergmann." The incident is also reported by Marie Volpe in her biography of Arnold Volpe (Miami, 1950) on the basis of the account in the *New York World*.

XLIV.
Moishe's thoughts on intervention
In this regrettable affair
Convey an overtone of tension,
Perhaps a note of real despair.
Indeed, the city that had fired
His hopes for work and had inspired
His trip away from Warsaw's slough
Appeared far less enchanting now.
His hopes no longer were ascendant,
The work he'd found had been a loss,
For used to being his own boss,
By nature, proud and independent,
It seemed that he could not adjust
To working for some giant trust

XLV.
Although Moisey had always prided
Himself on his tenacity,
On this occasion, he decided –
Albeit somewhat ruefully –
He was not meant to be a rover,
He could not bring his family over,
The new world way was full of bumps,
And he was really in the dumps.
He'd dug himself into a hole and
No longer had the slightest doubt
For him there was but one way out,
And that was – to return to Poland.
But where would youthful Richard go?
(Just wait! In Chapter Three, you'll know.)

CHAPTER THREE: YOUTH

For he is the artist of his own life...

–Dostoevsky

I.

"So where he go? Oy, such a worry!"
"Ach, Leib, I'm really in a state!"
"*Natürlich, Bruder, und* I'm sorry,
But what will be your Richard's fate?"
"Who knows?" "But Moishe, time is flying,
And what will you accomplish crying?"
"*Da nichevo*."[25] "I understand
Your fears, but take yourself in hand.
The first thing, listen what I'm saying,
You going home, and he *mit* you,
And there, you told me, *ist nicht* true?
He had success already, playing,
Did good and didn't break no rules?
They got *goot* teachers, music schools..."

II.

"I don't yet see to what you're getting?"
"Why Petersburg! That's what I'd choose."
"But Leib, you seem to be forgetting
The way things are there now for Jews –
Pogroms, and quotas..." "Ja, *und* Auer!
Don't he got there a lot of power?
Besides, he heard your Richard play
Already, and did you not say
He thought him *goot*? Well, now he's better!
So Moishe, why you look so grim?
Why don't you get in touch with him?"
"We're here, he's there." "So write a letter!"
"To Auer?" "Ja!" "Now?" "Right away!
My words you mark, he'll save the day!"

---

25 *Da nichego* = Well, nothing. (Russian). Leib's speech is peppered with German words, which are sufficiently close to English not to require translation.

III.
From Leib's fraternal exhortation
Moisey got back the pluck he'd lost,
Wrote Auer of the situation
And waited with his fingers crossed.
In six weeks came a letter saying,
"I do recall your Richard's playing,
And if he has not gotten worse,
I will accept him in my course.
To find that out he must audition;
So, I suggest your son you bring
To London, where I am each spring."
In hope that Leo's intuition
Foretold a better future soon,
Moisey and son set sail in June.

IV.
They sailed aboard the Lusitania
And disembarked at Liverpool.
The tension mounted, hemicrania
Had made my Richard's blood run cool.
His throat was dry, his heart beat faster,
He clenched his teeth to try to master
The fits and starts of fear inside
That seemed to orchestrate the ride
To London. Silent terror. Auer's
"When you feel ready, please begin."
He put his fiddle 'neath his chin;
Then, forty minutes lasting hours.
It's over. "Thank you." Flash of fright,
'I've failed.' But Auer said, "All right."

Richard Burgin in June 1908 before his return to Warsaw. The inscription on the back reads (in German): *To Uncle Leo, with fond memories on our New York days I remain your nephew, Richard Burgin 27.V.08.*

V.
So now I must be off to Peter
To recompose my hero's youth;
The city famed in Pushkin's meter
And Dostoevsky's prosey truth;
The city both mundane and magic,
Grotesquely comic, nobly tragic,
The source of Russian national myth,
Germanic, foreign, native, Scyth-
Ian, the real and legendary
Battleground of West and East,
Both New Jerusalem and Beast,
Was then in an extraordinary
Destructively creative stage,
The climax of the Silver Age.

VI.
An urgency apocalyptic,
A desperate yearning for the strange,
The new and ancient, mystic, cryptic,
Gripped Russia in the throes of change.
And everywhere raged controversy:
The bourgeoisie now pleaded mercy,
Now underwrote its reeling shock,
Supporting artists run amok
With innovations, real and phony,
Transgressing proper boundaries,
Destroying decent harmonies
With mystic chords and cacophony,
Expressing the creative molt
Of Russian culture in revolt

VII.
The eighteen nineties' dying flower
Of decadent aestheticism
Re-blossomed in Ivanov's* Tower
As symbolistic mysticism.
The poets seeking God and Gnosis
Saluted their apotheosis
In sound, from which the Word arose:
De la musique avant toute chose![26]
And striving for transcendence via
The myth *Prometheus Unbound*
In symphonies of light and sound
Scriabine* proclaimed himself Messiah,
Resolving all antitheses
In monumental syntheses.

VIII.
His music sang the aspiration
Of culture that was all at odds.
In spastic self-disintegration
It sought the twilight of the gods
That would consume reactionaries,
As well as revolutionaries
And reconcile Bolshevists
With anarchists and monarchists,
Resolve dichotomistic preachings –
Of Lev Tolstoy's arch-purity
And Saninesque* depravity –
And overreach the over-reachings
Of every artist's separate part
In one transcendent 'World of Art.'*

---

26 "To music before all else," the rallying cry of the French fin de siècle poets.

IX.

The world of Richard's youthful story
From nineteen eight to nineteen twelve,
The Petersburg Conservatory,
Was in the hands of Glazunov,
Composer and administrator,
Who made its reputation greater,
Increasing opportunities
For Jewish child prodigies.
Since many of them came to Auer,
My Richard got to know quite well
Poliakin, Piastro and Seidel,
And Heifetz, genius of the hour,
The "old professor's" pride and joy,
The Silver Age's golden boy.

X.

Although with jewels the age was rife, it's
Unlikely you will ever find
A more bedazzling one than Heifetz –
He truly was one of a kind.
But from the boyish superhero
I turn now to my youthful hero,
About to enter Petrograd
Chemu byl chrezvychaino rad.[27]
For Richard Petersburg was truly
A turning point in many ways.
At first, he wandered in a daze
As similar to any newly
Arrived, before his eyes unfurled
"A completely different world."[28]

---

[27] *Chemu byl chrezvychaino rad* = About which he was very glad (Russian).
[28] Richard Burgin (Dann tapes).

XI.
And Richard was "a different person"
Who had rethought and changed his goal.
Perhaps New York had put a curse on
The super virtuoso role;
Perhaps his nerves just couldn't take it,
Perhaps he feared he wouldn't make it,
And reconsidering his worth,
Resolved that an orchestral berth
Would suit him and his talents better;
Perhaps his overreaching sought
Relief from being overwrought;
Perhaps he felt he was a debtor
And hated leaving un-repaid
The sacrifice his father made.

XII.
But anyway, my hero, giving
Much thought to future and to fame,
Decided that to earn a living
Would henceforth be his primary aim.
He'd strive to be a good musician
And hope a permanent position
Would ultimately come his way,
So he could settle down one day.
And thus, he took the course pragmatic,
Or as he called it, "practical":
He shunned the theoretical,
Reversed the order axiomatic
That might describe his early start,
And put the horse back, fore the cart

XIII.
Perhaps you find this unromantic,
Or too mundanely true-to-life,
And you had visions of a frantic,
Exceptional youth, of storm and strife.
It's true the disciplined and stoic
May not evoke the mode heroic
And readers may prefer, of course,
A stallion to a good work horse;
But we can't all be lion tamers,
Defenders of the barricades,
Or heroes of the Light Brigades,
Impassioned, and quixotic gamers.
It's hard to live your life with dash
Unless you have some extra cash.

XIV.
As Byron noted, what's exciting
About perpetual poverty?
Or quintessentially indicting
About well-earned security?
I too have learned that annual earnings
Can help fulfill *some,* inner yearnings.

....
....
....
....
....
....
....
....

XV.
So Richard's worries over money
I understand entirely.
His passing up the milk and honey
Of fame, though, still amazes me.
When in my youth applause seemed manna
I'd never get, he'd say, "Diana,
My darling girl, why do you cry?
It's unimportant, *really*... I
Hate seeing you so pessimistic!"
And soothing his discomfiture,
He'd add, "I think you're too mature
For this, and being unrealistic."
"You say that," I'd retort, "because
All through your life you've heard applause!"

XVI.
I even thought he might be lying.
I now don't think so, but, like then,
His answer isn't satisfying
Although I do know why and when
His feelings underwent revision
Resulting in his proud decision
To view fame with insouciance
As "something of no consequence."
It helps to know his self-effacement
And widely noted modesty
Were ultimately traits that he
Developed, struggling, in replacement
For far less "saintly" ones inside –
Like arrogance and stubborn pride.

XVII.

And so it was in Peter's *gorod*[29]
Where stark ambivalencies surged,
Through winters frigid, summers torrid,
That Richard's double self emerged:
A dreamer of his dreaming leery,
A theorist debunking theory,
An artist often doubting art,
A reasoning but passionate heart,
A man of peace, in talk contentious,
A dogmatist and diplomat
Who could concede while standing pat,
A great pretender unpretentious
Who in the view of everyone
Was flattering but fawned on none.

XVIII.

But that's enough dichotomizing
Of Richard's character in youth,
Or I shall risk lobotomizing
A very complicated truth.
Besides, I really have neglected
To give those facts that you expected
About his teacher, friends, routine,
And the Conservatory scene.
I've overlooked the circumstantial,
Waxed on in generalities,
Intuited antimonies,
Which factually are insubstantial,
And so, I think it would be meet
To turn to matters more concrete.

---

29 *Gorod* = city (Russian).

XIX.

Let's start with Auer. He came to Russia
To play first chair for the Ballet.
He'd learned the violin in Prussia
And was Joachim's prodigé.
He made his reputation teaching
In Petersburg, forever preaching
The virtue of strict discipline
For mastering the violin:
"Auer always put importance
On diligence, assiduousness,
Hard work and conscientiousness;
He stressed appearance, health, endurance,
And twenty as the cut-off age
For big careers on the stage."[30]

XX.

These words about Professor Auer
Are from a monograph I read
By Raaben, Lev – a Soviet scholar.
They echo others in my head,
Which I shall versify verbatim
(In part at least), and *seriatim*
As Burgin, then an older man,
Recalled his youth to Mr. Dann
For tape-recorded reproduction.
"It was the opposite, you see,
From Lotto's way, and new to me.
With Auer, that was *class* instruction.
We each played individually
In class, which meant that usually,

---

[30] Quoted from Lev Raaben, *Leopold Auer* Moscow, 1962. Original in Russian, translation mine [DLB].

XXI.
"You could, at *most*, spend twenty minutes
To play whatever you'd prepared;
And everybody else was present –
To skip a class, few people dared.
Not that it was obligatory,
Just custom at Conservatory
Since what was really interesting
And valuable was *listening*
To one another at the lesson.
That's how we *learned*, and in my view,
My colleagues had much more to do
With what I learned than the professor.
But listening *was* a useful tool
Provided by the Auer school.

XXII.
"And also, I must give him credit
Especially for one other thing –
His great respect for the printed letter,
The letter – it meant everything!
One didn't dare to change the letter
Of the composer, 'who knew better
Than you,' he'd say, 'what should be heard,'
And that was in the printed word.
But it is helpful to a student
To discipline himself, you see,
And learn to have respect when he
Is young, professionally unproven.
Ja! Discipline was Auer's way
And a great asset, I must say.

XXIII.
"The rest, however, was a question
Of each one playing pretty much
The same as others. He made suggestions
But didn't really teach as such.
Of course, it's hard to be objective –
One has a different perspective
When one is actually studying
Than later, when considering;
You don't know really which conception
Is truer since you're influenced by
Your own ideas, and time, so I
Should say it is my own perception,
The only place where I could see
That Auer showed his artistry

XXIV.
"Was chamber music class, his passion.
Ja, he was wonderful in quartet!
Although at times as was his fashion,
He could get terribly upset.
His rages could be quite dismaying...
Once I remember, we were playing
Beethóven[31], Opus Fifty-Nine,
And everything was going fine.
We played, he stood there, made no comment,
Just listened, utterly absorbed,
You know, and looking at the score,
And at this very touching moment,
I play these insignificant –
Or so I thought – embellishments

---

31 As a native speaker of Russian, Burgin often stressed Beethoven's name on the second syllable.

XXV.
"When suddenly, his voice, like thunder,
Just roars at me, 'You carpenter!'[32]
Like hitting me in back. In wonder
I looked as if 'What is it, sir?!
What's wrong?' Then thunderous words came, saying,
*Do you know what you are playing?!
Those grace notes, carpenter, are tears!
Those are tears! He's crying here!...*'
He saw, it seems, a situation,
A feeling of emotions there...
But chamber music, that was where
He really gave you education –
You felt you had an artist, though
He could get very mean, you know.

XXVI.
"In fact, one time, when giving vent to
His fury at some student in
Quartet, he threw a score and meant to
Hit *him*, but hit his violin!
And that entailed a very major
Repair, and all because he raged at
Some little thing from his perspect-
ive, absolutely incorrect!"

....
....
....
....
....
....

---

[32] "Carpenter, in Russian, is the worst thing a violinist can be. I mean, that is the lowest you can go, when you can only saw wood, you know. It's like in German, *Schuster* [shoemaker], you know, although Hans Sachs was one. That's the lowest you can get in profession." (Richard Burgin, Dann Tapes).

XXVII.
Since Burgin's had the chance to air his
Opinions on his violin
Professor, it is only fairness
To give his teacher's views of him.
Of these I have two indications:
Remarks on his examinations
(Which Raaben mentions), and a note
From Auer to Moisey, I quote:
"I'm pleased to say your son is truly
Working very well, and he,
Both musically and technically,
Is one of my best pupils. Only,
His violin's not up to par,
Which could his solo career mar."[33]

XXVIII.
His comment on the examinations
As Raaben indicates, reflects
"His often-terse evaluations:
'Plays very well in all respects.'"
In sum, I'd say a strong A minus,
And that, my hero felt, was fine as
He worried less what grade he made
Than whether he would make the grade.
For him the pressure came from keeping
His promise to repay in kind
The debt that preyed upon his mind
And sometimes, hindered him from sleeping:
His father had made Richard's bed
Not so he'd sleep, but get ahead.

---

[33] Letter from Auer to M. Burgin, February 23, 1911. Original in Russian. Translation mine [DLB]

XXIX.
To Richard that meant education
Be utilized efficiently
As academic preparation
For practical activity.
So, what he learned in winter classes
He played in summer for the masses
At music festivals, to earn
The money necessary to learn.
He played in Kharkov, Kiev, Riga,
Gained valuable experience,
Met people of some influence,
Whom he impressed as able, eager,
Appreciative of work, and tips
On future concertmasterships.

XXX.
Since Richard saw no contradiction
Between his schooling and his life,
He did not suffer that affliction
With which *my* younger years were rife.
An alien to alienation,
Who could not stomach separation,
His motto was – participate,
Assimilate and integrate.
His goal in life was harmonizing,
And that is why he made the choice
To play his fiddle, single-voiced,
In concert, not in concertizing,
For group endeavor was the form
In which he would exceed the norm.

XXXI.
In groups, he shone as mediator
For other people's little rifts,
And in his own right as debater
Of rather formidable gifts.
The rule which guided his behavior,
In many arguments, the savior,
The apogee of *comme il faut*,
Was – always being in the know.
Like many bright young men in college,
Intolerant of stupidity,
And fearing most naivety,
He put a premium on knowledge,
And was respected by his peers,
As rather savvy for his years.

XXXII.
His main experience over others
Was all the traveling he'd done,
And to his more provincial brothers
He seemed most cosmopolitan.
He had a knack for storytelling,
Could spin a witty yarn as well in
His native Russian as *auf Deutsch,*
And even knew some English "voits".
In groups, he often was the speaker
But knew enough to listen too,
In conversation one of few,
Who used the force of being meeker.
He could defer and not get sore
And so, he never was a bore.

XXXIII.

In youth, he had in his possession
A quality he never lost,
For which our language lacks expression,
But Russians call *obschitel'nost'*.
The usual one-word translation
Does not convey its combination
Of joyous sociability
And unforced communality.
Yet as a youth, his democratic
Enjoyment of community
And preaching of equality
Revealed a source aristocratic:
As noble Excellence's liege
He exercised *noblesse oblige*.

XXXIV.

Or as he put it, he was "cocky,"
Believed himself to be mature,
Allowed occasional self-mockery
Without becoming insecure.
He didn't mind lighthearted teasing,
But he would rarely tease since pleasing
His *vis* à *vis* was more his need.
Yet he would not cajole or plead.
The thing he took the greatest pride in
Was, even when taken down a peg,
He never ever stooped to beg;
But here, dear reader, he was riding
For a fall since the above
Held true until… he fell in love.

XXXV.
How many kinds of love we suffer!
But I'm convinced by far the worst
In terms of being pride's rebuffer,
Has got to be the one called *first*.
Our hearts are never more afire
In red-hot ovens of desire,
We never more perversely shove
Our egos in, than in first love,
And never shall another passion
Remove the color from our cheeks
Or orphan us for weeks and weeks,
Like arson victims, faces ashen,
In shock, deprived of any sense,
And naked in our innocence.

XXXVI.
For us (and all the world) to ponder,
First love flays vanity alive
And stings the ego so, we wonder
If we'll our searing wounds survive,
Or just remain a mass of squealing,
Exposed, exacerbated feeling,
Whose lips occasionally spurt
One pained refrain, 'I'm hurt! I'm hurt!'
Against first love one lacks defenses:
It sickens, often breaks our hearts,
Torments some other body parts,
And crowning all of these offenses –
No other kind of love can be
So lacking in equality.

XXXVII.

F. Tiutchev*, in "Predestination,"
Affirms the inequality
Of hearts "in fateful combination" –
The softer dies, predictably.
Although he writes of all romances,
We cannot help but know the chances
Of being tossed a fatal glove,
Are greater when we're first in love.
Turgenev, in his poignant story,
Reveals how youthful love does in
The hero and the heroine
Through destinies non-amatory:
He loves her and defers therefore
To him she loves, a predator.

XXXVIII.

And what about the virgin Myshkin?
(I know I've used this rhyme before,
But for my proof I'll take the risk in
Recalling it to you once more.)
He loves Nastasya* but won't wrong her,
So she prefers his rival stronger,
And hates him since his love is pure,
And her 'first love' has ruined her.
O victims of first love! Nastasya,
Tatiana*, Lensky*, Anna K.,
Natasha*, Sonia, Prince Andrey*,
Bazarov, Mary, Bela, Asya* -
Your sufferers are everywhere
Convincing us first love's unfair.

XXXIX.

There is a method in the madness
Of this digressionary tract;
For me my hero's love and sadness
Is mostly fantasy, not fact.
Although I hate to be untruthful,
What can I do? For Richard's youthful
Romance I have no real-life source,
No memoirs, and must needs recourse
To books I know and pure invention.
And since the one fact I did get,
His first love's first name – Henriette[34] –
In what I'll tell, it's my intention
To shield my lovers' innocence
Behind fictitious incidents.

XL.

Perhaps not totally fictitious,
But based upon my own surmise.
I do not want to be capricious,
But oftentimes it seems unwise
To say what is true information
And what is real imagination.
Of what transpires in my plot,
Some things did happen, some did not,
But it's not spurious, rather *my* sense
 Of truth, despite reality.
At times, you know, I must be free
To exercise poetic license
Since I'm the artist of my *Life*
And Richard Burgin's after-life.

---

[34] Henrietta Borsh, pianist, laureate of St. Petersburg Conservatory, was married to Richard Burgin for about 4 years, c1912-17 (?)

XLI.

"In anything there should be freedom,
And more than anywhere in art,
But there's a point where this can't *be* done –
When you exaggerate your part,
You lose all sense of the proportion,
And freedom then becomes distortion.
As Goethe put it – *und bestimmt!* -
'Man merkt der Absicht, und wird verstimmt.'"[35]
The quoter of this thought shall guide me:
My story I shall freely tell
But try to stay in tune as well.
(Who is he? Reader, don't deride me
If I don't say, for I confess,
I think, dear reader, you can guess!

---

35 "One stretches the intention and feels out of tune."

CHAPTER FOUR: FIRST LOVE

And then SHE would appear.

–Tolstoy.

Oh, she no doubt will answer,
And maybe, she will kiss –

–Akhmatova

I. II. III.

IV.
The more I knew about my hero,
The less I had to make things up,
More thirstily drank down to zero,
The spirits of my Muse's cup.
Without resorting to deceiving
And biographical word-weaving,
We spun my hero's yarn till youth
To suit our pleasure and the truth;
But our strange quasi-life based diction,
Blown up like Epiphany's* Lives,
Unfortunately, only thrives
On facts inflatable with fiction,
And now deprived of her balloon,
My Muse has fallen in a swoon.

V.

How tedious to lack invention
And start to write a stanza out
Without belief in your pretension
To knowing what you'll write about.
How dull to check infertile rages
By crumpling up the half-filled pages
Which failed at telling what, if told,
Would doubtless, leave your readers cold.
How tiresome the self-reproaching,
The hopes and vows and timid dreams,
The crossed-out lines, rejected themes,
And stop-gap literary poaching –
Imagination overtaxed
By glaring paucities of facts.

VI.

This was my Slavist's situation
When starting her romantic tale.
She called her Muse for inspiration
But saw she looked distinctly pale.
By solid data clearly spoiled,
Her Muse instinctively recoiled
In horror at the mere surmise
That she would have to improvise –
But still, she tried. For days, she mumbled
The same three stanzas fifty times
With trite or simply missing rhymes,
And rhythm jagged, syntax jumbled,
Until about to lose her wits,
My Slavist cried, 'Let's call it quits!

VII.

'Enough of futile versifying,
My darling Muse! We'll work instead
On something far more gratifying
To you who have been born and bred
On modes and musings academic.'
'Your flattery is stratagemic,'
Her Muse replied, 'but for this breach
I owe you. Where's your Tolstoy speech?'
Thus, *Richard Burgin* was forgotten
For *Death and Women in Tolstoy:
A Jungian View.* My Slavist's ploy
Was happily not misbegotten.
Tolstoy revived her Muse's breath,
And thus, has saved my *Life* from death.

VIII.

But now that we have finally started
On Chapter Four, left Three behind
And in tetrameters have charted
The in-between, we must rewind
Our reel a bit to our depiction
Of Richard when first love's affliction
Infected him, and this, we glean,
Befell him at age seventeen.
So, reader, now we're off together
To early summer, nineteen ten;
My hero was in Pavlovsk* then,
Relaxing in the straw-hat weather,
A carefree youth until he met
A fellow student, Henriette.

IX.

A lovely day! I hear the trolling
Of birds and strings in summer air,
And there I see my Richard strolling
The wooded path without a care,
But now, he stops and starts to listen,
And smiles with his eyes a-glisten.
He murmurs, 'Yes, I know that sound,
The *Kreutzer*... but?' He looks around,
'But isn't that a *piano* playing
The part that Lotto played with me
On violin?! How can this be?'
He runs to see without delaying
And syncopates his gait with grins,
'I thought it's for two violins!'[36]

---

[36] " You know, when I first got acquainted with the *Kreutzer Sonata* I knew it as a piece for two violins because my teacher, Lotto, he played everything, all accompaniments, on the violin. And the first time I heard that with a piano was during the summer, out of town. I was in the country and there was some young violinist and a pianist who practiced there, and I happened to come in, when I heard the music, you know – and it impressed me enormously because I was crazy about that piece. Even for two violinists, I was crazy about it. It was a new world." (Richard Burgin, Dann tapes).

X.
He finds the *dacha*, knocks, all flushing.
"Why, Richard! What a nice surprise!"
"Boris! Oh, please forgive my rushing
In, but…" "Don't apologize.
Come in, come in. We're only playing
For fun. But tell me, where're you staying?"
"Nearby. I thought that I'd explore
A bit, and heard you. I adore
That piece, but thought, was I naïve! – it…,"
He blushed, "that it… I've never heard
It played with, isn't this absurd?!,
With *piano*!" "No, I can't believe it!
You're joking." "Yes, it's true, I swear,
So when I heard a piano there,

XI.
"I thought," he turned to Borya's pianist,
"I don't believe we've ever met?"
"Now I'm the one who's lacking manners,"
Laughed Borya, "Richard – Henriette,
Benois-Efron's* most gifted student!"
She smiled, "Borya, that's imprudent,
Suppose I can't live up to it?"
"Oh, I don't think you have a bit
To worry…" Richard interjected,
"What I heard you played beautifully.
I'm pleased to meet you." "Same for me."
A pause. Their smiles intersected;
Then Richard, gazing in her eyes,
Said, "Borya's praise was very wise."

XII.
He blushed and thought, 'Oh that was worthy
Of some banal Lothario.
She probably thinks I'm pretty nervy
Or awfully young. I'd better go.'
But his resolve was soon forgotten
When Borya said, "It's getting hot and
I feel as hungry as a horse!
Come on, let's eat! You'll stay of course?"
"I'd love to but…" "No buts accepted,
I hate them, like apologies."
He stayed. They lunched on rolls and cheese
And talked while Borya intercepted
A glance or two that we'd call vibes,
But graciously, refrained from jibes.

XIII.
Perhaps, dear reader, you are curious,
Not just about this Henriette,
But also, Richard's comrade, Boris.
They played together in quartet,
Had met through Mischa, Borya's brother,
And from the start they liked each other
And found some common interests
In chamber music, bridge and chess.
However, Borya, somewhat older,
And in some ways more worldly-wise
Occasionally would patronize.
This made my youthful Richard smolder,
But pride, of course, forbade him bend
Enough to say, 'Don't condescend.'

XIV.
Boris knew this and tried to curb his
Desire to play the despotist,
But seeing Henriette disturb his
Young friend, he just could not resist.
Next day, he said, as they were leaving
Rehearsal, "Could it be you're grieving?
Or sick? To look at you, you'd think
Last night you hadn't slept a wink!
She must have made a BIG impression!"
But Richard wouldn't be enticed
And simply smiled, "Yes, she's nice."
"Just nice? Come on, your wan expression
Says otherwise. Why Lord above,
Admit it brother, you're in love!"

XV.
"Oh Borya, stop! I've seen her once and
So what? It's stupid making such
A fuss, I..." "Richard, I'm no dunce and
It seems that you protest too much!"
"I'm not protesting, only saying,
I liked her and admired her playing,
And that is all, there's nothing more."
"But when've you looked like this before?"
And reader, that was the beginning.
Though Richard managed to escape
From Borya's taunts without a scrape,
The features he had found so winning
Tormented him again that night
And made him realize, 'Borya's right.'

XVI.
Indeed, it's true, my hero's smitten.
I don't know if that's good or bad,
Or both. The theme's been overwritten,
There's very little I can add.
I've said that fun is in the doing,
Perhaps, un-doing's in the wooing:
In love, when all's undone, unsaid,
One feels one might as well be dead,
Or failing that, there's always sleeping.
In sleep alone can love be fair,
For dreams knit lovers' sleeves of care
So well that waking leaves them weeping.
The more impossible love seems,
The more realizable in dreams.

XVII.
So, Richard spent his nights that summer
In high-fidelity reveries
While friends remarked upon his dumber
And very strange – for him – unease
At social gatherings, whenever
A *certain girl* was there. However,
They had no inkling how he shone
In dream-talk, home, with HER alone.
For all the social decrescendos
That left my Richard's tongue so tied
Would build again when it was plied
By HER to deafening crescendos
That climaxed, drowning out real life,
When SHE, in dreams, became his wife.

XVIII.
But who's this object of desire?
"Who is Sylvia? What is she?"
The light of Richard's youthful fire
Remains quite in the dark for me.
I've not, like Solomon*, uncovered
The mystery of his first beloved;
I've only found elusive clues,
And hence, her portrait's dusky hues.
Her origins were Polish-Jewish.
She was a Silver Laureate,
In nineteen ten a graduate,
A beauty (some say, cold and shrewish),
Intense, a bit imperious,
Intelligent, and virtuous.

XIX.
Informants told me she was older
Than Richard by a couple years.
Perhaps, that's why he wasn't bolder,
And had so many boyish fears.
An older woman's fascinating,
But surely it was devastating
To sense the more he sang her praise,
The more he sang his youthful ways.
But by her age he was attracted
And by her beauty, talent, taste –
Her virtue, though, was what laid waste
His heart in agonies protracted.
For what enticement can there be
 More virulent than purity?

XX.
I'll skip a lengthy dissertation
In praise of Virtue's attitude.
For me, it lacks all titillation
Though I despise the lewd and crude.
I note that it was not the siren
Who ultimately caught Lord Byron –
He sacrificed the lissome Lamb*
For 'Princess Parallelogram'* -
And also, bring to your attention
The strong and captivating hold
On Richard's peer group of the old
Tolstoy, who flailed about abstention
Against the *Kreutzer's* provenance
Of sinister concupiscence.

XXI.
Like others Richard venerated
The Yasnian-Polyanian sage
Because his thought encapsulated
The highest strivings of the age.
The aspiration to perfection,
The ethics of Tolstoy's rejection
Of false authorities for TRUTH,
Inspired idealistic youth.
And there was something in addition
That drew my Richard to Tolstoy
And made the *seer* seem *rodnóy*,[37]
A vague but deep-held supposition
Tolstoy had felt since childhood
Like him, a sense of orphanhood.

---

37 *Rodnóy* =near-and-dear, kin, native (Russian).

XXII.
Though Richard's parents still were living,
He felt detached, as if in Rome,
Completely Romanized, yet giving
Himself the lie that it was home.
And where was home? And "where was mother?"[38]
He felt before they'd known each other,
He'd been "ejected from the nest"
With one injunction: Do your best!
He missed his mother, and he worried
About her health. He'd dream at night
How he could still make things all right
For her before she… if he hurried
Back home to her – then SHE would get
Somehow confused with…Henriette.

XXIII.
Thus, summer dreams passed into autumn
Realities and sad good-byes,
And Richard, waking up, hit bottom
The day of parting, tearful eyes,
Since Henriette was off to Poland,
And Richard, feeling very low and
Convinced his destiny was cruel,
Would soon be going back to school.
But he resolved that his behavior
Would at the station not betray
A trace of sadness or dismay.
He wiped his tears and pride, his savior,
Rebuked him, saying 'Don't give in!
You have to have some discipline.'

---

[38] Quotations from Tolstoy's *Confession*.

XXIV.

He went with Boris to the station
And joined the muted milling throng's
Mixed chorus cadencing vacation
In whispered codas of so longs,
But just before the final killing
Farewell, he heard an alto trilling
Above his *ppp* "Proshcháy!"[39]
"Oh, I'll be back, it's not goodbye."
An unforeseen appoggiatura
Had lightly graced his parting note
And brought a lump to Richard's throat,
But also, made him feel securer
That with this movement's loss of heart
A more enlivening one would start.

XXV.

But when? And how? Throughout September,
As respite from the daily grind,
He'd fall to musing and remember
Her parting words to try and find
What kind of future they might presage:
Had they contained a hidden message
That she'd be back to be with him?
Or were the chances of that slim?
And so, he plucked his mental daisy
Of joyous/gloomy shifts in thought –
'She likes me, / No, she likes me not' –
Until what really drove him crazy
Was not the yesses or the no's,
But his concluding "I don't know's."

---

39 *Proshcháy* = farewell (Russian).

XXVI.

At last he realized this not knowing
The way she felt was killing him
And sensed determination growing –
You know the kind, we call it "grim" –
To make some sort of, well, confession
That would elicit an expression
From HER of how SHE felt about
The man her feelings left in doubt
So cruel, rejection would be better.
But should he risk it face-to-face?
No, that might mean complete disgrace –
But if?... Yes, if he ... wrote a letter??
'Why that,' he grinned, 'would save the day!
For once I'm glad that she's away.'

RICHARD'S LETTER TO HENRIETTE[40]
11.X.10

    Dear Henriette!
I'm writing you – don't be offended!
For what could cause me more regret?
I know, however you pretended,
You have the right to be upset,
But you, since you have condescended
To be my friend, will understand
That I must do my heart's command.
At first, I did not think of writing:
Believe me, had I kept my pride
You would have had no cause to chide,
Or known the battle I've been fighting.
The more I fight, the more I find
I just can't get you off my mind.

---

40 Richard's letter to Henriette adheres to the rhyme pattern and structure of Tatiana's letter to Onegin in Pushkin's *Eugene Onegin*.

Oh if, that morning at the station,
You'd only let your words reveal
More clearly how you really feel,
I might have stood our separation.
But what you said spawned endless doubt,
And so, I'm forced to write this letter
To tell you how I feel straight out.
I miss… and love you, Henrietta.

I wonder if I wasn't cursed
By overhearing that Sonata?
You took my breath away at first,
And I've been holding it *fermata*
Until this banal *serenata*…
Yet this I know – the piano part
Was but the least that I recovered,
For when you played it, I discovered
The missing pianist of my heart.

But now I've had enough of groping
For words to make my feelings clear.
And I am quite resigned to hoping
For a reply I also fear.
Boris (who often seems my rival)
Expects you back in just three weeks –
So, what will come with your arrival?
Shall you reject what Richard seeks?
Or will you … ? No! The mere suggestion
Of such enormous happiness
Might in itself subvert success.
Instead of finishing my question,
I think that I prefer to end
My letter in anticipation

With a collegial invitation
That I am making as a friend.
The Conservatory's dedicating
A chamber concert to Fauré,
And our quartet's participating.
There's no way of exaggerating
My joy if you could hear us play.
In fact, we all would be delighted!
In any case, you are invited –
November, the 13th, at two.
Borovsky's playing pianoforte –
Vtoroy kvartet.[41]   A pleasant sort, he
Plays well, but not as well as you.
Please come.
               And so, my Henrietta,
I'll close now hoping that my letter
Won't strike you as too "out of tune."
Forgive me if it sounds too sappy.
I hope we'll see each other soon
And that you've been both well and happy.
So all the best,
               I press your hand,
Your Richard (in the "fatherland")

---

41   *Vtoroy kvartet*=Second Quartet. The piece in question is Fauré's Second Quartet for Pianoforte, Violin, Viola and 'Cello in g minor, Op. 45.

XXVII. XXVIII. XXIX.

I've learned a lack of expectations –
The question 'Will she?' answer, 'Nope!' –
Is one of those expostulations
With which we mask a wealth of hope.
The poorer our predicted pleasure,
The richer are the hopes we treasure;
The more we say 'Impossible!'
The more we pray it's possible.
Thus Richard, having sent his letter,
Would tell himself each morning, 'I
Am certain she will not reply,
And in a way that may be better.'
Yet through the mail-less days and nights
He mutely prayed, 'I hope she writes.'

XXX.

Alas, dear reader, as expected
In situations of no hope,
She did not write. Although dejected,
My Richard tried his best to cope
With unacknowledged disappointment.
He soothed himself with work, an ointment
That may provide the sole relief
For disappointed lovers' grief.
He plunged into quartet rehearsals
And eagerly prepared for class,
Refused to think about the lass
Responsible for the reversals
In hopes he now could not ignore,
Although they made his ego sore.

XXXI.
Time fairly flew. Before he knew it,
The concert day was drawing nigh
And while to friends he would pooh-pooh it,
Inside, his hopes were riding high.
His overworked imagination,
Or what is called pure compensation,
Had led my Richard to opine
Her silence was a hopeful sign.
'If I were she,' he thought, 'I'd write me,
If what I'd say would make me sad,
But if my words would make me glad,
I'd want in person to delight me.
And so, the concert's my trump card!'
(O Lord, do youthful hopes die hard!)

XXXII.
The thirteenth. Rising in a hurry,
My Richard washed with special care
And dressed amid a furious flurry,
Though having but one suit to wear.
He rubbed the spots out, brushed it speckless,
Then blacked his shoes and shone them fleckless
Until the soles were free of dirt.
He donned (of four) his least-worn shirt,
Attached his newest, crispest collar,
Checked out his tie – 'thank God, no spot!' –
And fumbling for the perfect knot,
He heard his cousin (room-mate) holler,
"Hey, Richard! We have got to go.
It's almost one o' clock, you know!"

С.-Петербургская Консерваторія.

Воскресенье 31 Октября 1910 г.

МУЗЫКАЛЬНОЕ УТРО

въ честь директора Парижской Консерваторіи

КОМПОЗИТОРА Г. ФОРЭ.

Программа составлена исключительно изъ произведеній Г. Форэ.

ПРОГРАММА

1) 2-ой квартетъ для фортепіано, скрипки, альта и віолончели sol-min op. 45.
   - I. Allegro molto moderato.
   - II. Allegro molto.
   - III. Adagio non troppo.
   - VI. Allegro molto.

   Исп. уч-къ *Боровскій*, (кл. заслуж. проф. Есиповой).
   Буткинъ,
   Шиферблатъ, } (кл. заслуж. проф. Ауэра).
   Натусъ, (кл. проф. Зейферта).

2) Impromptu op. 25.
   Исп. уч-къ *Розенбергъ*, (кл. проф. Дубасова).

3) Элегія для віолончели и фортепіано, op. 24.
   Исп. уч-къ *Борисякъ*, (кл. заслуж. проф. Вержбиловича
   въ завѣд. проф. Зейферта).
   Захаровъ, (кл. заслуж. проф. Есиповой).

4) **Романсы:** a) Après un rêve.
   b) Sérénade Toscane.
   Исп. уч-ца *Виргъ*, (кл. заслуж. проф. Ирецкой).

5) a) „Improvisation"
   b) „Barcarolle"
   Исп. уч-ца *Гофманъ*, (кл. заслуж. проф. Есиповой).

6) a) Berceuse op. 16.
   b) Fileuse (extrait de Pelléas et Mélisande)
   Transcription pour violon par L. Auer.
   Исп. уч-къ *Полякинъ*, (кл. заслуж. проф. Ауэра).

Начато въ 2 часа дня.

Program of the Musical Matinee in honor of Gabriel Faure at the St. Petersburg Conservatory of Music on October 31 (old style), 1910.

Le Conservatoire de musique de St. Pétersbourg.

Dimanche 31 Octobre (13 Novembre) 1910

MATINÉE MUSICALE

en l'honneur de **M. Gabriel Fauré**,
Directeur du Conservatoire de musique de Paris.

Le programme est composé d'oeuvres de M. Gabriel Fauré.

PROGRAMME

1) **2-me Quatuor en sol-min pour piano, violon, alto et violoncelle op. 45.**
   - I. Allegro molto moderato.
   - II. Allegro molto.
   - III. Adagio non troppo.
   - IV. Allegro molto.
     - *M. Borovsky*, (classe de M-me Essipoff, prof. émérite).
     - *M. Bourguin,*
     - *M. Schifferblatt,* } (classe de M. Auer, prof. émérite).
     - *M. Natus*, (classe de M. Seiffert, prof.).

2) **Impromptu op. 25.**
   - *M. Rosenberg*, (classe de M. Doubassoff, prof.).

3) **Elégie pour violoncelle et piano op. 24.**
   - *M. Borissiak*, (classe de M. Wierzbilowicz, prof. émérite dirigée actuellement par M. Seiffert, prof.).
   - *M. Zakharoff*, (classe de M-me Essipoff, prof. émérite).

4) **Romances:** a) Après un Rêve.
   b) Sérénade Toscane.
   - M-elle *Viren*, (classe de M-me Iretsky, prof. émérite).

5) a) **Improvisation op. 84.**
   b) **Barcarolle op. 26.**
   - M-elle *Hofmann*, (classe de M-me Essipoff, prof. émérite).

6) a) **Berceuse op. 16.**
   b) **Fileuse** (extrait de Pelléas et Mélisande)
   Transcription pour violon par L. Auer.
   - M. *Poliakine*, (classe de M. Auer, prof. émérite).

On commencera à 1 heures.

Richard performed in the quartet which opens the program. The program is in Russian on the left and in French on the right.

XXXIII.
Expecting well-deserved berating,
He runs backstage and out of breath,
He greets his colleagues who are waiting
With anxious faces, pale as death.
"At last!" they gasp. "Thank God, what worry
You've caused us!" "Yes, I'm awfully sorry,
I ..." "Never mind, at least you're here
And that alone is cause for cheer."
"No time for talk! Let's go already."
With earnest faces, trembling hands,
They enter, bow, adjust their stands.
Then Richard, overcome by heady
Excitement, hears Borovsky's A,
Prepares to start and thinks, 'Fauré ...

XXXIV.
Will SHE? ...' He feels a flash of fright and
He steals a look around the hall...
And suddenly, his pupils brighten;
He smiles, staring and enthralled.
'She's here! Right over there, and smiling!
Is there a face that's more beguiling?'
He focuses his gaze ahead,
Straight at her, and ... she nods her head.
The concert is for him a mixture
Of trying hard to play his best
And seeking glances when at rest.
Four movements pass and paint a picture...
And just as from the sonorous mist
He sees emerge a lovers' tryst

XXXV.
Backstage, his dreams are interrupted!
No more of passionate pretend,
With loud applause, the hall's erupted.
Amazed that they have reached the end,
He seeks her eyes. Their sideways motion
Directs his exit, through commotion
Backstage, and pushing through the door,
He bursts into the corridor.
She waves her hand – 'Should I kiss it?'
Instead, his lips move to exclaim,
"Oh Henriette, I'm glad you came!"
"Why, Richard! Did you think I'd miss it?"
"Well ..." "Silly! But... let's take a walk.
It's noisy here and we ... must talk."

XXXVI.
Ah, walks and talks! I'm sure, dear reader,
Like me, you've had your share of them –
Both those when you're the verbal leader,
And those in which you haw and hem.
They range from arias sweet and charming
To portents dire and alarming:
Some walks and talks exhilarate
While other ones exasperate;
And like their moods, their tempo markings
Can vary, from *andante* strolls
To rigid à *la marche* patrols,
From *largo* drags t'*allegro* larkings,
And there are polyrhythmic ones
With syncopations, rests and runs.

XXXVII.
Some walks depend upon the setting
As much as on your general mood;
Some environs can be upsetting
While others make you feel quite good.
It's hard to pinpoint interactions
Between the place and one's reactions.
Does Nature feel our souls' dismay?
Or does she make us feel that way?
The question's mooter if a city
Is where you walk. It seems to be,
Or have, a personality
That's capable of hate and pity,
And oftentimes, exerts a force
Upon its walkers' future course.

XXXVIII.
Of this perhaps the prime example
Occurs in Russian literature.
A most unscientific sample
Of texts on Petersburg's allure –
So potently sublime, horrific,
Irrational and scientific –
Reveals how much that city's streets
Control successes and defeats
Of walkers: Dostoevsky's heroes,
The generous dreamers and the mean,
Pushkin's Hermann* and Eugene*,
And numerous Gogolian* zeroes –
In every case the city stalks
And orchestrates their walks and talks.

XXXIX.

Its snowy, wet November weather
Infects them, chills them to the bone;
In June's white nights they come together
Or stroll the desolate quays alone;
Its flooding river drives them crazy,
Its labyrinth traps smart, but lazy
Raskolnikov to dream of crimes;[42]
Its monuments inspire rhymes;
Its streetlamps, lighted by the Devil,[43]
Create illusions of pure love
Or mournful shadows of the Dove;[44]
Its youthful dreamers weep and revel;
And its broad prospects were the set
Of Richard's talk from Henriette.

---

42 Raskolnikov, the hero of *Crime and Punishment*, walks the streets of St. Petersburg, plotting his murder of the pawnbroker.
43 In "Nevsky Prospekt" by Nikolai Gogol, the two heroes pursue beautiful women who turn out to be not at all what they seem.
44 In Andrey Bely's *Petersburg,* the city streets are haunted by a shadowy, luminous figure suggestive of Christ.

XL.

It started as is customary:
"I hope you had a pleasant trip?"
"Yes, very nice, if ordinary.
And you? How goes the studentship,
[He winced], I mean, conservatory?"
"Oh, nothing new, the usual story;
Right now, it seems, we only talk
About Tolstoy..." "Yes, what a shock!"[45]
"It made me sad though now I'm better,
I guess because... because you're back,
And I ... but since I'm on this track,"
He paused, "well, did you get my letter?"
"I did." "You didn't answer, why?"
"I'd rather ... talk." She heaved a sigh.

---

[45] Leo Tolstoy died on November 7, 1910.

XLI.[46]

"I read, reread your every word and
I loved you ... for your honesty,
And yet, it also was a burden
Since you deserve the same from me.
To say this really isn't easy –
It even makes me feel, well, queasy –
I truly like you, quite a lot,
I do, but frankly, love it's not.
And now, I guess I mostly worry
That you'll not only be upset
But think I'm playing the coquette.
So please believe I'm truly sorry
That you and I don't feel the same,
But really, I am not to blame.

XLII.

"I've just not known yet that sensation,
That kind of ... love which you avow,
But if it's any consolation –
Though probably it won't be now –
If my heart were set afire
With love, and yearning, and... desire,
I couldn't find, I swear it's true,
A better man to love than you;
And though I do not feel the passion
That you must feel –and who knows why? –
To say I'm cold would be a lie,
For I do love you, in my fashion,
Not as a lover – why pretend? –
But as a sister and a friend.

---

[46] Just as Tatiana's letter to Onegin served as the model for Richard's to Henriette, so Onegin's verbal response to her (in chapter IV of *Eugene Onegin*) provides the model for Henriette's "talk" to Richard.

XLIII.
"I do not want to make you suffer,
But I have something else to say
That I'm afraid might make it tougher
For you to cope with your dismay
And put more strain on our relations
As colleagues here. Since graduation
I've had to think, as you must know,
About my plans and where I'll go.
Well, I've accepted an appointment
From Auer, as accompanist…
We'll see each other, if you wish,
But only if your disappointment
Will not prevent or interfere
With our continued friendship here."

XLIV.
With that my Henriette concluded.
They walked in silence till they reached
Her lodgings. Richard then exuded
A mournful sigh. His eyes beseeched,
But all their pleas remained unuttered.
He took her hand, with effort muttered
A faint "So long," then turned and left,
Trod home funereally, grave, bereft.
He'd never felt more hurt, dejected,
Downhearted, more disposed to brood,
Or in a more self-pitying mood.
"I guess," he moaned, "I've been rejected,
I'm full of sorrow, and in brief,
Not unacquainted now with grief."

XLV.

But don't be sad. Though unrequited
And unfulfilled his love and dream,
Unrealized all his hopes, un-plighted
His troth, unmanned his self-esteem;
Though un-consoled beyond all question,
Un-mollified by the suggestion
That's meant to calm, but most offends
Rejected lovers, - Let's be friends –
My hero has not long to languish,
For there's resiliency in youth,
And first love illustrates a truth
That gives a purpose to its anguish:
One has to drink its bitter cup
Way down in order to come up.

CHAPTER FIVE: THE FINNISH CONNECTION

And wanly dove-gray-bluish eyes
Similar to Finnish skies.

—Baratynsky

I.
A year went by, nineteen eleven,
And Richard spent it rather well:
His life was hardly seventh heaven
But neither had it been the hell
Predicted by the black depression
That followed Henriette's confession
Of friendly feelings, she was sure
Would cast a pall on her allure.
But then, how often our predictions,
Our efforts to control our fate,
Do not, in fact, anticipate
The unexpected contradictions
That actual living holds in store,
And no one can predict before.

II.
Thus, Henriette thought her appointment
Would only make relations worse,
And Richard feared his disappointment
Betokened that his love was cursed.
Yet, in the end, their being together
Did not exacerbate the weather
But actually, dispelled the gloom
That previously had forecast doom.
At first a certain discomposure
Was evident, their talk was strained,
But in a while they regained,
Because of mutual exposure,
The ease of shared experience
And overcame their reticence.

III.
The year had also had attractions
Within the realm professional
That counter-pointed the distractions
Of disengagements personal.
My Richard's life became so busy,
It left him feeling slightly dizzy,
But work's harmonious resonance
Drowned out romantic dissonance.
In March, still feeling in the pits, he
Received the opportunity
Of playing Scriabin's *Symphony
Of Fire* under Koussevitzky* –
It was the Petersburg premiere,
And greatly brightened his despair.

IV.
The summer brought a separation
From Henriette, which made him glum,
But as a kind of reparation
His work in Riga was a plum:
His solos with the Philharmonic
Of Warsaw were a potent tonic,
And though they left him quite fatigued,
They guaranteed he had "big-leagued"
And gave him little time to ponder
How much he missed his Henriette,
How much his heart could not forget,
And just how much it had grown fonder.
To be so tired one can't think,
Surpasses not to sleep a wink.

V.
He had returned to school assuming
They would continue as before –
As friends and colleagues, just resuming
Their work together, nothing more.
Yet while their everyday relations
Remained the same, in conversations
Her manner seemed ... more indirect.
On matters where he would expect
Straightforwardness, she played the hinter.
At first, he hardly was aware
Of her far more elusive air,
But as the fall passed into winter,
He sensed there really was a change –
In fact, she acted downright strange.

VI.
Before, she'd never been offended,
But now she often acted hurt;
Before, she never had pretended,
But now she openly would flirt.
Where formerly she'd been judicious,
She now at times became capricious
And would occasionally employ
Devices positively coy.
Where once she'd been enthusiastic
To join in group activity,
She now avoided company,
Retreated to a life monastic
And never let the truth be known
Why she preferred to be alone.

VII.
One needs but scant sophistication
To realize what these changes show,
But Richard lacked an education
In sentiment and did not know.
Her coyness made him feel unsettled.
By her caprices, he was nettled
And pushed to pleading self-defense
For words not meant to cause offense.
He found her presence most perturbing
And wished at times she'd go away,
But if she did, in just one day
He found her absence more disturbing!
He had no clue to what it meant...
(Oh reader, he was innocent.)

VIII.
Thus, not without some consternation,
My Richard greeted nineteen twelve,
And looked ahead. His graduation
In May loomed large: he had to shelve
His private worries since despairing
Was not conducive to preparing
For his profession's future chores,
His first real job, in Helsingfors.
(My goodness! I forgot to mention
The most important thing of all
The summer brought – a job next fall.
Oh, do forgive my inattention –
It must have been one of the times
When facts of life eluded rhymes.)

IX.
But I shall spare you long reflections
On why my memory mis-fared
And turn to Burgin's recollections
Of nineteen twelve when he prepared
To make the imminent transition
To his new Helsingfors position.

....
....
....
....
....
....
....
....

X.
"And my philosophy, I remember,
When going to a foreign land,
Was wanting to become a member
Of that new culture, understand
The language and the literary
Traditions. Literature was very
Important, interesting for me.
I also tended, musically,
Perhaps because I'd lived in Prussia
When I was young, you know, Berlin,
To be more cosmopolitan.
I sort of went outside of Russia,
You know, to find composers who
Were different from the ones we knew.

Richard Burgin in St. Petersburg, around the time of his graduation from the Conservatory in 1912.

XI.
"So, when I knew that it was certain
I'd go to Finland, I found out
About Sibelius's Concerto,
Which only then I learned about.
I practiced that and then I brought it
To class. And Auer' d never taught it.
Though Tseitlin* played it – that he knew –
For him it was completely new.
And also, Sinding, for example –
I brought to class and played his Third
Concerto which no one had heard,
And Auer, since he liked to sample
New music, had respect for me,
That I would bring it in, you see.

XII.
"And also, when I went to Finland
I learned – not Finnish actually –
But Swedish since there were in Finland
Still Swedish-speaking Finns, you see.
That was the strangest situation –
A city with a population
That was comparatively small,
A hundred fifty thousand in all,
And in a country of three million
That also isn't very large,
They had two symphony orchestras,
And each one gave a concert season.
No day would pass, in other words,
Without a concert in Helsingfors.

XIII.
"Those two full orchestras reflected
The country's ethnic rivalries:
The one that Kájanus* directed
Had nationalistic tendencies;
The one I was associated
With, Schnéevoigt's* (educated
In Germany although a Finn)
Was more inclined towards Berlin.
But due to this great competition,
Those special Finnish politics,
Helsinki's music life was rich,
And Finland's musical position
Was really way ahead, I'd say,
Of any countries of its day."

XIV.
I've quoted Burgin's recollections,
His look behind, to look ahead
And show the various connections
To which his education led,
But in the meantime, I've left pending
A situation far more rending
Than my young violinist's art –
The future of his tortured heart.
So now I'll do my own backtracking,
Pick up the still unwoven strand
I dropped with Richard, nothing planned,
Uncomprehendingly a-lacking,
Alassing, angered and upset
About the change in Henriette.

XV.
Her oddities did not diminish
But just grew odder in the spring,
And Richard saw his future Finnish
As finishing their future thing.
Again, the clouds of disillusion,
Annoyance and irresolution
Were gathering and seemed to blight
Professional horizons bright.
He tried to talk but met resistance:
Whenever he would ask, "What's wrong?"
She'd say, "I've got to go, so long."
And pleading proved of no assistance:
To his, "Oh please don't make a scene,"
She'd shrug, "I don't know what you mean?!"

XVI.
And yet, the more she drove him crazy,
The more, it seemed, he found her dear;
The more she left the future hazy,
The more he wished to make it clear.
At last, one night when he was pondering
Her oddities, he started wondering,
'What can I do? What should I say?
There simply has to be some way,
Some instrument at my disposal,
To solve this problem ... Let me see ...
Perhaps I'll make her ... [suddenly,
The answer sounded] ... a proposal!
That's it! If she says yes, it's great;
If no, well, still I'll know my fate.'

XVII.
Dear reader, I shall skip the details
Of his proposal. Why rehash
The sort of banal scene that retails
In Harlequins for petty cash?
He made it after graduation
And common to the situation
His eyes expressed both hope and dread,
He mumbled and his face was red.
She also blushed, demure, elated
To hear him get it out at last,
Then sighed and whispered, breathing fast,
Her answer, which you have awaited
For thirteen lines, but now must guess:
One word to rhyme my couplet: _____.

XVIII.
Nor will you hear from me effusions
About my lovers' happiness.
With all such blissful grand illusions
My Muse does not have much success.
She finds it telling that for *happy*
The most convenient rhyme is *sappy*;
It bores her that in English, *kiss*,
So glibly harmonizes *bliss*.
'In Russian, *kiss* is more amusing,'
She grinned, 'what rhymes with *potsel*úi?'
'Well what?' 'You know,' she whispered, '- - -'
(Forgive me, reader, for refusing
To write a word so crass and sick
It makes my conscience feel a prick.)

XIX.
But onward! What's the greatest hurdle
My youthful lovers have to face?
And what can make their hot blood curdle
With thoughts of scandal, shame, disgrace?
What wear-and-tear can snap the suture
With which they have sewn up their future?
What worry turns them into wrecks?
No, no, you're wrong, it isn't sex.
No, please don't think I'm being funny,
It isn't that, or their rapport,
Or problems of the mundane sort
Like housing, jobs, or even money.
There's something worse than all of these –
Their meetings with their families.

XX.
Perhaps you think I'm either joking
Or have completely lost my mind,
Or feel the need to be provoking
Because I have an axe to grind –
But you are wrong. It's not derangement
That moves me here, or some estrangement.
So, let me take a little space
And I shall try to make my case...

....
....
....
....

XXI.

If I am wrong, what child would grovel?
Or wish his home another one?
If I am wrong, what kind of novel
Was ever written or begun?
What plays or films would give enjoyment?
Where would we find enough employment
For counselors, psychiatrists,
Or lawyers, priests and therapists?
If I am wrong, who'd ever bother
To read the works of Sigmund Freud?
And who would ever get annoyed
Or want to fight with his/her mother?
If I am wrong – now, don't get sore –
All life would stop or be a bore.

XXII.

For all its worrisome detractions,
Its woes and tensions very real,
One's family still has great attractions,
Potential for one's own ideal
Of happiness. Who doesn't pander
To that beguiling propaganda
That there exists, and yours can be
(With luck) the perfect family?
And never is this feeling stronger
Than when you're coming home from school:
It seems your absence has been cruel,
It cannot last a moment longer,
You yearn for home, and hence your zeal
To make your visit there ideal.

XXIII.
And what's ideal, you ask? That question
Re families and other things
Quite frankly gives me indigestion,
And clips my Muse's soaring wings.
We can't give positive definitions,
But there are contexts and conditions
Where we'll suggest what, it is *not*:
It's *not* in general what you've got.
In striving, it is, *not* desiring
What is impossible to get,
In setting up, it's *not* upset;
In ending, it is, *not* expiring;
In blossoming, it's *not* to wilt;
In family life, it is, *not* guilt.

XXIV.
Ah guilt! Who'll offer me a reason
Why every family structure 's built,
When no one has committed treason,
On mutual do-not-blame- me silt?
Is there a way of understanding
The permanent self-reprimanding
That tips us from our cradle's tilt
And tears to bits our comfort quilt?
Why do our most sincere laudations
To families have a guilty lilt?
Why *is* the Golden Rule so gilt
With burnished self-recriminations?
Why, over milk by parents spilt,
Do children burst in tears from guilt?

XXV.

Like everyone, my Richard suffered
From guilt though he was not aware
Of this since early on he'd buffered
Himself against its wear-and-tear
By showing filial devotion,
Behavior based upon the notion,
That he could best avoid complaint
By acting out the role of saint.
He'd made his parents' mute injunction
His own: just always do your best,
Indeed, he never let it rest
And planned his future in conjunction
With what he knew they would expect,
And loved and showed them great respect.

XXVI.

The only time he could remember
When he had disappointed them
Was in that bleak New York November –
For that he did himself condemn.
But otherwise, his guilty flurries
Were hidden in what he called "worries"
That he would ever do again
What might entail his parents' pain.
He felt withal he'd been successful.
Through graduation – knock on wood! –
He had done well and had been good.
Yet lately, feelings most distressful
Disturbed his generally guiltless state
Whenever he would contemplate

XXVII.
His visit home. In consternation,
He tried to find the reason why,
From careful self-examination.
At first, it yielded no reply:
Indeed, what possible abrasion
Could mar this happiest occasion
Of sharing joys with kin he missed?
His being a Silver Medalist,
The job that he'd begin next season,
And then, the greatest news of all,
His plans to marry in the fall...
There seemed to be no earthly reason
Why he should be at all upset,
Unless... it might be... Henriette!

XXVIII.
And suddenly, the realization,
A-blush with guilt, had dawned on him,
That maybe out of sublimation,
Embarrassment, or by some whim,
Not once in person or by letter
Had he yet mentioned Henrietta.
So, it would come as quite a shock
When he and she, engaged, would walk
Into his home... O Lord, what terror!
Oh, why had he not paved the way
For bringing home his... fiancée?
And now that he had seen his error,
The happiness that lay ahead
Betokened nothing, if not dread.

XXIX.
So, reader, what's your expectation?
Has Richard's guilty prophecy
Foreseen the actual situation
He'll meet within his family?
Or will there be a contradiction
Of his most dread and sure prediction,
More proof of that phenomenon
That I affirmed in stanza One?
In other words, what's my intention?
Will I eventually undermine,
Or have my story stay in line
With my auctorial contention?
You ought to have some time to guess,
So, I shall once again digress,

XXX.
Just briefly, with some information
About the Burgin family scene
Where Richard hurried from the station
(With Henriette) on May nineteen.
You've met the missus and the mister,
His oldest brother and his sister,
And now I shall the others name:
In nineteen hundred Myron came,
And not too far behind him, Paula,
And then, Mateus-Teodor
And Juliusz (whom Ronia bore
Within a year of one another);
And that completes the Burgin eight
Who now await our graduate.

The Burgins, November 1911: Left to right: Moisey, Myron (seated in front), Julek and Mateus, Lilia, Ronia, Paulina (with baby carriage), Bernard, Richard.

XXXI.

With young Bernard and more so, Lily,
My Richard shared the closest ties.
They were the only siblings, really,
He'd lived with so that's no surprise.
Though when away he wondered whether
It would seem strange to be together,
"The family was so closely knit,"[47]
He rarely felt apart from it.
He shared close ties with all his siblings
From whom by travels he'd been cleft;
Once home, he felt he'd never left
And joined into their joys and quibbling
Spontaneously and magically,
A limb re-grown upon the tree.

XXXII.

Of course, the Burgins had their troubles.
Moisey and Ronia, you recall,
Were psychologically doubles –
At once enthralled and disenthralled
With one another. Yet, they rarely
Indulged in arguments unfairly
Before the children: he would cease,
Or she would tensely hold her peace.
In nineteen twelve, I ought to mention,
Moisey's finances had improved,
Which put him in a better mood.
Now optimistic, free from tension,
He had regained his former pluck,
His faith in self, and in his luck.

---

[47] Comment of Maria Wierna Burgin, widow of Juliusz Burgin, made to the author in August, 1981.

XXXIII.

And so, the home on Nowolipka[48]
When Richard crossed its threshold, rent
With guilt, *krasnéya, no s ulýbkoi*,[49]
Though not ideal, was quite content.
Arrival. Shouts of joy, embracing,
Excitement. With his pulse beat racing,
He raised his hand for silence: "Well,"
He paused, "I've got great news to tell!
Please meet...". Although the unexpected
Amazed and shocked them all at first,
There was no scandalous outburst.
Moisey and Ronia both respected
The rules of hospitality,
He noisily, she silently.

XXXIV. XXXV.

....
....
....
....

---

48 Nowolipka was a main street in the Jewish section of Warsaw.
49 *krasneya, no s ulybkoi* = blushing, but with a smile (Russian).

XXXVI.
Two weeks had passed. The visit, nearing
Its end, had settled into calm,
My couple outwardly appearing
Well-rested and without a qualm;
But surfaces can be deceiving,
And Richard found himself receiving,
Through all the noisy fun and sport,
A message of the silent sort.
For all the stories, banter, blather,
And chitchat, no one said a word
Pro éto,[50] till one night he heard
His mother whisper to his father,
"You know, Moisey, this is no whim.
You'd better have a talk with him."

XXXVII.
So, on the eve of his departure,
Moisey and Richard took a walk
To ... (oh, my reader, aren't you smart, you're
Quite right about the rhyme here) talk.
Around the neighborhood they ambled
As Moses nervously pre-ambled
The topic, feeling out of joint,
But finally, he approached the point:
"So, Richard, now you plan to marry?"
"I do. I love her very much."
"I know, my boy, but it is such
A ... serious step, a lot to carry,
I mean, responsibility... "
"I realize that." "You won't be free,

---

50 *Pro eto* (Russian) literally means, "about that." It can be used as a euphemism for "about love."

XXXVIII.
"So free, you know. I mean, it's harder...
A wife and ... children ... to support...
That's quite a job, to keep the larder
Well-stocked," he started to exhort,
"To make a living isn't easy!"
"I know that but don't be uneasy
On *that* score. I feel quite secure
My job in Finland will assure
Us stable income, and..." "Yes Richard,
Of course, and I'm so proud of you,
About the job ... your mother, too,
But son, we [words of warning which had
Eluded him, now reached his tongue]
We feel that you are ... just too young."

XXXIX.
"I'm not, I'm not," the youth insisted,
Too angrily to save his pride.
"We think you are," Moisey persisted
"And maybe we're unjustified,
Who knows? But wouldn't it be frightful
To end your visit, so delightful,
Somehow estranged?" He turned his eyes
To Richard, "So, let's compromise."
"How?" "Listen, I am not opposing
Your getting married, or your choice,
In fact, it makes my heart rejoice
To see you happy. I'm proposing
You ... put it off a year or two,
And then, my boy, good luck to you."

XL.

So once again my story hangs on
The guessing game of either-or,
But since I'm bored with tempos *langsam*,[51]
I won't suspend you as before.
He did agree to a postponement –
I don't know why – perhaps atonement?
Perhaps what Ronia left unsaid?
Or guilt? Or what his father said?
But he gave in, and at this juncture,
You may be thinking Richard's way
Will follow that of Prince Andrey.*
Such sharpness normally would puncture
My Muse, but her balloon is not
Inflated yet with such a thought.

XLI.

Unlike Natasha, Henrietta –
And everything depends on HER –
Herself believed it might be better
Somehow, if marriage were deferred.
It wasn't that she didn't love him,
Or maybe, held herself above him,
Or that she didn't want to wed,
Or that she hadn't lost her head,
Or was by nature too complacent.
She did not know quite what was wrong
Except that all the very strong
Emotions and desires, nascent
Within her sometimes strangely made
Her feel a little bit afraid.

---

51 *Langsam* = slow (German).

XLII.
And this confused and frightened feeling
Welled up in her and overtook
Her love when he, with eyes appealing,
Would radiate a certain look.
It seemed to her his look was gunning
Her down, it made her feel like running,
So much at times, it was a strain
To make the effort to remain.
That look, she knew, was not a sin and
She couldn't kill his happiness
For what she deemed her silliness,
But when she saw him off to Finland,
She sensed beneath her parting grief
An undercurrent of relief.

XLIII.
He journeyed forth, quite unaware of
The fears that plagued his darling's soul.
He had his own portentous share of
Anxieties about his goal.
The future alternately brightened
And then grew dim and left him frightened.
Had it been right for him to choose
To put things off? Or would he lose?
A year or two – that seemed forever!
Yes, clearly, he had been a fool
To let his father overrule
His own desires, and whenever
Impatient thoughts like these would nag,
It seemed that time would really drag.

XLIV.
But he became so very busy,
The weeks and months flew by so fast,
That time outstripped his private tizzy
About the year he wouldn't last,
That somehow passed before he knew it,
Or even how he'd gotten through it.
His old time-tested rule, "Don't shirk!"
And his devotion to his work
Not only made the time go faster,
They brought a second timely boon,
And really, not a bit too soon:
He was promoted concertmaster,[52]
Which he was sure would save the day
And put an end to all delay.

XLV.
And so, the Helsingfors connection,
Which Richard feared would be the death
Of his and Henriette's affection,
Turned out to give it second breath –
At least when viewed from his perspective
Since it attained his dual objective:
Material security,
And marital felicity.
He was all smiles when he told her
And gazed enraptured in her eyes
To see the love in their surprise
And with his eyes to try and hold her,
But her response to his great news
Had left him feeling quite confused.

---

52 In 1914 the two Helsingfors orchestras merged into one, the Helsingfors City Orchestra, in which Burgin served as concertmaster until 1916.

XLVI.

It's true that she had been excited,
Extremely proud and most impressed,
But asking her to marry blighted
Her mood, and she became distressed.
Her manner changed to slightly ruffled,
Her voice then sounded almost muffled,
And she appeared to hesitate
When he had tried to set the date.
Her attitude had been perplexing.
Although at last she did say yes,
The when was anybody's guess.
Her diffidence to him was vexing –
She seemed at once to dare and daunt –
'Good Lord,' he mused, 'what *does* she want?!'

XLVII.

Although he wouldn't have believed it,
She was as dumbfounded as he.
'To shy from bliss when you've achieved it!'
She thought. 'You're acting stupidly.'
And though with him I'm empathetic,
To her I'm also sympathetic:
When you yourself have made things worse,
It isn't any less a curse.
It's bad enough when others muddle
Things up for you or cause the strife
That discombobulates your life,
But it is worse when *you* befuddle
Yourself – the onus is the same,
But you yourself must take the blame.

XLVIII.
And endless futile lacerating
Yourself with blaming never solves,
But ends up just exacerbating
The guilt from which self-blame evolves.
And so, my heroine capricious
Would whip herself in circles vicious:
For days, she whirled, a spinning top
Until she tumbled to a stop
So dizzied by her self-derision
And nauseated by her pain,
She could not pull the string again
To spin some more in indecision.
She'd had enough of 'Let it ride,'
Her tailspin ended in 'Decide!'

XLIX.
Thank God. I too am sick of spinning
This dizzy lovers' tale of mine.
I never thought at Five's beginning
I'd get to stanza forty-nine;
But that's the way it is with "wimmin" –
They almost always leave you swimmin'!
(Although, it's also true with men
One can tread water, now and then).
But now my battle of the sexes –
To use a third stale metaphor
(A practice that I do abhor) –
With all its auguries and hexes,
Its plans and obstacles and frights,
Its feints and joinings and its flights

L.

Has ended, with both parties suing
For peace and future harmony,
And all their wearying, worried wooing
Resolves in conjugality.
Alas, no memory has carried
To me the date when they were married,
But I believe it might have been
In early spring, nineteen thirteen.
My guesswork rests upon a letter
The following year, from Glazunoff:
I quote his way of signing off -
For when they wed, there's no proof better –
"I wish you and your wife success,
Good fortune, health and happiness."[53]

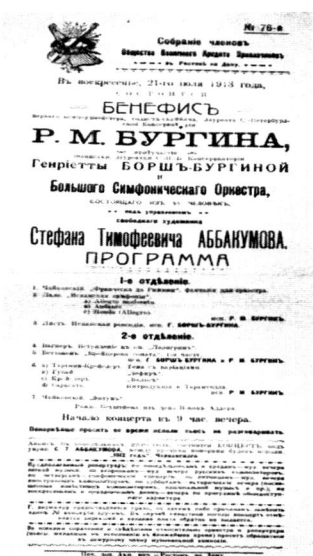

---

53 In the first edition of this poem (Slavica,1989), my guesswork was off by at least a year since I thought Richard and Henriette had been married in 1914. However, a recently discovered bit of memorabilia shown above, the Program of a Benefit Concert given by R.M. Burgin, violinist, and Henrietta Borsh-Burgina, pianist, in Rostov-on-Don on July 21, 1913, shows they were already married in summer of 1913.

CHAPTER SIX: THE SCANDINAVIAN SEPARATION

The only happiness is work.

— Briusov

I.
Once she had sent the joyful lovers
Abroad to Finnish happiness,
My Muse withdrew beneath the covers
To sleep and dream of their success.
Her absence soon had left me yawning
And fits of anxious boredom spawning.
From endless, dancing Chapter Five
I felt no more than half-alive
Creatively. So, sorely needing
A rest, I too turned down my bed –
Without a rhyme inside my head,
Without a bit of bedtime reading,
And with no "vision pure and deep,"
Exhausted, I lay down to sleep.

II.
And all was quiet. In the living-
Room, curled in satisfaction fat,
Her furry, faceless body heaving
Its noiseless breathing, slept the cat;
Within the gated galley-kitchen,
All horizontal, hardly twitching,
A knobby, moribund gray log,
In deathly stillness, slept the dog.
And though the ceiling from my neighbors'
Bombarding feet and stereo boom
Did not, for once, invade my room,
And night had quieted all labors –
To me sleep just refused to come;
I lay and stared in darkness, dumb.

III.
By *his* great joy, but half-expected,
And by the smiles in her eyes,
That still hid fears he'd not detected
But would to his chagrin surmise,
I was obsessed. I simply couldn't
Plot out the rest, my worry wouldn't
Allow my sleepy head to nod,
As if a sharp electric prod
Had shocked my brain, as if a measure-
Less chasm would blacken out my head…
'My *Life* shall die,' Diana said,
'Yet, grief from it is somehow pleasure.
"I'm not complaining: why complain?"
One can't create without some pain.'

IV.
So, onward, onward with my story!
A new direction now it takes
Through Scandinavian territory,
Pursuing Burgin as he makes
A movement west. My yarn unravels
The horizontal of his travels
Along the sixtieth latitude
To ten degrees of longitude.
From Finland, he goes west to Sweden,
But Stockholm residence is not
To be my concertmaster's lot.
His post there acted as a lead-in,
Conducting him to finally play
In Christiania, Norway.

V.

Good fortune charmed his westward movement:
A calm Hesperian destiny
Insured professional improvement,
And Burgin luckily broke free
From all the storms of destitution,
Pogroms, world war and revolution
That thundered from the risen Beast
Upon the European East.
My fate, alas, is less assuring:
To have to write a life so blessed
Can make biographers distressed,
But at the risk of being boring,
I still must tell, as best I can,
The story of "a lucky man."[54]

VI.

His luck was resonant of esses:
Herrn Schneevoigt, Strauss, Sibelius,
Successively insured successes,
Sagacity, and stimulus.
His Scandinavian story centers
On memories of these music mentors
But leaves unsung the silent strife
And *piano* of his private life.
My Scandinavian composition
Attaches to his key, *Es-dur*,[55]
The unrelated *H* of pure,
Though enharmonic, supposition.
My song shall hum the aitch's hush
Beneath his *Es-dur* saga's shush.

---

54 Burgin, at the end of his life, often would remark that he had been "a lucky man."
55 In German, *Es-dur* is E-flat major and *H* is B major. The key of *H* is only distantly related to *Es-dur* through the enharmonic equivalency of B and C-flat.

VII.
You'll hear in *Es* his half-official
Remembrances and anecdotes;
In *H*, some echoes interstitial
Which come from biographic notes
I've made. This programmatic mixture
Cannot, of course, create a picture
Of everything that happened then
Since much remains beyond my ken;
It only can suggest impressions –
Researched, remembered, fixed and free –
That stayed with him, occurred to me,
My hunches and his self-expressions
Of six years when he'd separate,
Assimilate and emigrate.

VIII.
"In Stockholm, Helsingfors and Oslo
I held the concertmasterships
And formed a string quartet, and also
Made yearly concertizing trips."
His soloistic reputation
Was built on his interpretation
Of Jan Sibelius, whose advice
He sought, to make it more precise.
His wife, HB, was also active,
Performing under Burgin's name
To widespread critical acclaim
That deemed her gifted and attractive.
The Burgins seemed to be that rare
Example of an ideal pair.

IX.
Our public and our private image,
However, oftentimes diverge,
And only at the line of scrimmage
At home, do they attempt to merge.
The work arena's hustle-bustle
Out-sounds our muffled private tussle,
And thus, to others it may seem
We both are playing on one team
When actually we are opponents
Who struggle, maybe over-much,
To give ourselves the lie we touch,
Pretending that we are exponents
Of teamed up unity ideal,
While teeming with dissension real.

X.
This game, of course, requires players
Of idiosyncratic stamp –
It's not for hotheads or dismayers,
The braggart lover or the vamp;
It's not for people who can handle
Or have a flair for public scandal,
Or openly to friends express
Their inner anger and distress.
This game appears designed for persons
Who cannot let their feelings out,
Who feel ashamed to rave or shout,
Who blush at even mild cursings,
Who have to cover up the taint
Of grievous hurt with self-restraint.

XI.
A person who in conversations
Will rarely air his private beefs
And shuns as banal, recitations
Of secret troubles, woes, and griefs.
He usually refrains from stoking
His angry fire by chain smoking
And manifests the stubborn quirk
Of calming down through anxious work.
This person often is divided
Between the selves he shows the world
And keeps inside so tightly furled,
That others think him too one-sided;
This is a person who pretends
To everyone, including friends.

XII.
And such a man was Richard Burgin,
And such a woman – Henriette –
To friends their marriage was an erg in
The desert of their *tête-à-tête*,
And if their private life eluded
Their intimates, you'd be deluded
To think that after all this time
I would uncover it through rhyme.
According to the testimony
Of Törnquist, Burgin's closest friend
In Stockholm, "only toward the end"
Of his mysterious matrimony
"Did Richard seem to be upset,
Perhaps, because of Henriette.

XIII.
"I thought that maybe he was seeking
Divorce, perhaps it came about
In Stockholm." Here, he finished speaking,
And left the matter in much doubt.
Supporting Törnquist's information
About the time of separation
Are several disparate facts that came
Through research: under Burgin's name
Our Henrietta, post-December
Of nineteen sixteen, did not play;
And then, some relatives conveyed
Their feeling that they could remember
The marriage lasted just three years,
But nothing more had reached their ears.

XIV.
In sum, although this may be stretching
Imagination on my part
And blur the demarcation sketching
The boundary of life and art,
I still will quote to you, in view of
My skimpy proof, from a review of
A March 1st concert, 'seventeen.
You too may read beneath, between
These lines: "...A rather agitated
Interpretation was given us
By Burgin of Sibelius..."[56]
I wonder, has the critic stated
Unknowingly, by chance, some kind
Of clue to Burgin's state of mind?

---

56 *Stockholms-Tidningen*, Friday, March 2, 1917.

XV.
Who knows? I've clearly no solution;
I think the break-up with his wife
Occurred around the Revolution.
It caused my Richard psychic strife
That really was quite devastating.
I'm sure, though, further perorating
On this, is hardly anything
That he'd consider "interesting,"
And so, enough of my reflections,
Of trying my divining rod
On Burgin's Swedish period.
He too had "vivid recollections,"
Not of the break-up in his house,
But of his meeting Richard Strauss.

XVI.
"Strauss came to guest conduct in Stockholm,[57]
And had a first-rate orchestra –
That was the only place that offered
Good food in those days, not *ersatz*.
That's why we had the best, and sundry
Musicians there, from every country,
And Strauss was happy too, you see,
To come there and eat decently.
Ja! I've a vivid recollection –
Oh, his conducting was superb!
But he was really quite reserved;
He won respect but not affection.
I had there, though it makes me wince,
An interesting experience.

---

57 At the end of February, 1917 (DLB).

XVII.
"I then was in my early twenties,
And pretty cocky too, you know,
And I spoke very well in German –
That was a great advantage – so
I played *Ein Heldenleben,* ánd he,
Though silent, let me understand he
Was happy since he could be quite
Outspoken if some thing weren't right
When someone played. Well, I was cocky
And very much less nervous than
I am now, or have been since then.
So, somehow, I got up the courage
To ask him – hoping I'd exposed
Some unclear thing that he'd composed –

XVIII.
"About that phrase in *Heldenleben*
That's double for the violins
And for, if I am not mistaken,
Bass clarinet. The phrase begins:
A-sharp, inverted F-sharp major
Chord, resolving to D-major –
Exactly as one would expect,
All very simple and correct.
But the inversion has the bass note,
F-sharp, which goes below our G,
And that was very strange to me!
So, I'd the nerve to ask the maestro –
It was in German that we spoke –
'How, maestro, should we play this note?'

XIX.
"As if to ask for his suggestion.
His answer put me in my place:
'You know,' he said, 'this stupid question
Is put so often to my face
That I am sick and tired of it,
But seeing you are not above it,
And such a young man, very young,
I'll ask you, what should I have done?
Should I have written – incorrectly –
G-natural since you can't play
F-sharp? Then, you'd be right to say
"That's wrong." Besides, you can't expect me
To let *your* lowest string confine
And mar this lovely curvy line.'

XX.
"You know, for me, brought up to honor
Each note, for so aspiring
A young musician, well, his answer,
Quite frankly, was discouraging.
I felt confused. I said, 'I'm sorry,'
But seeing that there was no more he
Would say, I left. But still, you know,
His answer had disturbed me so,
For years, I looked for a solution.
The F-sharp's played by clarinet,
The violins don't play it, yet,
They try creating the illusion
That there's an F-sharp there, and so
They move their hands somewhere below

XXI.

"The G-string, make believe they're playing;
And that effect, you see, a kind
Of unintended *gliss*, I'm saying,
Is what, I think, he had in mind.
I do not blame him for refraining
From telling me since such explaining
Should not be necessary; yet,
That's something I will not forget!
You know, I've always found composers
Enigmas. How do they create?
And how do they communicate
Outside of music with musicians
They need to have their work performed,
So their intentions aren't deformed?

XXII.

"In this respect, three great composers
Impressed me more than anyone –
Stravinsky, Hindemith and Schoenberg –
And I had contact with each one,
But that was when I was in Boston,
And it's a little bit exhausting
To tell these stories all at once;
Besides, it must be time for lunch."
A good idea. I'll end this portion
Of Burgin's memories on tape;
My poem must retain its shape,
And I'd be guilty of distortion
To have him sing his Boston air
Before I'd even got him there.

XXIII.
And that is yet another story
That contrapuntally we'll tell,
Resounding to his greater glory
Upon the echoes of the knell
That tolled divorce and desolation,
Dejection and disconsolation,
The dolorous feelings that he heard
Though never spoke of them a word.
The year when Burgin was divorcing
Does not in concert dates abound,
But he was able to rebound
In nineteen eighteen by re-coursing
To teaching, playing symphony
And chamber group activity.

XXIV.
The latter was a gainful reason
To fight his loss of Henriette;
The nineteen-eighteen nineteen season
Enhanced the Burgin String Quartet.
It toured and played all over Sweden
And Scandinavia as a leading
Contemporary chamber group.
The motley members of the troupe –
Ernst Törnquist, Burgin's fellow
Fiddler, Russian-speaking Mann,
A little-known violist, and
The Finnish Kinkulin on 'cello –
Played well together, greatly hiked
The group's success, and were "well-liked."[58]

---

[58] Törnquist commented that "The Quartet was successful and well-liked."

The Burgin String Quartet, Stockholm, ca. 1918
Left to right: Abram Kinkullin, Tor Mann,
Ernst Törnquist, Richard Burgin.

XXV.
The steady rise of Burgin's fortunes
In Sweden helped to ease the strain
Of other family misfortunes
That must have also caused him pain,
And these, like many other troubles,
As often noted, came in doubles:
An unexpected tragedy -
Paulina's death from bone TB;
And next, the news about his mother –
Her health had steadily declined
Until she was to bed confined.
For Richard, there could be no other
Anxiety so torture-some;
Oh, how he wanted to go home!

XXVI.
But for the moment there was naught he
Could do but hope that she would mend
And work his hardest with the thought he
Was earning money he would send
To Warsaw; hence, his spring decision
To try to find a new position
So he could send more home each week.
He did not have too long to seek,
For once again, the old "S-Factor"
Combined with talent, will and pluck
To bring another bit of luck.
His chef-d'orchestre/benefactor,
Herr Schnéevoigt, sighted virgin land
To found a new orchestral band.

XXVII.
A man of energy unbounded
For whom there was no last hurrah,
In nineteen-nineteen, Schnéevoigt founded
The Oslo Symphony Orchestra,
And as before in Finland, Sweden,
So now in Norway, Schnéevoigt, needing
A concertmaster, forthwith thought
Of Richard Burgin for the spot.
"I came to Oslo in the autumn
And learned Norwegian so well
That most Norwegians couldn't tell
I wasn't born there. Hamsun, Thörson
And Ibsen – every word they wrote
I read and almost knew by rote.

XXVIII.
"When I left Russia for some country,
It always was my attitude
To think my stay in that new country
Would not just be an interlude,
And so, I tried assimilating
To that new culture, speculating
That for some length of time, you see,
I'd settle down there, hopefully."
In Oslo, though, his expectation
Of permanence was not fulfilled.
Some Chance apparently had willed
A second sudden separation
That was by nineteen-twenty near;
He stayed in Norway just one year.

XXIX.
"I had been working now with Schnéevoigt
In Oslo, Stockholm, Helsingfors,
And we'd been many years together
And knew each other well, of course.
Well, in the summers he would often
Conduct in Scheveningen, Holland.
Among the guest conductors there
In nineteen-twenty, was Monteux,
And he, as it turned out, was booking
For Boston. Fradkin[59] had resigned –
A union fracas of some kind –
But anyway, Monteux was looking
And spoke to Schnéevoigt there, you see,
And Schnéevoigt recommended me.

XXX.
"He wrote – I was in London – saying,
'Although I hate to let you go,
I told Monteux about your playing;
If I'd not done that much, you know,
My conscience never would forget it.
Of course, this doesn't mean you'll get it,
But such a chance is really rare,
And so, I ought to do my share.'
Well, that was really very nice and
He wrote, 'Till such-and-such a date
Monteux's in Paris. Don't delay.'
And so, I took Schnéevoigt's advice and
I went to Paris right away –
Some friends invited me to stay –

---

[59] Fredric Fradkin (1892-1963) was the concertmaster of the Boston Symphony Orchestra until he was forced to resign at the end of the 1919-20 season due to his role in union strife. Monteux's appointment as conductor of the orchestra was to begin in the fall, 1920.

XXXI.

"They'd just arrived from Russia, lately.
I played for Monteux in his home;
He told me that unfortunately,
On piano, he can just play some,
Well, harmonies, once in a while
Since he plays badly. Then he smiled
And asked, 'What would you like to play?
Tchaikovsky? Beethoven? Please, say.'
You know, the standard repertory.
I played this, that, then this, you see,
For forty minutes, and, well, he
Chose not to bother me or worry
About orchestral music since
He knew I'd had experience

XXXII.

"With Schnéevoigt many years already.
I ought to tell him, though, I thought,
Till then I had performed a steady
Germanic repertoire. 'I'm not,'
I said, 'Outside of Strauss, not very
Familiar with contemporary
Composers,' and that there were few
French works or modern things I knew.
He said, 'That isn't too alarming.
I too don't know them, but I hope
Together we'll enlarge our scope.'
Well, that was very nice and charming!
He clearly liked the way I played
And told me, 'Go back right away

XXXIII.
"'To London, and see Mr. Bremen,
The manager.' I had to sign
A contract, once I got a permit,
Which was not easy at that time.
Somehow, however, I succeeded.
I went to London, signed the needed
Agreements and that was the way
Monteux engaged me there to play."

....
....
....
....
....
....

XXXIV.
Since we have now approached the moment
When Burgin's future die was cast,
Perhaps the time has come to comment
In general, on the life that's past.
His marriage and his youth now over,
My Burgin, once again a rover,
Aboard the Bergensfjord, awaits
A new life in the United States.
So, as he sails across the ocean,
Let's scan the past he's left behind
(Which he might too have called to mind):
The joys and sorrows, calms, commotion,
The ordinary and bizarre
Events that marked his life thus far.

XXXV.
Before I turn reflection inward
And dabble in psychology
(A ticklish business!) I'll begin with
A try at physiognomy.
His red-cheeked face, complected fairish,
Was oval-chinned, high-browed and squarish,
Half circled in brown wavy hair;
His nose curved down below the flare
Of nostrils with its base inverting
In shape his chiseled upper lip,
Its pointed peaks and center dip;
The lower lip, more self-asserting
And thicker, often would jut out
When he would concentrate or pout.

XXXVI.
But Burgin's most attractive feature
Was deep-set eyes of hazel gray;
Their glances were a silent teacher
Of what he said and didn't say:
They opened wide to share your pleasure,
In narrowed calm, they took your measure,
Their distant stare would often seem
To tell about some private dream;
A downcast glance conveyed, 'How vile,'
A gentle glow expressed, 'You're dear,'
A glaze – 'I'm bored,' a dimming – fear;
But best of all, those eyes could smile –
No other eyes could shine so bright
With joy, surprise or pure delight.

XXXVII.

So when, a ripened twenty-seven,
He pondered all he'd undergone,
What happenings would memory leaven?
Who would he smile back upon?
Winetzky, Lotto and Joachim -
The day that Auer "thundered" at him –
Young Jascha's *pizzicato* scales,[60]
Boris's quips and Mischa's tales –
Pavlovsk, that day that he "discovered,"
When he had thought he was so smart,
The *Kreutzer* had a piano part!
And all the music he'd uncovered
That no one else had heard as yet –
The fine success of his quartet,

XXXVIII.

His marvelous luck in Scandinavia,
The charming people he had met,
Like Schnéevoigt, colleague, friend and savior,
'How many jobs he helped me get!'
And Törnquist, Stenhammer*, Grevillius*,
Hannikainnen*, Sitt*, Sibellius,
And Strauss – 'I never will forget ...'
(His smile tinged now with regret)
'The strange F-sharp in Heldenleben,
A real enigma! ... But, why fret?
I'll find an explanation yet,
It's not like ... Oh, hör auf zu beben!'[61]
(He stared, then lit a cigarette) ...
It isn't like ... my ... Henriette.'

---

60 A reference to one of Burgin's reminiscences to Professor Dann when he recalled a lesson of the young Jascha Heifetz when the *Wunderkind* astounded Auer with his "flying pizzicato."
61 *Hör auf zu beben* ("Cease trembling"), from the final movement of Mahler's Second Symphony. For more information on Burgin's attitude to Mahler, see Memoralia.

XXXIX.
He smiled as the tears were welling
And felt a lump inside his throat
As if some inner voice were quelling
The urge to sing so sad a note.
It was a very strange sensation,
Half-solace and half-desolation,
To keep on smiling as you sigh
And feel like laughing when you cry.
He felt so tragic, yet the comic
Would sometimes syncopate his grief;
From sadness smiles brought relief.
To this mixed motion metronomic
Came memories of *those* three years,
With rueful smiles through the tears.

XL.
If one can contemplate the wreck of
One's happiness with smiling gaze,
One's playing right in tune with Chekhov
And might be acting out his plays,
In which, they say, hearts break from battle
Behind the teacups' muted rattle,
And where the lovelorn have the quirk
Of burying sadness in their work.
The selfsame smiles mark his stories
Wherever wrongs have no redress,
And people cope with their distress
By pasting smiles on their worries –
They rise, work hard and go to bed,
Survive their woes and look ahead.

XLI.

They hope the future will be better.
Like Dr. Astrov[62] they avow,
The human race will break its fetters
About two hundred years from now.
Their present woes have no solution,
But they have hope – in evolution:
In nature, there is permanence,
A pledge of life's continuance.
Their only comfort comes from working:
One plants one's garden, helps it grow,
And though its progress may be slow,
There's no excuse in that for shirking,
For if one quits, gives into gloom,
One's plants will surely never bloom.

XLII.

Some say that Chekhov is depressing;
They find his viewpoint a dead-end,
Dislike him for his not expressing
The faith that mortals will transcend,
That there's a heaven for achievers,
Eternal life for true believers,
A comforting embrace above
For those betrayed by earthly love.
Some readers think it meretricious,
And for a Russian writer odd,
To put more hope in work than God,
While others just find work suspicious,
Or cannot cope, or lack all hope
And thus, resort to doing dope.

---

[62] A character in Chekhov's play, *Uncle Vanya*, who is disappointed in love and puts his energies into reforestation.

XLIII.

But Chekhov also has defenders –
I count myself among their group –
Who run to work from their offenders
And somehow manage to recoup,
Who try to focus on the antic
In youthful debacles romantic,
And realize, once they've had their cry,
That life goes on (though who knows why?);
Who have no doubt that on the trek of
Existence, everyone has woes,
Youth flowers and away it goes,
And through their tears they read their Chekhov
And smile, 'How wonderfully he
Depicts my own reality!'

XLIV.

It may appear that this digression
Has taken me quite far a-field,
But I just had to give expression
To certain thoughts I hope will yield
Some inner truths about my hero.
Of course, it's possible that zero
In Chekhov's writing, will obtain
To Burgin and I've waxed in vain.
Yet still, I have this stubborn notion –
A sign of madness to be sure –
That somehow Russian literature
Will serve me up a magic potion
Which if I drink sufficiently
Shall make my hero known to me.

XLV.

And that is why Tolstoy provided
The aims and atmosphere of *Youth*;
By Dostoevsky I was guided
In hearing Burgin's silent truth;
First Love combined Tolstoy's Irteniev[63]
With Pushkin's Tania and Turgenev;
And poets of the Silver Age
Conveyed the ambience of each stage.
And now, on Burgin's separation
From youth and Europe, on the brink
Of his maturity, I think
His real and bookish maturation
Have formed a new American
Of character Chekhovian.

XLVI.

But that's to come. Though I sincerely
Am moved to tell my hero's fate,
My Muse has fixed her mute and clearly
For now, his *Life* will have to wait.
Towards academic prose inclining,
A deadline's dampening my rhyming,
And I – with some regret, it's true –
"More lazily my verse pursue."[64]
I do not feel the old desires
For scribbling these Onegin reams
Since other frigid, numbing dreams
And other choking, smoking fires,
In light of day and night's black hole
Disturb the harmony of my soul.

---

63 Nikolai Irteniev is the hero of Tolstoy's autobiographical novel, *Youth*.
64 Quoted from Pushkin, *Eugene Onegin*, Chapter Six, XLIII. In general, the stanzas at the end of Chapter Six here follow those at the end of Pushkin's Chapter Six and in fact, parody them.

XLVII.
I've felt the gasp of jerky measures,
I've heard a new unstable key,
Arrhythmia pants of fewer pleasures
And rues the old tonality.
Oh Harmony, where is your rigor?
And where its perfect-rhyming *vigor*?
Can it be really true at last
Its joyful season now is past?
Can it be factually attested
Without august encomion
The springtime of my life is gone
(As often up till now I've jested)?
And can it be there's no return?
And I shall shortly forty turn?

XLVIII.
Well then, complaints are unbecoming
My Apollonian design,
For life's a balance – going, coming –
So, fare thee well, oh youth of mine!
I thank you for your sweet euphorias,
Your nightmarish phantasmagorias,
Your larks and lulls, your lows and lifts;
For all your losses and your gifts
You have my gratitude. With you I
Had many a worry and a thrill,
Of Dionysus drank my fill …
Enough! Now curious for the new I
Set out again to try my best
And from your storms, to get some rest.

XLIX.

Just one look back. Goodbye, scenarios,
In which I've acted to the hilt
The second-stringers, impresarios,
My dreams, anxieties and guilt.
But you, capricious inspiration,
Excite my poor imagination,
Buy me a new Ball-Liner pen
And come to visit in my den.
Don't leave the poet in destitution
To sit and scribble all alone,
Or worse, embittered, turn to stone
In some dream-deadening Institution
Of Learning where, like all my friends,
I must earn means to gain your ends.

CHAPTER SEVEN: IN THE NEW WORLD

My city and country as I am Antonius,
Is Rome; as a man, the whole world.

– Marcus Aurelius

Die liebe Erde allüber all
Blüht auf im Lenz und grunt aus neu!
Allüberall und ewig blauenlicht die Fernen!
Ewig, ewig. . .ewig, ewig. . .

– Gustav Mahler

How saddened am I by your coming,
Oh Spring, Spring! Time of love!

– A.S. Pushkin

I.

Chased out by sultry southwest breezes,
Cool April suddenly retreats.
The first May warming Cambridge seizes
To dress in green its naked streets.
And overnight without a warning,
The bud eyes pop to greet year's morning;
Just washed, but still half-dressed, the trees
Urge on their sleepy limbs, 'Oh please!
You're late, so hurry with your greening!
Forsythia's already out,
Clipped lawns and waxy hedges shout,
In geometric patterns preening:
"The Spring is here."[65] Its painful birth
Revives from dreams the song of earth.

II.

How saddened am I by your coming,
Oh spring, the season of farewell!
What deathly memories stir the humming
Of *ewig* that your songs foretell!
With what mute grief, I mishear *never*
In the repeated faint "forever"
Of your "horizon glimmering blue"
And of your earth, "grown green anew."
What is it? Can it be your pleasures
And everything that freshens, gives
To earthly life delight, relives
The pulse of Mahler's dying measures
I heard conducted long ago
By one whose death bereaved me so?

---

65 "The Spring is here," from "The Drunkard in Spring," *The Song of the Earth* by Gustav Mahler.

III.
Or is it, ruing the renewal
Of verdure, soon to fade in fall,
I find ironic spring too cruel
And wonder why it blooms at all?
 Or is my longing just endemic
To my profession academic,
The springtime urge for having fun
Reminding me my work's undone?
Perhaps too often I remember,
In moments lackadaisical
The start of my sabbatical,
My *Life's* beginning in November,
And now that it is nearly grown,
Recall the spring when it was sown.

IV.
That was the April he lay dying,
But when his daughter came to life –
Belatedly, there's no denying –
And jogged the memory of his wife,
Preserved the stories she had lost and
Returned to start research in Boston.
Spring called me to the archives then!
A time of studious regimen,
A time of gathering information,
Of taking notes, transcribing tapes,
And dreaming out the narrative shapes
For facts, surmises, inspiration.
That springtime blossomed with a task
Allowing grief to wear a mask.

V.
The future makes my Muse downhearted.
Indulge her fondness for the past,
My patient reader! Let's get started!
I'm ready to begin at last.
Let's go to where my Muse feels freer
To rhyme a musical career,
To Massachusetts Avenue,
To Symphony Hall, where Burgin, new
When he arrived in nineteen twenty,
Became a fixture on the stage –
Conducting, playing, till the age
Of sixty-nine; where he left plenty
Of gifts behind for those he got,
But where today, alas, he's not.

VI.
It's April, 'eighty-one, we're taking
A special, very private tour
Of Symphony Hall for which we're making
Our entrance by the side stage door.
Descending deeply to the basements,
We walk beneath the window casements,
Circuitously fathoming
The cellars of the newest wing.
There in a room, alone, surrounded
By dusty tomes, my Slavist sits,
Scans old reviews for novel bits,
Her vigor seemingly unbounded,
And tape-records the ones she needs;
Let's take a look at what she reads:

VII.

"SYMPHONY'S NEW CONCERTMASTER,
Violinist of Renown,
Richard Burgin, Born in Warsaw,
Joins Orchestra. By Olin Downes."[66]
(I swear, to rhyme gazette descriptions
Is worse than Latinate prescriptions
That Byron managed to enshrine –
But then, he had a longer line!)
The critic gave his first impression:
"Precocity he has survived
Quite well indeed; he's frank, blue-eyed,
Brown-haired, and has a fair complexion."
Downes then described his interview,
Which here, I'll re-enact for you.

---

[66] *The Boston Post*, October 1, 1920.

Richard Burgin at the time of his arrival in the United States.

VIII.[67]

D: America, does it seem different
    On this your second visit, here?
B: "Oh yes! It's really very different,
    It's now – how does one say? – so dear!"
D: Of course. The dollar dwindles faster
    Each day... Well, you're a concertmaster
    Of broadly-based experience,
    I'm sure the Boston audience
    Would like to know your tastes in music.
B: "For me, there only are two kinds –
    Good and bad. I also find
    I like some music that's not music,
    Perhaps. I'm fascinated by
    The late works of Ravel, but I

IX.

  "Would say that's color more than music.
  I like some Strauss but do not care
  For *Don Quixote*, *Zarathustra*,
  Or the *Domestica*, for there
  His music is too programmatic.
  Don Quixote tells dramatic
  Adventures, and if you mistake
  Which scene he wants to illustrate,
  Then you're all wrong. Then you are kissing
  The wrong girl in the dark. To me,
  That's moving pictures which we see
  By hearing them. I'm not dismissing
  Such music, but its place withal
  Is scarcely in a concert hall."

---

[67] In this version of the interview, Downes' (D) questions are imagined and Burgin's (B) answers are quotations of Downes' quotation of them.

X.

D: But don't you think there's some reflection
   In music, though perhaps impure,
   Of other arts? Or some connection
   With painting, or with literature?
B: "Of course, there is. But influences
   Which art or writing evidences
   At one time, say, are felt by us
   In music, much, much later. Thus,
   The nineties saw a generation
   Of painters like Ravel, and though
   We have now so-called Cubists, no
   Composer-Cubist has emerged yet.
   No doubt he'll come, although, to ask
   If he'll be welcome's not our task."

XI.

D: Indeed! Well, since we've started speaking
   Of Europe, more specifically,
   What country do you think is seeking
   The most advancement musically?
B: "Undoubtedly, I should say Russia.
   No other country now has such a
   Large group of innovators who
   Are looking forward. This is true,
   As well, of Finland's Jean Sibelius,
   Whose 1914 symphony,
   The *Fifth*, revised quite recently,
   Is even more impressionistic,
   More striking, newer and so forth
   Than his extraordinary *Fourth*."

XII.

D: And what of France? B: "Well, certain Frenchmen
    Are showing new, astonishing
    Perceptions worthy of attention."
D: This really has been interesting.
    Do you have time for one more question?
B: "Of course!" D: Well, what is your impression
    Of Europe's orchestras, today?
B: "Well, since the war, I'd have to say,
    There's just not any that can cope with
    America's. In Germany,
    They are old men now principally,
    And there is nothing any longer
    In Europe like the BSO."
D: Well, on that note, I'll let you go.

XIII.

Then, once such questions had been fielded,
My Burgin started to perform.
The Boston archives also yielded
Reviews, which judged above the norm
His early efforts soloistic;
But nothing can be less artistic
In music *Lives* than quoting such
Reviews of concerts overmuch,
And it would really be too boring
To cite in full the praise and blame
Evaluating Burgin's fame
In every critical outpouring;
So, I'll be brief and give instead
A summary of those I read.

XIV.
The Boston critics' view composite
Of Burgin, up to 'twenty-nine
Allows my teacher-self to posit
The final judgment, "Very fine!"
This does include consideration
Of Burgin's bearing, intonation,
Technique, enthusiasm, zeal
And his musicianly appeal,
As indicated by his playing
The violin concertos of
Tchaikovsky, Brahms and Glazunov –
(The latter two to the inveighing
Of some who thought them "jaded" then) –
Sibelius and Beethoven.

XV.
About his tone there's disagreement:
Some call it "lustrous," others – "wan,"
But there is positive agreement
On his "musicianly élan."
They deemed him "noble," "enthusiastic,"
"Temperamental," not bombastic,
"Convincing," "musical" and "free
Of crass sentimentality";
Of bearing "youthful," "unpretentious,"
He sounds "the Golden pleasant mean,"
Is technically "accomplished," "clean,"
And always "thoughtful, conscientious,"
"Subordinates his efforts to
Produce ensemble playing true."

XVI.
In sum, a violinist "tasteful,"
"Unwaveringly accurate,"
"Refined," "authoritative," "graceful,"
"Unmanneredly delicate";
"Romantic," but "not egoistic,"
"Not virtuosic," but "artistic,"
"Sincere," "painstaking," "very clear,"
"Euphonious," "pleasing to the ear,"
"Effective," "virile," "deft," "resilient,"
"Straightforward," "energetic," "light,"
"Incisive," "unaffected," "bright,"
"Unclouded," "polished," "sterling," "brilliant,"
"Remarkable," "intelligent,"
"Scholarly" and "excellent."

XVII.
I'm sure there's no one who could rival,
Now that my appraisal's done,
Its subject and its adjectival
Assessing prolegomenon.
Despite the scholarly abuses –
Quotes out of context – it has uses:
My catalog of adjectives,
Although a bit one-sided, gives
To any teacher who is frantic
About the "recs" he has to write –
A task of dubious delight –
A list of positive semantic
Descriptive qualities to choose,
With which no applicant can lose.

XVIII.
Before you chide me as a cynic,
Just ponder the descriptive word:
It is by nature polygynic –
One finds it marrying a herd
Of substantives, from whose quintessence
It swells and puffers, an excrescence
(In essence, there is little doubt)
Nine-tenths its mates can do without.
A virile adjective is handy
For sprucing a lackluster house,
Or livening a barren spouse,
But every one of them's a dandy,
Attracting twins to its renown
And overburdening its noun.

XIX.
And *the* most burdensome and fickle
Are adjectives of fulsome praise:
Their object's vanity they tickle,
But leave its essence in a haze.
Although it's meant to be upraising,
There is an irony in praising –
It isn't funny when it's sparse,
But in excess, it seems a farce.
Still more ironic is invective:
We're tickled by laconic, sharp
Assaults, but if the critics harp,
We find we want to be protective
Of egos they obliterate,
And we defend the second-rate.

XX.
But to continue this digression,
Ironically might undermine
The praises that received expression
In Burgin's case and misalign
My reader's trust. I need not mention
That it was never my intention
To drown in adjective excess
My hero's talent and success.
From his Bostonian beginning
The critics wrote, "When he appeared
As soloist, his colleagues cheered."
And soon the audiences, grinning,
"Would repeatedly recall
Him to the stage of Symphony Hall."

XXI.
Yet, solos were for him a sideline;
His most important function was,
As concertmaster, helping guide fine
Performance with the orchestra's
Conductor, thus effecting concert
Of boss and men, some more than once hurt
By moody leaders' vents of spleen –
Rehearsing, maestros can get mean.
The concertmaster is a leader,
Content to seem as if he's led,
Who plays two parts to get ahead –
The promulgator and the pleader,
Withal, the dauntless diplomat,
Which Burgin was a master at.

XXII.
Throughout his forty years of service
With three conductors Burgin worked,
And though at moments he was nervous,
He rarely showed them he was irked.
First came Monteux, then Koussevitzky –
The latter, prone to temper fits, he
Relied quite often on the balm
Of Burgin's friendship to calm down –
And finally, Munch, less roused to anger,
Who hated to rehearse and fought
His battles mainly at *ballot*,
But could express a peevish languor
When a rehearsal would begin
If Burgin hadn't let him win.

XXIII.
But archives don't give information,
Or at the most, not very much,
About professional relations,
Dependent on a personal touch.
So, having reaped her public harvest
Of adjectives and dates, my Slavist,
Bemoaning that her primary horse
Mouthed words no longer, sought a source
To plow his work life's inner furrows.
Books failed her, but by happenstance,
October brought those tapes of Dann's,
And in their memories, she burrows.
Those tapes as anyone can see
Have been a lifesaver for me.

XXIV.
"Monteux," so Burgin recollected,
"Could not play any instrument,
But had his inner ear perfected
And heard just how the music went.
The score he'd studied really só well,
That even at the first rehearsal
Of something new, we'd be amazed –
He'd spot the tiniest mistakes. . .
I still recall how I reacted,
In 'twenty-two when he put on
Stravinsky's *Sacre de Printemps*,
And I first played it. Well, I acted
For weeks, as if I didn't know
What happened in the world, you know.

XXV.
"It was as if a revolution
Had taken place in me, but I
Was in a state of dissolution
And could not pinpoint, how or why.
I realized it was just tremendous –
Life's not the same now, those stupendous
Sounds, those rhythms, the polý-
Tonality were new to me.
The general drive, oh, every measure
Just stirred me! Not that I could say
I liked or disliked it. It's way
Beyond a case of feeling pleasure;
It was – some thing phenomenal
Had happened in the music world.

XXVI.

"We had a lot of preparation.
Monteux knew *Sacre* inside out.[68]
And then, before our unionization,
Nobody gave a thought about
Rehearsal time. He had the power
To keep us daily seven hours;
You simply did it, no one dared
To say a word because we shared
The sense this manner of presenting
A piece of music was a first –
In fact, we felt we could rehearse
It even longer, not resenting
The extra time, that it was so,
A very major thing, you know."

XXVII.

And so, symphonic revolution
In 'twenty-two was made by spring;
And then orchestral evolution
The fall of 'twenty-four did bring.
Monteux resigned from his position
And was replaced by a musician
Of early virtuoso fame,
A bassist who achieved a name
As impresario and conductor,
First off, in Russia, then, in France,
A man of great exuberance
And very powerful *kharákter*,[69]
A charismatic demiurge
Whose name was: Koussevitzky, Serge.

---

68 Monteux conducted the world premiere of *Sacre de Printemps (The Rite of Spring)* in Paris, 1913.
69 *kharákter* = character, personality (Russian).

XXVIII.

"When Koussevitzky came to Boston,
He needed quite a bit of help –
His brilliant gift depended *most* on
His intuition, not a wealth
Of learning in his own profession.
And in a way, it's my impression
That that's what really made him great.
He really could communicate
In spite of lacks in education.
He had shortcomings like us all,
But more important overall,
He had conviction, imagination.
For players, such a man's a czar,
Despite how cynical they are.

XXIX.

"He really tried to take good care of
The members of the orchestra
And always tried to be aware of
What each musician's worries are.
He had a sort of father's pride in
His players, always took their side in
Their gripes with management, so they
Would try to go out of their way
To do whatever he'd require.
The give and take, despite his whims
Between the orchestra and him
Was just the best one could desire,
And very few conductors guested
Because he called us his *orkestr*."

XXX.

And Burgin was *his* concertmaster,
At least when all was said and done.
He took the part his life had casted
And played the role of Koussey's son,
A role in which he had much training,
Some thirty years now of restraining
His temperament from reckless rants
To gain in harmony his wants;
A trying role since he was "cocky"
And clearly wanted to impress
The new conductor with his success.
Thus, their relations had a rocky
Start, and got so out of joint
That Burgin, proud, "was on the point

XXXI.

"Of handing in his resignation
During that first season, but
Arrived at reconciliation,"[70]
According to the scuttle-butt.
How like the love-and-hate attractions
And sometimes troubled interactions
With fathers of those moderate sons,
Not like Bazarov*, but the ones
Who being softer, like Arkady,*
At first rebel and foment strife
But soon reject the rebel's life.
He made his peace, and working hard, he
Was quite content to settle down
And help finesse his chief's renown.

---

70 Quoted from Moses Smith, *Koussevitzky*.

XXXII.

So, Burgin "reached an understanding
With his new chief and from then on,"
In cases of misunderstanding,
"He was the effective liaison
Between the boss and the musicians."
His talent, tact, shrewd intuitions
And skill bore fruit when "he became
In fact, as he'd become in name,
Assistant BSO Conductor."[71]
(I'd add, my hero had to thank
Besides his tact, for this new rank,
That ineluctable instructor
Who had, so many years before,
Conduced to *takt*[72] a child of four.)

XXXIII.

For surely, reader, you remember
How Richard's talent was found out –
That Warsaw concert where a member
Of the public pointed out
To Moses that his son was waving
His arms in rhythm and behaving
"As if he were conducting too."
(If not, you should One/V review!)
Thus, after years of observation,
Redress in concertmaster's guise,
And as his library testifies,
Considerable self-education,
His old conducting gifts unfurled
In Boston's musical new world.

---

71 Moses Smith, *Ibid*.
72 *takt* = beat, time, measure (Russian).

XXXIV.
The growth, however, of Assistant
Conductors spreads at gentle pace,
Since with the maestro's co-existent,
They must not crowd that flower's space.
"My programs had to pass inspection
By Koussevitzky. My selection
Of works was always fitted to
The ones that he desired to do."
Adapting to environmental
Restrictions, hardy Burgin's bloom,
In search no doubt of *Lebens*-room,
Grew out in some experimental
Directions, bringing to the air
New works such as *Pierrot Lunnaire*.

XXXV.
"By Schoenberg I was just awestricken,
Both by the man and by his work.
I studied hard what he had written, -
That was, you know, a whole new world.
In nineteen twenty-eight, some patrons
Of art, elite Bostonian matrons,
Would sponsor *private* concerts of
New works, worthwhile works above
The ordinary. I succeeded
In getting them to work with me
To put *Lunnaire* on *publicly*.
They gave me the support I needed,
And after having weeks rehearsed,
We put that on – a Boston first."

XXXVI.

As you, dear reader, have expected
Because of what has gone before,
There is an anecdote connected
With this event. "In 'thirty-four,
When Schoenberg came," said my recounter,[73]
"I had with him my first encounter.
Before the Cambridge concert he
Sent up and asked to speak with me.
I thought, 'Perhaps it's last instructions
To give before we shall begin.'
I quickly took my violin,
Went down and based on my deductions,
I asked, 'What would you have me say?'
He says, 'It's not about today's

XXXVII.

"'Performance. I just heard you've done my
Pierrot Lunnaire some time ago?'
'Yes.' 'Was it difficult to put on?' 'Why,
Of course, it's hard, as you must know.'
'How much rehearsal?' 'More than twenty.'
'Where was it?' 'Jordan Hall.' 'How many
Can fill that hall?' 'Twelve hundred in all.'
'Oh, that was much too big a hall!'
And now comes what I must consider
My, *the* most stupid repartee
That anyone could give, you see,
Because I was by him awestricken,
I said, to be agreeable,
'Maestro, *es war nur halb-voll!*'[74]

---

73 Schoenberg was invited to Boston by the BSO to conduct the orchestra, and his first concert was in Sanders Theater, Cambridge [DLB].
74 *Es war nur halb-voll* = It was just half-full (German).

XXXVIII.
"'Thank goodness!' he replied, thus easing
My obvious embarrassment.
'But how is it you find so pleasing
A half-filled house?' 'Yes, I'm content.
You know, I doubt quite truly whether
More than six hundred altogether
Would like that piece. Twelve hundred there
Would mean that half would hate *Lunnaire*,
And let me tell you, nothing's worse than
To sit beside a person who
Just hates what's interesting to you.
I've sat beside that type of person
Who hates my work with all his might –
It almost ended in a fight!'"

XXXIX.
Your ears, dear reader, were accosted
By Burgin's anecdote to keep
My promises, but I'm exhausted,
With strophes to go before I sleep.
My Slavist has at length reflected
On Burgin's work but has neglected
His private life and views. Perhaps,
She ought to try to fill these gaps.
Of little help her usual sources –
Her library books and transcribed tapes –
And she must look some other place.
So like Tatiana* she recourses
To Burgin's library where she looks
For him by leafing through his books.

XL.
The many scores, I need not mention,
To her but little did impart;
Nor did she pay too much attention
To textbooks on conducting art.
The search seemed futile, and Diana
Did doubt the methods of Tatiana,
And wondered, 'Why this bookish fuss?'
But then, she found . . . Aurelius.
Whole sections of his *Meditations*
On nature, feeling and the mind,
Our Burgin once had underlined
And made some marginal notations,
Like rules to which he would adhere,
E. g. 'In thoughts be clean and clear.'

XLI.
Encouraged, she continued searching,
And in Descartes's philosophy
Again, she saw his pencil lurching
Beneath the thoughts on clarity,
And found more marginal inscriptions,
Her father's earnest self-prescriptions –
When positively he'd react,
He'd make a note on how to act.
But though she felt that she was nearing
Her father's thinking, not Descartes,
Nor Marcus could reveal his heart.
She knew some family tales, but fearing
She might in telling them, abuse
His privacy, she sought my Muse.

XLII.
My Muse, not generally jealous
Of privacy, persuaded her
That she was being over-zealous.
'It won't disgrace his character,'
She mocked, 'to talk about his worries,
Or even loves, or tell some stories
About his friends and family!
You're being too damn scholarly!'
'Perhaps,' my Slavist said, retiring.
'So, maybe I'll allow you to
Relate such things, at least a few?'
'I'm happy to.' 'But be inspiring,
Or failing that, just do your best.'
'*Mais certainement*! Now, go and rest.'

XLIII.
Though Burgin was a workaholic –
No doubt, a family disease –
He was not alien to frolic
And knew what made him feel at ease.
When pressures or rebukes would harass,
He found relief from them in Paris,
Where he would spend his summers in
The twenties, playing violin
And also (Juliusz said) the dandy,[75]
And most successfully, roulette.
The winnings he would often get
Delighted him and came in handy.
(He played his "system" as a rule
And never ever lost his cool.)

---

75 Juliusz Burgin, Richard's youngest brother, was the source of this information.

XLIV.
"In 'twenty-five,'" recalled Marysia,[76]
"Your father took Maman and me
To Paris, and we met there this, ah,
A woman friend of his, you see,
A millionairess with a fancy
Estate and daughter my age, Nancy.
Their garden had, to my surprise,
Stuffed animals of real-life size!
Yes, she had millions, and her villa
Was absolutely élé*gant* . . .
They'd serve us supper on a long
And splendid table, all on silver,
And after supper, Mam would go
With Richard to the *casino*."

XLV.
Aha! I hear my love-starved readers –
Ils pour l'amour toujours ont faim –
Becoming hankering, hungry pleaders,
Beseeching me, *Cherchez la femme*!
And since I share their pangs completely
(Albeit, somewhat more discretely),
I'll tell you her identity:
Louisa Fletcher Connely.*
From Indiana, she was carried
(To go to school) away to Smith,[77]
And after that, to marriage with
Booth Tarkington. Their match miscarried,
And four years after their divorce,
She married Connely* (of course).

---

76 Marysia Morawski, daughter of Burgin's sister, Lily, was born in 1922 in Warsaw. After World War II she emigrated to Austria and settled in Vienna where the author interviewed her in August 1981.
77 Louisa Fletcher graduated from Smith College in 1900. She was ten years older than Wilfred Connely, her second husband, and fifteen years older than Burgin.

XLVI.
Louisa liked creative, vital,
Intelligent and younger men.
A Boston poetess, her title,
The Land of Beginning Again,[78]
Appeared in print when Burgin's history
Began with her – now there's a mystery!
It's clear, however, she was rich
Until the Crash, because of which
She lost ten thousand she'd invested
In houses Burgin's uncle built.[79]
And Burgin paid her back, from guilt,
Or just because he so detested
To be in anybody's debt,
Especially someone he'd upset.

XLVII.
For it's a fact that she was crazy
About our hero and pursued
Him, calling forth in him a hazy
Remembrance of his attitude
To Henriette and of his torment
When his beloved's love lay dormant,
Because, you see, it's also clear,
Though disappointing to you, I fear,
While Mrs. Connely was frantic
And absolutely engagée
Our Mr. Burgin could not repay
The principle of her romantic
Investment in him or pretend
To interest more than for a friend.

---

78 *The Land of Beginning Again* was published in Boston in 1921.
79 Burgin's uncle, Leib (Leo) Burgin, built several duplexes on the Jamaicaway in Jamaica Plain, in which Burgin invested heavily and persuaded Mrs. Connely to invest in.

XLVIII.
Was he aware of this reversal,
So true in matters of the heart,
By which first love is one's rehearsal
For playing someone else's part?
Had his failed love with Henrietta
Convinced him passion was a fetter,
So he Louisa's heart refused
To keep his own from being bruised?
Or did he seek from her another
And unerotic kind of love
To compensate his wanting of
The missing woman, namely, mother?
Or did he somehow wish to hide,
The moreso after Ronia died

XLIX.
In 'twenty-six, the greatest sadness
Of all his thirty-three odd years
In agape's platonic gladness,
Which calmed for him his orphan fears?
It could be one, or all these reasons
Or just Love's ever-changing seasons.
I only know he told his son[80]
"The best thing I have ever done
Was being almost ever-present
Around my mother's bedside for
The week before she died." (Oh Lord,
Must death in love be omnipresent?)
Enough! I've gotten back again
To that sad land where I began.

---

80 Burgin's son, Richard Weston Burgin, was born in June, 1947.

L.
But I shall end with Burgin living,
In 'thirty, on Jamaicaway.
If he were home, he might be giving
A lesson, pacing, engagé . . .
I see him stop and while explaining,
Light up beside the stand containing
His Chesterfields, a large supply
De-packed because he likes them dry;
Or maybe he is in the kitchen
With Myron,[81] just returned from class,
Debating hotly over a glass
Of steaming tea, his eyebrows twitching,
The national economy,
And what it means, politically.

LI.
If he weren't home, and it were morning
Or afternoon, you'd find him at
The Hall, with diligence performing
His musical trade, or failing that,
Catch up with him at the dispersal,
Enroute to a quartet rehearsal;
And evenings, were he concert-free,
And not with friends or family,
Our very busy concertmaster
Would be inside the Cavendish,[82]
Fulfilling there his secret wish
To be an amateur Grand Master.
And so in life he moved along,
Content on cards, strong tea and song.

---

81 Myron Burgin immigrated to the US in 1925 and lived with Richard in Jamaica Plain while he earned his Ph.D. in Economics at Harvard University.
82 The Cavendish was the bridge club in Boston to which Burgin, a championship-level player, belonged.

LII.

I'll leave you with this new-world picture
Of Burgin, newly naturalized
In 'twenty-eight, an old-new mixture
Of callings newly synthesized:
Conductor, concertmaster, teacher,
Bridge player, veteran overreacher,
Debater, didact, *raconteur*,
Paternalistic bachelor,
Survivor of some quite distressful
But ordinary growing pains –
Some losses, but a lot more gains –
He'd been so lucky and successful,
What kind of further happiness
Would lie ahead? He couldn't guess. . .

Richard Burgin, 1930's

CHAPTER EIGHT: DOUBLE CONCERTO

*The Seventh Annual Meeting of Friends
of the BSO on Nov. 5, 1940 at 4 p.m.
featured Bach's Concerto For Two Violins...*

– BSO Program Book

*My ballad's theme is he and she –
Not terribly new of me.*

– Mayakovsky, *Pro èto*

I.
Those were the days when I was living
On Plympton Street and was at peace,
Had gotten tenure, and was giving
My joy in teacherly release;
Those were the days when preparations
For classes – versified translations
Of Russian lyric poetry –
First conjured up my Muse to me.
My small apartment (not idyllic!)
Expanded with her bubbly wit,
At first, she parodied a bit,
Burlesqued Tolstoy in rhymes dactylic,
Then into verse perversely chose
To put my academic prose.

II.
With idiosyncratic "Myshkin"
To Howard Keller we laid siege;
To our surprise, he took the risk in
Accepting it for print in SEEJ.[83]

....
....
....

---

[83] SEEJ = *The Slavic and East European Journal,* of which Howard Keller was editor in 1980-81.

III.
Last autumn we began the present
Half-humorous, half-serious work;
At first my Muse was rather hesitant
To show the world my latest quirk,
But vanity at last induced her
To strut her stuff. I introduced her
Amidst the friendly noise and glee
Of Friday Night society,[84]
And like a tippler she cavorted
And sang a chapter over wine.
The faces of those friends of mine
With tearful laughter were contorted.
Oh, I admit that I was proud
To share her with the Friday crowd!

IV.
However, feeling we would bore them,
We sought seclusion in my den.
Her songs grew faint, and to restore them
I pushed my academic pen.
No luck. Oh, I was feeling tragic
When suddenly, as if by magic,
She came and took me on a spin
To Pávlovsk, then turned west to Fin-
Land, toured all over Scandinavia,
Attending concerts here and there,
Sang work's delight and love's despair,
Then sojourned briefly in *Norvegia*,
And played the *cosmopolitaine*
As well as the *Varsovienne*.

---

[84] The Friday Night Club was a gathering of the author's friends and colleagues that met every two months or so for dinner, conversation and the presentation of original parodies.

V.
Then quitting northern Europe's cities
With their successes and their woes,
In new-world Boston, fiddling ditties,
She played how a career grows
In new assignments and appointments.
She drowned romantic disappointments,
Forgot her fiddle's tenderer notes
For new professional anecdotes
And songs to working energetic.
Impassioned suits she would disdain,
And settled in Jamaica Plain
To play the bachelor hermetic,
With eyes of wistful self-command,
Baton and playing cards in hand.

VI.
At Burgin's she has been sequestered
For five years now. He's said to shun
The female sex by whom he's pestered,
Preferring hands of bridge for fun.
Though he'll admit that he is lonely,
With each potential one-and-only,
He simply cannot get in stride,
Or fears, perhaps, a loss of pride.
He often jokes to friends that he's a
Great lover . . . of the game of whist
And not a *real* misogynist.
From time to time he sees Louisa
Who lives above him and despairs
That just her photo stays downstairs.

VII.

He's used to bachelor existence,
Its orderly disorder free
From the perturbing inconsistence
Of "silly" femininity.
But wait! Who is that lovely creature,
As blessed by talent as by feature,
Who just put down her instrument
And heard from him a compliment
He'd never pay to any student:
"I've never heard, it seems to me,
Tchaikovsky played more beautifully!"
Dear Muse, who is this blonde intruder
Who's won our Burgin's praise heartfelt?
'Why, don't you know?! That's Ruth Possèlt,

VIII.

The famed American violinist,
Nedávno sdélavshaia furór[85]
In Soviet Russia where she finished
Her latest European tour.
March 25th she'll be appearing
At Symphony, and slightly fearing
Serge Koussevitzky's temper, she
Called Burgin up to ask if he
Would hear her play and maybe offer
Suggestions. So, she came today,
And after he had heard her play,
He stood in admiration of her.'
'How interesting! Bravissimo!
What more about her do you know?

---

[85] *Nedavno sdelavshaia furor* = who recently made a sensation (Russian). Ruth Posselt (1911-2007) was the first American woman violinist to play in Soviet Russia. She returned from her tour there in January 1935.

IX.
Her pa, Emile, musician, preacher
Of German values, had a fierce
Attraction to an English teacher
And singer, Ida Lewis Pierce,
Whose family came from old New Bedford.
They married, settled down in Medford,
Had Gladys, multiplied apace
With Molly, Marjorie, Emil, Grace,
Naomi, and the last of seven
To join her sisterly quintet,
Was Ruth; with talent rarely met,
She came in nineteen hundred 'leven
And was a child prodigy
Who started violin at three.

X.
How blessed the child who is childish,
Blessed she who can on time mature,
Who as a girl is free and wildish
And then grows up to feel secure;
Who by her gift's not isolated,
And from her peers not alienated;
Who wows the boys at sweet sixteen
And marries happily her dream-
Boat, wins, at forty, liberation
From children and the kitchen sink
To garden, work, or simply think;
Who gets success and relaxation
And hears through life how people choir:
'Jane Doe's a woman I admire!'

XI.
But it is sad to think of *Kinder*
Whose *Wunder* robs them of their youth,
Incinerates their growth to cinder
And cheats them of its booty – truth;
Whose bright, prodigious aspirations,
Whose ringing, glistening ovations
Are dulled by Wonder's double spoils:
Excessive pampering, and toils.
Unbearable to see them shoulder
Adult responsibilities,
While overwhelmed with "childese";
Eternal children growing older,
They tempt a doubly banal fate –
Too much too soon, too little – late.

XII.
Ruth's childhood, or so I gather,
Was torn by a parental rift:
Her mother dreamed of fame; her father
Would not commercialize her gift.
At six, she made her first appearance
As *Child Wonder Violinist*,
In Steinert Hall; and after her debut
In Jordan, Carnegie ensued.
The raves made Ida more ambitious
While Emil wished to hold Ruth back
From traveling the public path,
Which he considered meretricious:
He would not have his daughter roam
Since girls, he thought, should stay at home.

XIII.

Sweet "Baby Ruth" found bravos pleasing
And loved to play ("It was a game!"),
But feared enormously displeasing
"Strict" Emil with her yen for fame.
She felt within a double longing,
Desired uniqueness and belonging;
She strove to be unusual
And at the same time, typical.
The split grew worse when in December
Of 'twenty-four her father died.
It left her feeling terrified,
And all her life she would remember,
Awash in guilt and fear of death,
His last, tormented gasps for breath.

XIV:

The next ten years brought vacillations
Between the common and extreme
As Ruth received her educations
In striving for her double dream.
In school, she read the usual titles,
On stage, earned laurels for recitals;
She rose in play up to the best,
She fell in love like all the rest.
In 'twenty-nine she's nominated
For "Typical American Girl,"[86]
Then concertized around the world,
And recently, the headlines stated:
"MISS POSSELT IS CROWNED QUEEN IN
AMERICA, ON VIOLIN."[87]

---

86 *Boston Evening American,* April 2, 1929
87 *Boston Globe*, March 15, 1935.

Ruth Posselt in 1929, published in the *Boston American's* contest: 'Is She the Typical American Girl?'

XV.
'Well, that is all that I can tell you
Of Pósselt up until today,
But if you want to know her well, you
Should really go to hear her play.'
'I'd love to, but . . .' I answered sadly,
'I have no ticket.' 'Oh, I'll gladly
Ask Burgin,' said my gracious Muse,
'I'm almost sure he won't refuse,
And maybe we can sit together.'
'How very nice of you,' I praised.
'Well, thanks, but do not be amazed,
I know we've had some stormy weather,
But let's calm down, make up and kiss,
I'm bored with solitary bliss.'

XVI.
So, acting for our double pleasure,
My Muse took me to Symphony
To hear Tchaikovsky and to measure
RB's reaction to RP.
It seemed to us her playing captured
Him from the start: he sat enraptured,
Of every single note, aware,
In spite of his impassive stare;
And when she started the cadenza,
He noticed how some bow hairs broke,
Then waited for a paused up-stroke,
And acting out of Providence or
A sense she did not want to stop,
He rose and deftly plucked them off.

XVII.
My Muse gave me a nudge and winking,
She smiled in her knowing way;
Of course, I knew what she was thinking,
And as we clapped, she bent to say,
'Well, that was very nice and charming!'
I grinned, 'And typically disarming.'
'Exactly,' she affirmed, 'the start
Of Richard Burgin's change of heart.'
As usual, I feigned protesting,
'Oh Muse, I can't believe that's true!
For several years now, haven't you,
His friends and he all been attesting
That he's a bachelor confirmed?'
'Indeed, confirmedly mis-termed!'

XVIII.
'Dear Muse! You're really too capricious!'
'What makes you say that? 'Tisn't so.'
'If not, then I'm a bit suspicious
You know some things that I don't know.'
'Perhaps,' she cooed. 'Well, stop your teasing,
I thought you'd promised to be pleasing.'
'Okay, okay, I'll tell you this –
The day she played for him, that Miss
Possèlt, as she was leaving, mentioned
That she was looking for a place
To play with piano. Burgin's face
Lit up with smiles well-intentioned:
"You know, I have a great idea!
Why don't you come and practice here?"'

XIX.

I shrugged, 'That's just a friendly offer,
You know, collegiality . . .'
'*Don't* be dumb and play the scoffer,
I know when I've seen chemistry,
And so, I'll make a small prediction,
And it will brook no contradiction,
That B and P's bilabial fate
Is binary and they will mate.
However, there are circumstances
Around her that will take some time
To overcome, but we won't rhyme.
There're always secrets in romances;
Though you, of course, I would indulge,
We'll skip the things I can't divulge.'

XX.

'Oh, you're a mystifying creature,
A real provocateur in skirts!'
'Perhaps my most exciting feature,'
She purred, 'some mystery never hurts!'
'No doubt, but don't we have a duty
To truth?' 'Not if it mars the beauty
Of our real-life romantic tale
With some dispensable detail.'
'But I don't want to be deceptive.'
'Okay. Feel free to give some clues;
Your readers aren't all ingénues,
And those of them who are perceptive
Will put together two and two;
The others shouldn't worry you.'

XXI.

I found my Muse's view convincing,
But more convincing I must say,
My sense that you have been evincing
Impatience at this long delay.
So, onward, onward. In a blink, we
Fast-forward, locate to Helsinki,
Where B connected years before,
And P is now on concert tour.
She waits backstage. The concertmaster,
B's colleague, Hannikainnen, comes
And proffers a bouquet of mums.
She reads the card, her heart beats faster:
"I know that you'll play beautifully,
In admiration, Your R.B."

XXII.

"I think those mums were the beginning
Of our romance," she'd recollect
As he would listen, silent, grinning,
In his machismo, circumspect.
Indeed, though often separated,
Their double longing escalated
Until by nineteen thirty-eight,
They were in love and feeling great.
Theirs *was* most surely an attraction
Of opposites where each one feeds
The hunger of the other's needs
In satisfying interaction –
There was some dissonance, of course,
But harmony proved the stronger force.

XXIII.
Despite the difference in their ages,
Their pasts and personalities,
They'd both survived the harrowing stages
Of growing up as prodigies;
Despite the obvious disjunctions
Between their backgrounds, by injunctions
Of parents, they had both been ruled –
In duteousness, both were well-schooled;
Despite the many oppositions,
They both had suffered guilt from loss
Of parents they revered as boss;
Despite their different dispositions,
They both had known the anguish of
A heart-tormenting youthful love.

XXIV.
Although each was a fine musician,
They were not rivals but help-meets,
For she admired his erudition
And he – her virtuosic feats.
True complements in education,
Two tones in double intonation,
Professionally, one could not find
More unity of heart and mind.
And personally? Though I be slighting
The complex truth of what's unheard
To put attraction in one word,
I think that he found her "exciting,"
And she was fired up with vim
To make a married man of him.

XXV.
And marriage was where they were tending,
Or should be, so the grapevine felt,
Reporting Mr. B was spending
A lot of time with Miss Possèlt.
Now quite adept at illustrating
The programme of American dating,
He'd drive her home to Medford, park,
And kiss the right girl in the dark;
And as these private moving pictures
Became an ever later show,
The Boston matrons were not slow
To whisper their vicarious strictures:
'You know, dear, Ruthie's never in!'
'They're living, so I've heard. . . in sin!!'

XXVI.
But Ida had another worry
When seeing Ruth come in at night
On tiptoe, in a fearful flurry
To hide the signs of her delight.
She understood Ruth's dreams and passion
And did not want to quell or dash 'em,
But she'd by love and life been taught
The wisdom of the second thought
Especially concerning marriage;
She knew a woman needs must make
A choice, for dream's or passion's sake.
Though wedded bliss she'd not disparage,
She knew the burdens it begat
And thought with Ruth she ought to chat.

XXVII.

"Is that you, Ruthie dear?" "Why mother!"
Ruth flushed, "Are you still up? So late?"
"I couldn't sleep. It's such a bother,
But well, you know, I often wait . . .
Until you're home." "Oh Ma, I'm sorry.
I really hate for you to worry!"
"I know, but that's what mothers do.
When you're a mother, you will too.
But Ruth, if you don't feel too tired. . ."
"I'm wide awake." "I'd love to hear
About your evening." "Mama dear,
I...I simply couldn't have desired
A better one, it's like a dream...."
She sighed and said, her eyes agleam,

XXVIII.

"We're so in love. . ." "And your ambitions?
Remember how it was . . . before . . ."
"Oh, Ma! This time we're both musicians,
He understands me, and what's more,
He doesn't find my working stressful
And wants for me to be successful,
For when I have a big success,
It always gives him happiness."
"Well . . ." Ida clasped her daughter's shoulder,
"I have to say, I love him too –
He's tender, soft and kind to you.
I worry though, he's so . . . much older. . .
And that is something that could get,
Well, that you later might regret."

XXIX.
Ruth usually listened to her mother,
But this time felt that she was wrong;
Her ear was captured by another,
Less worried-for-the-future song.
Despite his being forty-seven,
She was convinced that seventh heaven
In nineteen forty was the thing
The difference in their age would bring.
And to that bliss she soon was carried
In May when Richard spoke the word:
"These nights of ours are just absurd!
You're free now, so why not get married?
If not, I'm worried if we keep
This up, we'll never get to sleep!"

XXX.
And so, that summer, naught regretting,
July the third, they tied the knot,
In an extraordinary setting,
Or so at least I've always thought.
For several hours, they'd been riding
The Berkshire country roads deciding
That neither of them wished to cope
With ceremonies, but elope,
When Richard, in some excitation,
By chance glanced at the dash. Alas!
The car was almost out of gas.
"I hope that we can find a station,"
He said, his heart about to sink.
"West Stockbridge has one, dear, I think."

XXXI.
They found it but it looked deserted
Until the owner, all in grease,
Approached them: "Help ya?" Burgin blurted,
In some relief, "Yes, fill it, please."
"You folks from round here?" "No, just driving,"
They chimed in unison, and striving
To damper their excitedness.
He felt her tiny fingers' press,
And quickly turning to the owner,
"Is there . . ." (he heard his heartbeat sound)
"A Justice of the Peace around?"
"You really are an out-of-towner,"
The man grinned imperceptibly,
"The Justice of the Peace is me."

XXXII.
"Can we be married?" "Sure, I'll only
Just go wash up. Please step inside." (. . .)
"Now, you would like, which ceremony?"
"The fastest." "Fine. Well, who's the bride?"
"I'm Ruth Posselt." "Groom?" "Richard Burgin."
"Your occupations?" "We're musicians..."
"And could I have the wedding bands?"
"We don't . . ." "No matter. Just join hands."
Thus, in a station few in service
Could ever have surpassed, they wed,
Filled up with gas and drove ahead,
In haste, but feeling much less nervous,
To celebrate their marriage with
The Speyers and the Hindemiths.

XXXIII.

'Dear Muse, that *was* a charming story!'
'And every word of it was true.'
'It also was commendatory
How at the end you managed to
Effect a rather deft transition
To Hindemith, whose composition
Involved the early married life
Of Richard Burgin and his wife.'
'I thought that you'd appreciate that,'
She beamed with pride, 'but I need rest,
So, don't you think it would be best
To have RB himself relate that?
You help him tell about his friend
While I prepare our poem's end.'

XXXIV.

"Well, Hindemith was a terrific
Personality, and he –
His knowledge being so prolific –
Was very interesting to me.
I had extraordinary luck in
Both playing under him, conducting
His works and then premiering in
America his Violin
Concerto.[88] Then my wife took over.
She played so beautifully that work
That she performed it in New York,
For him, and everywhere, all over.
And yet, the way it came about
Was very strange and roundabout.

---

88 Richard Burgin gave the first American performance of the Hindemith Violin Concerto in Boston, April 19/20, 1940 before he and Ruth Posselt were married. She played it for the first time in New York on January 9, 1941. It ultimately became one of her signature pieces and she performed it with major orchestras all over the US during the next two decades.

XXXV.
"When he first came here, to this country,
In 'thirty-nine (I think), although
He was reserved, we got quite friendly.
I'd often argue with him, so
When I had got to know him better,
I said once, 'Paul, I like your *Kammer-
Musik* and have been practicing...'
He said, 'Why bother studying
What isn't worth your time?' I felt he,
That this was strange. 'I don't agree.
I like this piece, but I don't see
Why do you write so difficultly
For violin?' He said again,
'Why should you bother with it then?'

XXXVI.
"I couldn't sway him, but a comment
I made did stop the argument.
I said, 'You know, Paul, from the moment
You have composed a piece and sent
It off, you lose all jurisdiction
Because without your benediction
Anyone can take it and
Has got the right to understand
It as he wants.' My little sermon
Hit home: he said, 'Well, that is true.
You know, I think I'll send to you
My new concerto,' then in German,
'*Wenige Noten, aber schön*,'[89]
And therefore, easier to learn.

---

[89] *Wenige Noten, aber schön* = fewer notes, but beautiful.

XXXVII.

"' I'm sorry, though, the first performance
Has been arranged, for Amsterdam.'
'It's not about the first performance,
Just let me see it if you can.'
Time passed. In May when he was leaving
For Germany, still not receiving
This new concerto that's supposed
To be so *schön* with fewer notes,
I thought at first, 'Well, that's another
Of those nice things composers can
Well, promise but. . .' Then I began
To think, 'Why really does he bother
To send it? I can buy it, after all.'
I went to him and told him, 'Paul,

XXXVIII.

"'Why bother sending that concerto?
Who is your publisher?' 'Why, Schott.
But you can't buy that yet, I'm certain.'
'How come?' 'Because, you see, it's not
Yet printed.' 'Could you let me see a,
A manuscript?' I was so eager,
I loved his music long before
I had known him. He said, 'I'm sor-
Ry but I simply haven't got one
Because it isn't written down.'
'How is that possible?' I frowned.
'It now is May, the first performance
In just four months from now is set,
And you have not composed it yet?'

XXXIX.
"'It is composed,' he answered, growing
A bit impatient, 'every note.
It's just not *written*, but I'm going
To Europe, as you know, by boat –
Six days with nothing else to do when
I'll write it down, and when I'm through, then
My publisher will be informed,
It will be printed and performed.'
And that's a fact which I attested:
Like J.S. Bach and Mozart, he
Could just compose from memory.
Since I was always interested
In how composers do create,
He was, for me, a special case.

XL.
"In fact, he finished (in Jamaica
Plain) the last three pages of
His Symphony in E-flat Major
Right in my home, at five o'clock...
I finally got, in February,
His new concerto. It *is* very
Beautiful, and there are far,
Far fewer notes. So his remark
Was true and also characteristic:
There were too many notes, you see,
In all his early works, but he,
As most composers do, got rid of
Those barnacles that seem to grow
Unneeded on the host, you know."

XL.
'I hope, dear Muse, by now you've rested
And shall be able to expend
Your energies, as you suggested,
To bring our story to an end.'
'I guess you're feeling awfully tired?'
'Not awfully, but my tale's expired,
So, you take over now for me,
I know you'll play it beautifully.'
'I'll try my best.' She whispered, yawning,
Got up and rubbed her sleepy eyes.
'I've planned for you a small surprise,
Which, while I slept, my dreams were spawning,
And at the end, I'm sure, will give
New life to our long narrative.'

XLII.
Our newlyweds, their true love proving,
Throughout the Berkshire summer thrive;
The fall of 'forty finds them moving
To 57 Larchwood Drive
In Cambridge, there, without the trouble
Of dawn goodbyes, to start the Double
Concerto of their lives and hearts,
Their contrapuntal minds and arts.
November's BSO Friends listen,
Their faces lit with major grins,
To Bach's d-minor violins,
And January premiers Piston[90]
With her new virtuosic feat
Conducted by his steady beat.

---

90 Walter Piston composed his violin concerto for Miss Posselt in the summer of 1939. She played it with the BSO, Richard Burgin conducting, on January 31 / February 1, 1941.

Conductor Richard Burgin kisses soloist Ruth Posselt's hand after her performance of the Piston Violin Concerto in Boston, February 1, 1941.

XLIII.

Then summer. Strolling through the arbor,
We spread our blanket in the sun
At Tanglewood, to hear her Barber[91]
In August, nineteen forty-one.
The season changes. In more sober
Attire, chilled by late October,
We warm our souls in Symphony Hall,
By her Dvorak held in thrall.[92]
But on the heels of that ovation,
She leaves to tour the great mid-west
While he, quite lonely, copes as best
He can with weeks of separation:
In work, he muffles his dismay
And writes her letters every day.

XLIV.

In 'forty-two he is promoted,
Conducted to Associate[93] . . .
But we have dutifully noted
Career growth and shan't relate
The ups and downs of each performance,
Their aspirations and their torments.
There are some kinds of happiness
Besides professional success.
Thus she, one night that fall, said, "Maybe,
My bobkins, something's missing in
Our lives. I love my violin
But. . . would you like to have a. . . baby?"
His eyes beamed wide with pleasure full,
"I think that would be wonderful!"

---

91 Posselt premiered the Barber Violin Concerto with the BSO at Tanglewood on August 16, 1941.
92 Posselt played the Dvorak Violin Concerto with the BSO on October 31/November 1, 1941.
93 Richard Burgin began the 1942-43 season as Associate Conductor of the BSO, a position he held until 1967.

XLV.
So was it by some intuition,
Some prescience or some shared romance,
Or was it just the imposition
On Burgin's programming of Chance,
That January's symphoniana
Was overtured by *Donna Diana*
And dramatized the *Don* of Strauss[94]
Who sought so long the ideal spouse?
And by what chance was it constructed
That on that venerable stage,
In March, still at a pre-birth age,
As P performed and B conducted,
By both unseen, perhaps D heard
Dukelsky's *First* and Mahler's *Third*.[95]

XLVI.
Who knows what memories human beings
Might form while still inside the womb?
What murky hearings, stirrings, seeings
Might reach them in that liquid gloom?
Who knows if deeply-felt perceptions
Might not recall some faint receptions
Of major joy and minor blight
Before we saw or heard the light?
I only know his urge paternal,
So often stymied in his life,
Has blossomed through his second wife,
Combining with her dream maternal,
And my Life's ballad, He and She,
Shall end with their creation – me.

---

94 Burgin's program for January 15/16, 1943 included Reznicek's *Overture to Donna Diana* and Richard Strauss's *Don Quixote*.
95 On March 19/20, 1943, Ruth Posselt gave the first performance of Vladimir Dukelsky's first violin concerto and Richard Burgin concluded the program with the first Boston performance of the First Part of Mahler's Third Symphony.

XLVII.
On August third, in nervous torment,
Our Ruth put down her violin,
Unneeded in this first performance,
And left for Boston Lying-In.
There, after eighteen hours' labor
(Details of which I shan't belabor),
She heard a yell in spinal pause,
Then rested up and got applause
From Richard, Ida, friends, relations,
A mighty chorus of hurrays
Amid a flurry of bouquets,
And "heartiest congratulations"
Esteeming her bravura's worth –
Diana Lewis Burgin's birth.

XLVIII.
The baby's home. Our Burgin, happy,
As if immersed in the sublime,
Is feeding her, his shoulder nappy
All readied as from time to time,
He puts the bottle down to hold her,
His left-hand patting, to his shoulder . . .
But as he smiling waits to hear
The burp that's music to his ear,
We'll leave him, reader, for a while –
Perhaps for good. Enough our whim
We've satisfied in following him
Around the world. Let's share his smile
In having found a home at last –
The time for us to go is past!

XLIX.
Whoever you are, my reader, whether
You're hostile, friendly, false or true,
Right now, as friends let's come together
To say goodbye. Whatever you
May seek in these eight motley chapters –
Remembrances of stormy raptures,
Some peace from life's imbroglio,
Tableaux vivants or sharp *bons mots*,
Contorted syntax or misspellings,
I hope that in this book you'll find,
For your distraction, for your mind,
Your deepest yearnings or your yellings –
Some morsel that will satisfy,
And on that hope, we part: goodbye.

L.
Goodbye, my *muzykant* aspiring,
And you, my virtuoso-mom,
And you, enlivening and tiring
Unfinished *Life*. With you I've come
A long way in my versifying,
Now fretting and now satisfying
My Muse's worried, loving gaze.
So many, many grueling days
Have passed since that obscure November
When dreaming, I first caught the beat
Of Burgin in Onegin feet,
And in the distance, I remember,
I stared as in a crystal ball
But could not see their end at all.

LI.

Those friends of mine with whom it mattered
So much to share these stanzas first . . .
Some remain, but others have scattered,
The Friday Night Club has dispersed.
Without it most of this was written;
And he with whom I was so smitten,
Who formed my fatherly ideal . . .
It's hard to say goodbye for real.
And blessed the one who, growing older,
Has learned that just the past is dead,
And smiling, eager, looks ahead,
A burping baby on his shoulder,
And can't foresee their parting strife
Like me, with Burgin's half-lived *Life*.

Second, revised version.
Housatonic, Massachusetts
November, 2016

Unfinished proof of photo of Ruth, Diana, and Richard Burgin, c 1945 (*Royal Atelier*, Brookline Massachusetts).

GLOSSARY OF NAMES

Arkady	Bazarov's friend in Turgenev's *Fathers and Children* who starts out as a fellow traveler of the nihilists (radicals of the 1860's) but ends up marrying and settling down to a life very much like his father's, only more productive and financially secure.
Asya	The heroine of Turgenev's novella of the same name who is a victim of an unreciprocated first love.
Bazarov	The gifted, but tragic young nihilist hero of Turgenev's novel, *Fathers and Children*. An example of the 19th century "superfluous man" in Russian literature, Bazarov is undermined by his unreciprocated passion for an attractive, but passionless widow, Odintsova.
Benois-Efron	Professor of piano at the St. Petersburg Consevatory before the 1917 Revolution.
Connely, Wilfred	1888-1967. American educator and author, born in Atlantic City, N.J., married Louisa Fletcher (Tarkington) in 1915.
Dann, Elias	Professor of music at Florida State University. In June 1974, he did a lengthy taped interview with Richard Burgin at Burgin's home in Tallahassee, Fla.
Elman, Mischa	1881-1967. Russian-Jewish violinist and older contemporary of Richard Burgin. Elman was one of the first in a long line of child prodigies who studied with Leopold

	Auer (1845-1930) at the St. Petersburg Conservatory. Elman's sensational debut in London in 1904 secured Auer's reputation as a pedagog.
Epiphanius (the Wise)	A 15th century Russian monk and hagiographer known for his ornamental style called "word-weaving."
Eugene (Evgenii)	The poor-clerk hero of Pushkin's narrative poem, *The Bronze Horseman*, who loses his mind and runs crazed through the streets of St. Petersburg after the flood of 1824 kills his fiancée and ruins his modest dreams of happiness.
Fletcher, Louisa	1878-1957. American writer born in Indianapolis, graduate of Smith College (1900), married to Booth Tarkington (1902-11), had a daughter, Nancy, from her second marriage (to Wilfred Connely).
Gentle Creature	A story by Dostoevsky, published first in *Diary of A Writer*, 1876.
"Gogolian zeroes"	Nikolai Gogol (1809-52) was a major 19th century Russian novelist, playwright and short-story writer. The heroes of his Petersburg stories tend to be mediocre poor clerks and spiritually bankrupt non- entities. The city exerts a magical, often demonic influence on their lives.
Grevillius, Nils	1893-1970. Scandinavian conductor who frequently directed the Stockholm Symphony Orchestra during Burgin's concertmastership there (1916-18). Both Bur-

	gin and his first wife, Henrietta, appeared as soloists under Grevillius' baton.
Hannikainen, Toivo Ilmari	1892-1955. Finnish composer and violinist with whom Burgin became acquainted during his years in Helsingfors.
Hermann	The hero of Pushkin's short story, *The Queen of Spades*. Hermann senses the city of St. Petersburg as a fateful force that leads him, when he is out walking one day, to the house of an old countess, who, he has been told, possesses a magic card trick that could, if he learns what it is, win him a fortune at faro.
Ivanov, Vyacheslav	1866-1949. A symbolist poet and theoretician, Ivanov lived in an apartment in St. Petersburg known as the Tower. It was a leading, very chic pre-revolutionary gathering place for Symbolist poets and other Russian Silver Age (1893-1917) notables in the arts.
Kajanus, Robert	1856-1933. Finnish composer and conductor.
Karamazov, Ivan	The tortured, self-lacerating intellectual rebel of Dostoevsky's novel, *The Brothers Karamazov*, 1880.
Kavalerov	The hero of Yuri Olesha's novel, *Envy* (1927), who is obsessed with achieving old-fashioned, Western- style glory (his name means "cavalier") and envies the mundane achievements of the new "Soviet men." Like many of his 19th century forebears in Russian literature, the "superfluous men," Kavalerov fails to realize his poten-

tial, both for lack of a social outlet congenial to his talents and ideals and for a manifold weakness of character and will. He chooses to wallow in his failure rather than betray his ideal of glory with ordinary success.

Koussevitzky, Serge	1874-1951. Russian double-bass virtuoso, impresario and conductor, who led the Boston Symphony Orchestra from 1924 to 1950. During his pre-revolutionary years in Russia, Koussevitzky had his own orchestra which was based in Moscow. Whenever the orchestra performed in St. Petersburg and the demands of the work required additional players, as was the case with the premiere of Scriabin's *Prometheus*, Koussevitzky would hire Conservatory students as extras.
Kreutzer Sonata	A late story (1889) by Tolstoy which contains one of the writer's most vociferous attacks against the sensuality of music, specifically, Beethoven's famous *Kreutzer Sonata*, against women, doctors, the conventions of courtship and marriage and the evils of sexuality, in general.
Lady Caroline Lamb	The woman with whom Lord Byron had one of his most scandalous and passionate love affairs.
Lensky	The secondary hero of Pushkin's *Eugene Onegin*, who is killed (by his "friend," Eugene) in a duel which he fights to defend the honor of his first love, Olga.
Lotto, Izydor	1844-1936. Polish-Jewish violinist and composer who studied at the Paris Conservatory under Massart, con-

	certized as a virtuoso and retired from the stage after suffering a nervous breakdown. He became Professor of violin at the Music Institute in Warsaw and also taught privately.
Nastasya Filippovna	The tragic heroine and "femme fatale" of Dostoevsky's *The Idiot*. She ends up being murdered by one of the two men who are madly and truly in love with her.
Nastenka	The young heroine of Dostoevsky's early story *White Nights* (1849). A spunky young woman, she lives in St. Petersburg with her grandmother, who is blind. To keep track of Nastenka's whereabouts, the grandmother pins Nastenka to her skirts.
Natasha, Pierre & Prince Andrey	The three main characters in Tolstoy's novel *War and Peace* who constitute the work's central love triangle. Natasha's first serious love is for Prince Andrey. It ends unhappily and contributes to Andrey's lack of interest in life and rejection of earthly love for the perfect love of God. Pierre's first love for a society belle, Princess Helene, leads him into existential despair. At the end of the mammoth epic, Pierre finds true happiness with Natasha.
Pechorin	The Byronic hero and archetypal "superfluous man" in Mikhail Lermontov's novel, *A Hero of Our Time,* 1840
Prince Andrey	One of the two main heroes of *War and Peace*. He proposes to Natasha Rostova, who accepts him but agrees to postpone their marriage for a year in deference to his

father's wishes. The postponement turns out to be Andrey's undoing since Natasha grows restive in her beloved's absence, begins to doubt his love, and almost is carried away, literally and figuratively, by another man, thus making marriage to Andrey impossible. Although Natasha acts imprudently, the onus is on Andrey who, in Tolstoy's view, acts unnaturally in agreeing to postpone happiness and halt the flow of life.

Prince Myshkin	The tragic hero and "positively beautiful man" of Dostoevsky's *The Idiot*, whose first love for Nastasya Filippovna is rejected by her with the most dire consequences for everyone involved, including Myshkin's rival, the rich merchant Rogozhin, and his "second" love, Aglaya.
Princess Parallelogram	Byron's sobriquet for his wife, Annabella Milbanke, because of her intelligence and interest in mathematics.
"Oblomovitizing"	A neologism of the author's [DLB] based on the character and attitudes of Oblomov, the eponymous hero of the novel by Ivan Goncharov. Oblomov's main "occupation" is indolent dreaming. His antipode and close friend in the novel is a young, entrepreneurial Russian of German background, Stolz, the incarnation of the energetic, striving spirit.
Rubenstein, Anton	1829-1894. Russian composer, pianist, and the first rector, from 1860, of the Moscow Conservatory of Music.
Salieri, Antonio	The composer and legendary poisoner of his contem-

	porary, Mozart, as interpreted by Pushkin in his "little tragedy," *Mozart and Salieri*.
Sanin	The eponymous hero of a decadent novel by the otherwise little known Russian writer, Artsybashev, which caused a scandal when it first appeared in 1907 because of its erotic theme.
Schnéevoigt, Georg	1872-1947. Finnish conductor and impresario, founder of the Helsingfors City Orchestra (1912), director of the Stockholm Konsertforening (1915- 1924), and founder of the Oslo Symphony in 1919.
Scriabin, Aleksandr	1878-1915. Russian composer and virtuoso pianist. By the time of his death, Scriabin had achieved mythic status in Russian intellectual and artistic circles as the self-proclaimed "musical messiah" of the Silver Age. Strongly influenced by Wagner and the idea of the *Gesamftkunstwerke,* he strove for musical compositions that would unify all the arts.
Silver Age	The name applied to the turn-of-the-century symbolist-modernist period in Russian culture from 1893 to the Revolution of 1917.
Silvio	The pseudo-Romantic, envious and vengeance- obsessed hero of Pushkin's short story, "The Shot."
Sitt, Anton	1847-1929. A violinist in the Helsingfors Orchestra and Burgin's chair companion when he joined the orchestra in 1912.

Solomon, Maynard	A 20th century biographer of Beethoven who is credited with discovering the identity of the composer's "Immortal Beloved."
Stenhammar, K.W.	1871-1917. Swedish composer, pianist and conductor whose series of 6 quartets was considered unique in Swedish music at the time they were composed.
"superfluous man"	The name applied in Russian literary criticism to the main type of 19th century Russian literary hero. The superfluous man reflects Russian authors' fascination with Stendhal's Julien Sorel and Shakespeare's Hamlet.
Tatiana	The heroine of Pushkin's *Eugene Onegin* who is roundly rejected by Eugene in her love for him but recoups and in the end, rejects him when he finally falls in love with her. After Eugene leaves the country, having killed his friend Lensky in a duel, Tatiana visits his estate and looks through the books in his library, searching for clues to his character.
Tiutchev, Fyodor	1803-1873. A major 19th century Russian poet.
Tolstoy's "arch-purity"	The puritanical tendency in Russian letters reached its apogee in the late, dogmatic preachments of Tolstoy, who died in early November 1910, and whose obsession with the moral need for sexual abstinence, together with his philosophy of non-resistance to evil by force, were tremendously influential on a large segment of Russian educated youth.

Volpe, Arnold	1869-1940. Russian-American conductor. In 1902, he founded the Young Men's Symphony of New York and also conducted a group called the Volpe Symphony Orchestra, 1904-14.
Vronsky and Anna	The star-cross'd lovers of Tolstoy's novel, *Anna Karenina*.
Warsaw Philharmonic	This orchestra, founded in 1901 and called "the pride of Poland," gave an annual summer festival at Riga (Latvia) during the pre-war years.
White Nights	Dostoevsky's early story which uses the magical atmosphere of the white nights in St. Petersburg to orchestrate the bittersweet romance between the hero, a dreamer, and his first love, Nastenka.
World of Art	A movement in the visual arts led by the artist, Benois, which began in St. Petersburg in the late 1890's. The members of this group, like Scriabin in music, sought artistic expression that aimed at synthesis of various art forms.
Zimbalist, Efrem	1889-1985. Russian violinist and student of Auer, active in America. He made his debut in 1907.

SOURCE MATERIALS

I. BOOKS CONSULTED

Aldrich, Richard. *Concert Life in New York 1902-1923* (New York, 1941)

Alexeyev, A.D. *Russkie pianisty* (Moscow, 1948).

Auer, Leopold. *My Long Life in Music* (New York, 1923).

Camner, James, ed. *The Great Instrumentalists in Historic Photographs* (Dover, New York, 1980).

Connely, Louisa. *The Land of Beginning Again* (Boston, 1921).

Ganina, M., ed. *A Glazunov: pis'ma, stat'i, vospominaniia* (Moscow, 1958).

Golebiowski, M. *Filharmonia w Warszawie 1901-76* (Krakow, 1976).

Johnson, H. E. *Sibelius* (London, 1959).

Jusefovich. *David Oistrakh* (Cassel, London, 1979).

Kupferberg, Harold. *Tanglewood* (McGraw Hill, 1976).

Kowalski, Jozef. *Trudne lata* (Warsaw, 1966).

Kremlev, Yu. *Leningradskaia gosudarstvennaia konservatoriia 1861-1937* (Moscow, 1938).

Levas, Santeri. *Jarven paan mestari,* Vol. 2 (Helsinki, 1960).

Malinowski, Marian. *PPS-Lewica 1926-31 (Warsaw, 1963) Geneza PPR* (Warsaw, 1975).

Puzyrevskii, *Ocherk piatidesiatiletiia deiatel'nosti S.P. konservatorii* (Petrograd, 1912).

Raaben, Lev. *Leopol'd Auer* (Moscow, 1962).

Ringbom, Nils E. *Helsingfors orkesterföretag 1881-1921* (Helsinki, 1932).

Rudakova, ed. *A.N. Scriabin* (Moscow, 1979).

Smith, Moses. *Koussevitzky* (New York, 1947).

Ungar-Hamilton, C., ed. *The Music Makers* (New York, 1979).

II. NEWSPAPERS

A. Obituaries of Richard Burgin

Boston Globe, April 30, 1981
Boston Herald American, April 30, 1981
The St. Petersburg Times, April 30, 1981
The Berkshire Eagle, April 30, 1981
New York Times, May 1, 1981
Brookline Chronical Citizen, May 21, 1981
BSO Newsletter, Summer, 1981
International Musician, October, 1981

B. Articles

BSO Press Office, *Fact Sheet* on Richard Burgin

Downes, Olin, Interview with Richard Burgin, *Boston Post,* October 1, 1920.

Dyer, Richard, "Colleagues pay tribute to a musical giant," *Boston Sunday Globe*, May 10, 1981.

Ehlers, Sabine, "Music Is His World," *Tampa Tribune*, October 1, 1971.

Good Listening, "First Chair: Richard Burgin," Vol 2, No. 4, September, 1953.

Harris, McLaren, "Professor Burgin Chats on Music," *Boston Sunday Herald*, November 6, 1966.

Sabin, Robert, "Richard Burgin, Veteran in Two Careers," *Musical American,* 1962.

Taylor, Robert, "A Seeker of Truth," *Boston Globe*, June 4, 1981.

C. Reviews of Concerts

1. Russian

Zapadnyi golos (Warsaw), December 23, 1904.
Golos Warshavy (Warsaw), December 29, 1904.

Warshavskii dnevnik (Warsaw), December 30, 1904.
Russkaia muzykal'naia gazeta: 1910 (no. 20-21); 1912 (no. 21-22); 1914 (no. 17-18).

2. Swedish

Dagens Nyheter, December 11, 1916.
Nya Dagligt Allehande: October 6, 1916; March 2, 1917; November 23, 1917; March 5, 1918; January 10, 1919.
Stockholms Tidningen: October 6, 1916; October 30, 1916; December 11, 1916; March 2, 1917; November 23, 1917; January 25, 1919; April 7, 1919.
Svenska Dagbladet: October 6, 1916; December 11, 1916; October 5, 1917; November 23, 1917; January 10, 1919; January 24, 1919.

3. American

New York Sun: November 22, 1907; March 16, 1923
New York Times: March 17, 1907; April 14, 1907; April 15, 1907; November 22, 1907; March 20, 1921; March 6, 1923; March 16, 1923; February 16, 1947; February 10, 1948; February 22, 1948; January 13, 1949; February 18, 1951; January 14, 1954; January 10, 1957; January 28, 1962; November 18, 1966
New York Herald: March 20, 1921
New York Tribune: March 20, 1921
Brooklyn Standard Union: March 17, 1923; April 9, 1927
Brooklyn Times: April 9, 1927; March 9, 1929
Boston Advertiser: March 19, 1927
Boston American: December 18, 1920; March 24, 1923; March 2, 1929
Boston Globe: December 18, 1920; March 24, 1923; March 19, 1927; February 1, 1941
Boston Herald: December 18, 1920; March 24, 1923; March 19, 1927; February 1, 1941

Boston Transcript: December 17, 1920; December 18, 1920; April 11, 1922; February 9, 1923; March 2, 1929; March 15, 1929

Boston Traveler: March 2, 1929

Christian Science Monitor: December 18, 1920; April 11, 1922; March 2, 1929; February 1, 1941

Providence Journal: January 26, 1921

III. UNPUBLISHED MATERIALS

1. Interviews

Professor Elias Dann of Florida State University with Richard Burgin, Tallahassee, May-June, 1974.

Professor Diana Burgin with Maria Wierna Burgin, former Minister of Foreign Affairs for Socialist Countries in Poland and widow of Juliusz Burgin, in Amsterdam, August 1981.

Mr. George Lawlor (Research Assistant) with Professor Ernst Törnquist, former member of the Burgin String Quartet in Stockholm (1916-19), in Stockholm, June 1981.

Professor Diana Burgin with Nora Burgin, daughter of Leo Burgin, Richard Burgin's uncle, in Brookline, spring, 1981.

Professor Diana Burgin with Maria Morawski, daughter of Lily Burgin, Richard Burgin's sister, in Vienna, August, 1981.

2. Letters

To Richard Burgin from various musicians, 1902-1966. Richard Burgin Archive. Housatonic, Massachusetts.

To Diana Burgin from Richard Burgin.

To Diana Burgin from Maria Morawski concerning Burgin family history.

Richard Burgin: A Life in Verse
Copyright © 2017 by Diana Burgin

All rights reserved. No part of this book may be used or reproduced in any form, electronic or mechanical, including photocopying, recording, or scanning into any information storage and retrieval system, without written permission from the author except in the case of brief quotation embodied in critical articles and reviews.

Book design by Jessika Hazelton

Printed in the United States of America
The Troy Book Makers • Troy, New York • thetroybookmakers.com

To order additional copies of this title, contact your favorite local bookstore or visit www.tbmbooks.com. Also available through amazon.com.

ISBN: 978-1-61468-390-2

RICHARD BURGIN
a life in verse